Law Office Automation
for Paralegals, Administrators,
and Legal Secretaries

Law Office Automation for Paralegals, Administrators, and Legal Secretaries

Ashley Saunders Lipson, B.A., M.A., LL.M., J.D., As.D.

PRENTICE HALL
Englewood Cliffs, New Jersey 07632

Prentice-Hall International (UK) Limited, *London*
Prentice-Hall of Australia Pty. Limited, *Sydney*
Prentice-Hall Canada, Inc., *Toronto*
Prentice-Hall Hispanoamericana, S.A., *Mexico*
Prentice-Hall of India Private Limited, *New Delhi*
Prentice-Hall of Japan, Inc., *Tokyo*
Simon & Schuster Asia Pte. Ltd., *Singapore*
Editora Prentice-Hall do Brasil, Ltda., *Rio de Janeiro*

10 9 8 7 6 5 4 3 2 1

Library of Congress Cataloging-in-Publication Data

Lipson, Ashley S.
Law office automation for paralegals, administrators, and legal secretaries/Ashley Saunders Lipson.
p. cm.
Includes index.
ISBN 0-13-526583-5
1. Law offices—United States—Automation. I. Title.
KF320.A9L57 1989
651.8'4'024344—dc20 89-34403
CIP

ISBN 0-13-526583-5

PRENTICE HALL
BUSINESS & PROFESSIONAL DIVISION
A division of Simon & Schuster
Englewood Cliffs, New Jersey 07632

Printed in the United States of America

ABOUT THE AUTHOR

ASHLEY S. LIPSON is the managing partner of the law firm of Coleman, Lipson and Bradford, Professional Corporation, of Farmington Hills, Michigan. He is a member of the California Bar Association, the Michigan Bar Association, and is certified to practice law by the New York Committee of Bar Examiners; he is also licensed before various Federal Bars, including Tax Court and The Supreme Court. His other professional memberships include the American Bar Association, the American Trial Lawyers Association, Mensa Lawyers, Volunteer Lawyers for the Arts, and The College of Computer Lawyers.

Mr. Lipson was educated at Michigan State University where he earned a B.A. in Telecommunications in 1966, and St. Johns University where he earned his Law Degree (with Awards) in 1970. His list of degrees continue to include a M.A. in Mathematics, an LL.M. in Tax Law, and an As.D. in Computer Science.

His areas of expertise have covered the widest range, touching upon virtually every major area of law during his 18 years as a practitioner. He is an acknowledged expert in the area of law office systems and computerization. His articles (in excess of 20) and systems have been published by virtually every major Bar in the United States.

Articles in professional journals include *Legal Economics* (American Bar Association), *Trial Magazine* (American Trial Lawyers Association), *Law Office Management, The Profitable Lawyer, Of Counsel, The California Lawyer* (Bar Journal), *The New York Bar Journal, The Michigan Bar Journal, The Docket* (International Association of Legal Secretaries), *The Maryland Bar Journal, The Hawaii Bar Journal,* et al.

Preface

Producing data is the Legal Profession's primary pastime, and its most important. Control of information and "paper" is equally critical. Many firms are devoted exclusively to the production of Agreements, Wills, Trusts, Retirement Plans, and other forms of paper data. And those that are not, must nevertheless rely upon writings. Even the few practitioners who claim to be full-time trial lawyers cannot step into a courtroom, unless preceded by pleadings and briefs, not to mention the data required for procedural matters concerning schedules, dockets, and billings. It is therefore safe to say, that a firm's profitability must be inseparably linked to the quality and quantity of data that it can produce and control within a fixed amount of time.

This book is designed to bring together into a flexible, unified operation some revolutionary techniques for Client File Management, Form Creation and Storage, Document Preparation, Billing, and Management of Data in general. It is designed to make new use of the hardware and equipment that your firm has already selected. Suggestions for new purchases are also presented.

With the relatively simple, but scientific techniques presented in this book, you can turn your person and firm into a document production powerhouse. Productivity and efficiency can be multiplied far beyond what most law office personnel would imagine possible. Lengthy personalized documents, briefs, trusts, and wills, once requiring many hours, or days, can now be produced in a matter of minutes. Perhaps what is more significant, is the fact that the lawyer's time is no longer the primary focal point of the document production process. This means that the non-lawyers can increase their values significantly by multiplying data productivity well beyond that of the classically time-limited attorney, who is normally encumbered by standard dictation methods.

THIS BOOK IS FOR ALL LAW OFFICES

The Secretaries, Paralegals, and Administrators of *every* law firm in the United States can benefit. When initial descriptions of the methods and conventions (contained herein) first appeared in the major law journals, the inquiries ranged from a sole practitioner in Guam to the office of The Attorney General for the State of California. The systems are designed for every law firm, *regardless* of *size, regardless* of *specialty,* and *regardless* of *current equipment.*

HOW THIS BOOK CAN HELP YOU

Regardless of whether you are an administrator, paralegal, or secretary, your personal productivity and efficiency can be multiplied, not *just* increased, and your firm can follow suit. The methods are simple, proven, and logic-based. They will allow you to produce output that previously would have required a team of drafters, typists, proofreaders, and researchers; and at the same time the system will teach you how each piece of paper and data fits into the overall legal process.

Never before have the Paralegal, Administrator, and skilled Legal Secretary been in such a position of unrecognized value and power. Quite simply, the ability to control, retrieve, expand, and multiply data is a skill that can make any one of them the most valuable person in the firm. In truth, these skills have been with all of us, at least as long as the legal profession's love affair with wasted searches and duplications of effort. It took the advent of the microprocessor to make us fully aware of the non-lawyer's full potential. But the computer is not the only tool to be used to develop our capabilities.

Our methods are revolutionary, and yet proven. They are comprehensive, yet simple. The systems are standardized, yet flexible.

- If you are a LEGAL ADMINISTRATOR, this book can be used as a basis for efficiently structuring your entire firm, from the color of its file labels to the employment of its most sophisticated software.
- If you are a PARALEGAL, you can use it to increase your work output and billing potential, well above that of most lawyers.
- If you are a LEGAL SECRETARY, you can increase your value, and productivity, while at the same time slashing your overall workload significantly.

An important by-product of learning and using these methods will be the insight that you can gain into the legal system in general. For the first time, you will be provided with a comprehensive scheme that will show how each procedure, document, and "piece of text" fits into that once-vague concept known as "law."

WITH OR WITHOUT A COMPUTER

By now every law firm should have at least one computer; not only can that tool maximize the benefits to be derived from our methods, it can *multiply* those benefits. While the book is designed to take fullest advantage of the latest equipment and technologies, it is recognized that there are a few of you who may never buy a computer. There are, perhaps, many more who are in a transitional state, or who, some time in-the-future, plan to buy a computer. *Regardless* of which pattern you fit, this book will tell you how to develop a dynamic, structured document system, that will operate with or without a computer. Of course, we will make every effort to convince you to buy one; but even if you do not, this book should nevertheless increase your productivity significantly. It will *also* make your office computer-ready, should you decide to purchase one. With the computer added, the potency of your system will multiply. But keep in mind that the only *mandatory* requirements are some labels, folders, and the ability to count. The computer-oriented aspects of this book (together with the "paper control" methods) will apply to *any* brand of hardware, software, or computer configuration.

To assist your particular focus, several topics are divided up by what we later refer to as "Levels of Sophistication." Those *with* a computer will be able to take advantage of *all five* levels; those without, will be targeted toward the first two. But it is important to emphasize that *all* firms should benefit from all levels of discussion. Those without a computer will want their systems to be computer-like, nevertheless. When an outline of the original system first appeared in the journals, back before micro-mania started, it was titled—"File Your Forms as a Computer Would—Without the Computer." Those who *are* computerized, will likewise benefit from discussions pertaining to the first two levels. For they not only provide important building blocks for the higher levels, they also cover some indispensable office tools that you cannot scrap, regardless of your degree of computerization.

IT ISN'T NECESSARY TO SCRAP ALL EXISTING SYSTEMS

The methods are extremely flexible. They may be implemented slowly, gradually, or all at once. But, there is no need to shut down an operation for even a minute. Nor is there any need to alter those aspects of your office that are operating to your satisfaction. We do, however, plan to expand significantly your requirements for "satisfaction."

AN ORIGINAL SYSTEM

This is, perhaps, the only standardized logic-based system in existence. The methods have already been tested, and proven. Brief descriptions have appeared in many of the major bar journals throughout the United States. The concepts have been carefully thought-out.

You will find that most of the material is unique and will not be found in any other book. You may even find that restructuring your office by using it, can be an enjoyable process due to its novelty. The structures do not require expensive machinery or consultants. I will rough-in the frame; you can either adopt my finishing touches, or supply your own—as you wish.

THE TYPE OF INFORMATION YOU'LL FIND

There is a wide range of ''how-to-do-its,'' stretching from rudimentary instructions on how to prepare your client-folder labels, to lessons about training your computer so that it will ''think'' and prepare documents for you. We have omitted no item that should be of help to you and the efficiency of your law office. Plenty of examples and answered questions accompany the material.

Those of you who like variety, will find plenty of it. We are going to cover all sorts of systems, equipment, software, and methods for improving your office efficiency and profitability. But, if you expect to be dipped headlong into pools of computerese, don't worry. A pair of scissors, some nicely colored labels, and some three-ring binders will give you all of the tools that are necessary to create a powerful text base. Add your own components, as you wish. We will, of course, devote substantial time to the microprocessor; for it is the undisputed king of data movement and control. But there are *other* tools that you will be encouraged to add to your own flexibly created system.

STEP-BY-STEP TREATMENT

After providing a Basic Framework (Chapter 1), we are going to deliver a foolproof set of methods for labeling, constructing, arranging, and numbering your clients' files (Chapter 2). It will allow you to find them faster, locate papers more efficiently, and keep things neatly organized. As a by-product, requiring no additional work or thought, it will provide a closed file system that is *automatically* arranged categorically and chronologically.

The Form-Text Storage methods that follow (Chapters 3, 4, and 5) will show you how to store, retrieve, and create personalized briefs, pleadings, wills, agreements, letters, writings, and even ''pieces of text,'' at speeds that you never thought possible. A typical brief, for example, might normally require days of lawyer research, and hours of paralegal writing, in addition to repetitive secretarial typing. You will do it all by yourself, in minutes.

Your expectations about forms and ''cabinet drawer searches'' should change dramatically. Would *you,* for example, ever expect to be able to pull an obscure, rarely used form (from among thousands) out of your file cabinet, in seconds? Without ever referring to an index? And without even knowing the form's name or title? Finding such forms will become "second nature."

Our basic premise is a simple one. If you can store and find text rapidly regardless of quantity, then you should be able to save, store, and retrieve virtually anything. And once you can do that, you will never have to re-create, re-do, or re-draft anything again. Typing long documents "from scratch" should become obsolete.

Before you finish this book, you will not only *expect* your office to provide the mentioned conveniences, but you will require comparable speed and efficiency from *all* of your office equipment (Chapter 6) and accompanying functions—billing, docket control (Chapter 7), and research (Chapter 8), to name a few. Perhaps what is most significant, is the fact that you will do it yourself *without* expensive consultants.

Your goal will be to work toward a perfectly automated law office by constructing your own tailor-made system to suit your particular needs. If you can *not* dictate your firm's equipment purchases, you *can* nevertheless trim existing machinery to serve the purpose (Chapter 6). But even if you have authority to buy machinery, your objective will *not* be to fill your office with every new gimmick, but rather to free-up the time required to get your original thoughts from brain to paper, via your machinery. Equipment *alone* can never accomplish this task efficiently; but used properly, it can provide some quite powerful help, particularly if that equipment includes at least one computer station.

The remaining chapters will provide information about some important skills for the law office of the future, that you can use *now*. Teaching your computer to "think" and draft documents *automatically* (while you relax), for example, is a capability that is *currently* within your grasp (Chapter 9). Other important skills, designed to multiply your personal worth, will be briefly mentioned (Chapter 10).

Those of you who are concerned about "automating" your "hourly billing" law firms into poverty, should read Appendix B before worrying unnecessarily. Your firm is *not* ethically bound to bill on a strict hourly basis. If that were the case, with your new methods in hand, your firm's document preparation fees would have to be measured on a "micro-secondly," not "hourly" basis.

The systems are going to touch up every aspect of your firm's practice. The following chart briefly shows how the remaining chapters relate to those aspects. Notice that the first two elements come together, but only when a product is being produced; the first and the third then meet to generate income and control the various office processes. A key goal involves *maximizing* the

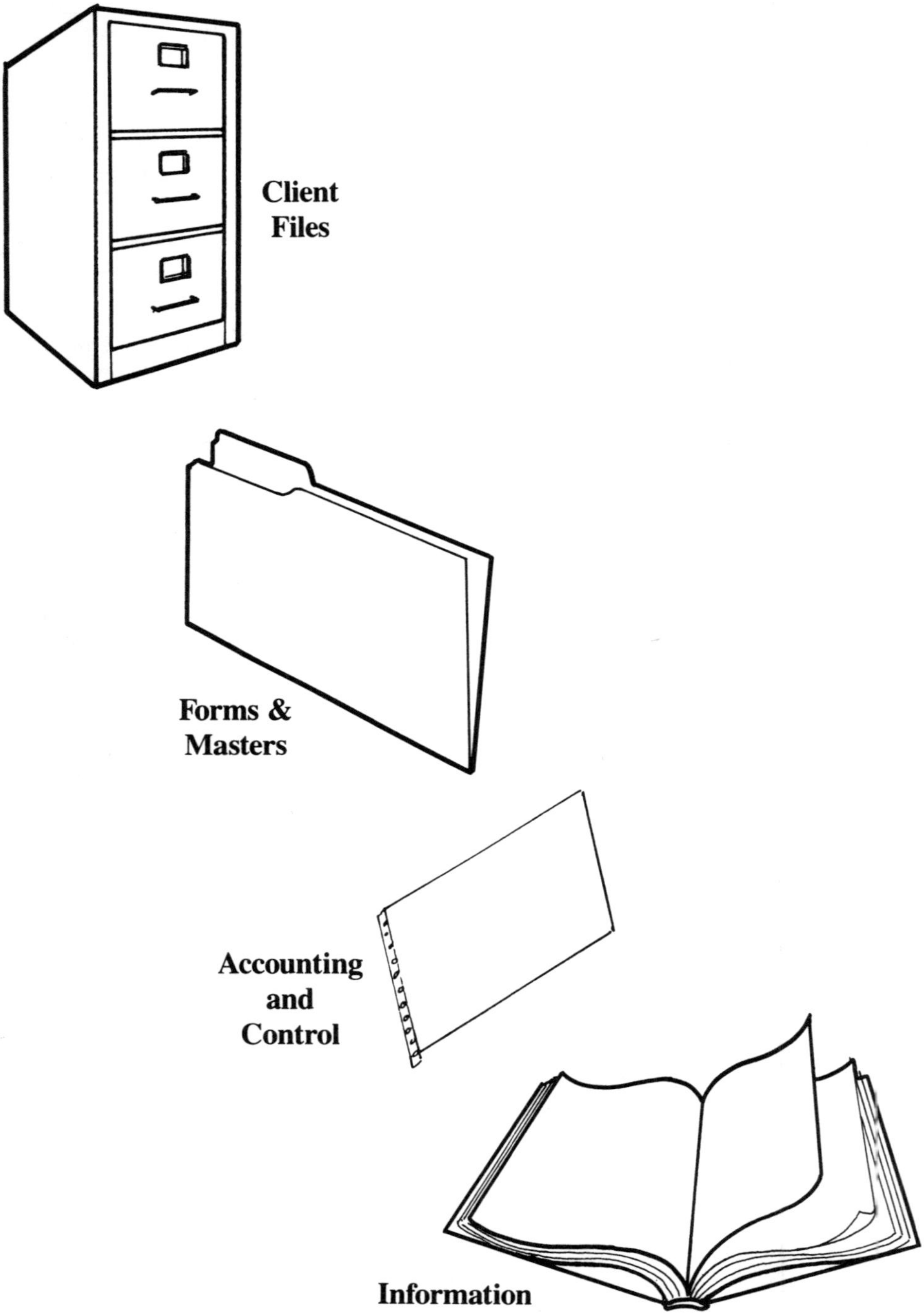
Client
Files
Forms &
Masters
Accounting
and
Control
Information

Figure 1-1

flow from element 4 into 2, thereby *minimizing* the otherwise duplicative and repetitious flow from element 4 into 1.

Ashley Saunders Lipson

ACKNOWLEDGMENTS

I would first like to thank my Managing Editor, Gerald Galbo, for his personal assistance and guidance. His cooperation made this comprehensive project run smoothly.

I want to thank my consulting expert, Joseph H. Clancy, Esq. of Farmington Hills, for his assistance and guidance in developing those categories of law pertaining to Probate, Corporate and Business, Real Estate, and Tax. I also want to thank my partner, Jerome S. Coleman, an acknowledged expert in the field of Labor law.

Artist: ***Marcie Millard***

Table of Illustrations

Table of Contents

1

The Advantages of Categorizing

A STRUCTURE DESIGNED FOR EFFICIENCY

Your structure will be simple, but nevertheless, *extremely* important; it will tie into the other methods, equipment, and devices discussed in the remaining chapters. The system will be very flexible; but even the most flexible system needs a stable foundation. For that foundation is the glue that gives unity and simplicity to an otherwise uncoordinated array of papers, files, and magnetic impulses. With a base foundation firmly in place, you may then proceed to use, modify, or expand your office equipment to suit your needs, with *no* disruption whatsoever to your system's base. Rest assured that from the base that follows, you will be able to develop the structures for handling matters that range from your simplest forms to your most sophisticated equipment, and office systems.

* * *

The law is often confusing, to be sure; and it seems that every exception to every rule has its own set of exceptions. But there does exist some *structure* and *order*. And just because judicial rulings happen to be inconsistent and often disorganized, does not mean that your office structures must follow suit.

So we start by accepting the proposition that the law *does have* a ''natural'' structure and division about it. Everything else seems to have a classification system (most notably plants and animals). The concept is not particularly radical; nor is it nearly as complex as it may sound. For every science, social study, or discipline works in a related fashion; i.e., you must divide, separate, and classify before you can hope to analyze. You might relate our method to the manner in which biologists arrange all living species into groups with headings such as ''Genus,'' ''Order,'' ''Class,'' etc. With that in mind, our *entire legal system* will be separated into nine parts which we will refer to as ''Major Categories,'' or sometimes, just ''Categories'':

Arranging The Nine Major Categories

Our nine *Major Categories* should be immediately recognizable as ''Areas of Practice.'' Later, we will take each Category, one by one, and divide *it* up into ten or less elements. These ''elements'' may not immediately be familiar to non-specialists, but neither should they be totally foreign. They will then be broken down into Subgroups, and some Subgroups will further be broken down into Divisions. As we proceed, you will see that the process sounds far more complicated than it is.

First consider the ''Major Nine'':

LITIGATION
PROBATE
CORPORATE AND BUSINESS
REAL ESTATE
TAX

WORKERS' RIGHTS
MOTOR VEHICLE
ADMINISTRATIVE AGENCY
ET AL.

Like a good constitution, a good model must be both rigid in some respects,and yet flexible in others. The basic structure should be sound and unchanging to allow standardization, rapid reference, and universal recognition. The flexible portions will be considered later. However, at the core of *our unchanging* structure is the principle that *all* of the law is divisible into the above nine major categories. It is therefore important to know these categories, and know them "cold."

The small price to pay for being able to locate files, forms, and other items instantly, involves this very small amount of rote memorization. With it, the rest of the system will mentally fall into place, by use. So with that in mind, the nine elements should be memorized, and very carefully, so that they become second nature. They should be memorized *in the order presented* so that the position number may be recalled immediately. Though not mandatory, it may also help to learn the associated colors; they will be used for labeling purposes. No other rote memorization is required.

Major Categories

1. **L**itigation (Black)
2. **P**robate (Red)
3. **C**orporate and Business (Green)
4. **R**eal Estate (Brown)
5. **T**ax (Yellow)
6. **W**orkers' Rights—Labor (Blue)
7. **M**otor Vehicle (Purple)
8. **A**dministrative Agency (Orange)
9. **E**t Al.—Other

Figure 1-2

Your first reaction to the above list may be one of curiosity about what we are going to do with it; if so, your questions will be answered shortly. If you already know, and can accept the list, so much the better. If, however, being the creative thinker that you are, there is a desire to rearrange or change the basic structure, the next few paragraphs should dissuade you.

Your urge to alter is normal, particularly if your office's practice is limited to only one or two of the items listed. You may have an uncontrollable desire to delete Categories that you feel may never be used, or you may wish to add specialties that you think have been omitted; you may even have an urge to rearrange the order of the list. Please consider the following reasons why you should *not:*

The list of categories is:

- *Carefully Planned* and has been slowly developed; a lot of thinking went into the structure, which provided the system with some not-so-obvious characteristics, shortly to be considered. The list is also the product of many hours of testing, user feedback, and adjustment.
- *It Is Comprehensive,* notwithstanding its simple appearance; this will become clear in later chapters. For example, if you are wondering why ''Estate Planning'' is missing—it is not; it will later be explained why it has been included within the ''Probate'' Category. And those of you who specialize in Workers' Compensation, will find *that* item included within the scope of a state ''Administrative Agency.'' We could continue with dozens of additional examples to make the point; but there is no need. Enough examples will be provided soon. Suffice it to say that in all of the years that the system has been employed at our office, there has never once been a need to employ the Et Al. (''other'') Category.
- *The Elements Are Necessary,* although it may seem that some elements will never be used by your office. Testing made it clear that because of the propensity of legal topics to overlap one another, all of the elements *are* needed. Even the most specialized litigation attorney, for example, will have occasion to represent people. People die; and when they do, estates must be set up (Category 2). Likewise, Litigation may involve Real Estate (Category 4); or Real Estate may involve Corporations (Category 3); or Probate, etc., etc.
- *The List Is Available,* to serve the needs of your firm in the event of expansion or change. Often, a firm's future course may not be predictable. You don't want to have to go back and change your system's roots every time that your practice takes an unanticipated turn.
- *The Arrangement Is Standardized,* and for this reason, perhaps more than any other, the Categories should remain intact. Inter-firm and inter-state identification of forms may depend upon a common structure or ''convention.''

For those of you who want to tailor the System to your own particular practice, there will be more than adequate opportunity to do so. A foundation, however, should be firm and unchanging, so that it can be consistently relied upon.

Decimal Systems Organize as They Identify

A Decimal Numbering System is a method by which numbers are assigned to objects in such a manner that each digit (of those numbers) represents a different characteristic of the objects. In other words, instead of merely assigning random or consecutive numbers, the user ''constructs'' the digits of each number to conform to some trait of the numbered object, person, or item. The benefits to be derived from decimal systems are many; but there are two overriding ones. *First,* by knowing the item's identifying number, and nothing else, one can determine its major characteristics. *Conversely,* by knowing its characteristics, one can determine its number. This becomes quite important, particularly if the items are arranged in numerical order; for they can *then* be located without reference to any external guides or indexes. At this point, please note that the term ''decimal'' does not necessarily mean that a decimal point is to be used; rather, that term refers to the natural ''base ten'' structure inherent in our Natural Number System.

Consider a good example of a *non*-decimal numbering system—Your social security number probably consists of nine digits which say next to nothing about you. Take 378-99-8309, for example. It is a number assigned by someone, at random. It provides little, if any, useful information without reference to some external documents.

Similarly consider another rather clumsy (*non*-decimal) example. We've all seen the types of numbers that banks use. I once received a loan application number that ran something like this:

3K-09357612090735-087-85-CL035

The number is bulky, easy to foul up, takes a weekend to pronounce, and cannot possibly make sensible use of all of the digits—at least not until 10 trillion people show up to apply for a loan. Only a sick person (such as the one who assigns your credit card numbers) would use so many digits without a single comma of relief.

The preceding loan number was presumably issued pursuant to some random 26 digit-letter combination system. Those who issue such numbers on a regular basis probably assume that we enjoy wasting as much time as possible reading them over the telephone. There simply are not enough borrowers to justify such a structure.

But assume for the moment that we used a *decimal system* whereby the first two digits represented the number of the Bank's branch and the next digit denoted one of the following: (1) female, single at time of issuance, (2) female, married at time of issuance, (3) male, single at time of issuance, (4) male, married at time of issuance. Moving right, the next two digits could denote a 50-state numbering code, representing the applicant's state of residence at the time of the loan (assume 01 = California).

Let the next digit in the sequence indicate the type of the loan (mortgage, home improvement, auto, bill-payer, etc.). Then let the following two represent the range of the amount of the loan; and, finally, the remaining few digits could be randomly assigned. Consider this loan number, for example:

2 5, 1 0 1, 2 0 5, 3 8 7

With the above number and *nothing else,* the banker would expect the applicant to be a single female (1), from the State of California (01), who applied at Branch 25, for a home improvement loan (2), for between $4,000 and $5,000 (05). All of this information would be available without referring to any indexes, or external information. And if, in place of the 3 trailing digits, the applicant's Social Security number were used, one could obtain a person's loan number without referring to *any* external source whatsoever (of course, so could anyone else having access to her Social Security number). The file could be pulled immediately, since *it* would be in simple numeric order.

The example is quite oversimplified, and not nearly as beneficial as the one that we are about to construct. For unlike forms and files, you cannot line up all of the loan applicants of the world by numeric order. It is the ability to order or ''line up'' that gives your soon-to-be created system a double-barrel benefit.

How Your Decimal Systems Will Work

We are going to be using *two* separate, pure decimal systems. One will be used to store, arrange, and label all of your Forms, Sample Pleadings, Prototypes, Masters, Etc. (Chapter 3). The other system will be used for performing cataloguing functions, but for your Client File System (Chapter 2). While the number structures for the two systems may differ, the denotation of the first, (far left) digit will be the same. That digit, *regardless* of whether it is part of a Form Number or Client File Number, will always denote a particular MAJOR CATEGORY.

Consider this example of a folder label that might be used for one of your *forms:*

Summons Federal Court	131,001

Figure 1-3

The first digit (farthest left) is a ''1,'' denoting ''Litigation.'' The rest of the form's number tells us some things about that form, but has nothing to do with that of the Client File Numbering Structure, even though all Litigation *client* files will also have a ''1'' for the first digit of their labels.

Now consider an example of a typical *client file* label. The first digit, as indicated, is "1," denoting "Litigation," but the remainder of the number is part of a different structure; its *remaining* digits mean something entirely different than the *remaining* digits in Figure 1-3:

Smith v. Jones	181,025

Figure 1-4

In essence, each element (be it client file or form number) will be assigned a pure integer (whole number). There will be no letters, dashes, or other symbols to confuse the matter.

The key characteristic of this system, or any decimal system, is that *each separate digit provides unique and important information about the item that is being numbered*. Numbers are *not* assigned at random nor are they necessarily assigned consecutively. Rather, the items are arranged and numbered according to their most significant characteristics. Of course, after the numbers are assigned, *then* the forms or files are put in consecutive numerical order.

Form Sophistication Levels

Chapter 3 will introduce you to The Direct Reference *Form* Filing System. It will divide your forms, masters, prototypes, and drafting aids according to the NINE MAJOR CATEGORIES. And, as we stated, within each MAJOR CATEGORY, a decimal sub-structure will be presented (that is *different* from your Client Filing System). As we shall see, Chapter 4 then extends the *Form* Filing System to your computer. But let's leave the subject of Decimal Systems for a moment.

As part of your overall *form* system, a simple, completely separate classification scheme will brand the physical make-up of each of your forms; one of five *Roman* numbers (to keep it distinguished from *form* numbers), will tell you *where* your form is and what it looks like. We refer to these *Five* Roman Numbers as the "Levels of Technology" used to construct the form. It might help to summarize them briefly before we get started, even though they are thoroughly developed in subsequent chapters. For example, Chapter 5 will tell you how to create a single Master Book for locating *all* forms *regardless* of Level, shape, or species. Each index entry will display the form's Level:

Level I— *Supplied* forms, printed forms, multi-part carbons, impression forms, summonses, sample pleadings, and prototypes—These forms are stored in the file cabinet.

Level II— Photocopier-*created* forms—These ''pull page'' forms are also stored in the file cabinet.

NOTE—Even though the next three levels concern computers, they are *still* of importance to those of you who are not yet computerized. They provide the framework for a simple transition, when the computer arrives. And those few who will never buy a computer may nevertheless purchase a typewriter, or other machine, with microprocessor storage capabilities.

Level III— Computer-*stored* forms and text—These may be stored on a hard disk, floppy disk, or both.

Level IV— Computer-*generated* forms—These are generated by programs, which are disk-stored.

Level V— Documents *devised* by Artificial Intelligence—The programs used to create these reside in the computer's memory.

LEVEL I is the simplest. When a multi-part carbon or impression-copy form is to be stored, it will invariably go into your file cabinet, *regardless* of whether or not you have a computer. Likewise, official forms and printed forms will also be stored in the form file cabinet. Where another firm serves your office with a particularly brilliant brief, or where a Judge's Opinion may have some value in future matters, you may also want to store copies in your file cabinet. No skill or ''Technology'' is involved with respect to this type of form; you merely copy and file it, or, in some cases, file without copying.

LEVEL II forms will also be found in the file cabinet; but there is more involved than the mere stuffing of papers into a folder. Level II forms are designed and tailored for your specific requirements, then multiplied on your photocopier for immediate use as the need arises.

They would commonly include ''ministerial'' forms such as time sheets, client status sheets, and questionnaires. But with a little thinking and creativity, they could also include ''pull'' pages of repeatedly used text for Wills, Trusts, Agreements, and even Briefs of Law (for those of you who refuse to computerize).

LEVEL III will be found in your computer's hard disc, or stored on a floppy disc or ''micro-floppy.'' The Level III text will be stored as ''files'' that are created by your word processing software. Some typewriters come equipped with built-in microprocessors that permit storage of text. To distinguish files that are stored on such a typewriter's micro-floppy discs, we may use the designation ''iii'' instead of ''III,'' to indicate a ''baby'' Level Three.

LEVEL IV involves something more than mere storage, or data base entries. It consists of Programs or ''Scripts'' that the computer will use to generate and *create its own* documents (see Chapter 9).

LEVEL V will actually consist of impulses or thoughts. The computer will eventually generate its own intelligence, and draft its own documents.

Major Category Descriptions

1. **L**itigation (Black)
2. **P**robate (Red)
3. **C**orporate and Business (Green)
4. **R**eal Estate (Brown)
5. **T**ax (Yellow)
6. **W**orkers' Rights—Labor (Blue)
7. **M**otor Vehicle (Purple)
8. **A**dministrative Agency (Orange)
9. **E**t Al.—Other

Figure 1-5

We start with the list of Categories, as our base of operations. The fact that the law "divides itself" along those lines should be accepted as axiomatic. To gain a sound footing, study Figure 1-5 and *note carefully* the following structural characteristics:

- *First*—The elements appear to be discrete and easily identifiable, even though the lines of demarcation are not always obvious. The broad-based general practitioner may see the individual items as separate, specialized areas. There will always be overlap, to be sure; and later we will carefully deal with this. But in forming the basic Category elements, focusing upon the overlaps instead of the distinctions would serve only to confuse and blur those areas that are otherwise clear. So for the time being, we will treat *each element* as a very separate universe or practice unto itself.
- *Second*—Notice, that to some extent, the divisions not only separate and classify areas of Law, but also *areas of practice,* and even lawyers. Litigators, for example, are *different* than Tax attorneys. And the client files of a Corporate attorney may not look the same as those of an attorney who handles only Real Estate closings or Estate Planning matters. The demarcations are by no means absolute; but they are recognizable.
- *Third*—Notice that the first letter of each Category is distinct. This may relieve your curiosity as to why "Labor" is designated as Workers' Rights. (Litigation has already claimed the "L.")
- *Fourth*—The "Other" Category is provided as a catch-all; however, in the years that the system has been in our office, it has caught nothing. Everything

should fit into one of the given Eight Major Categories. I use the designation Et Al. (Latin for "and others") instead of "O" (for "others"), which is too easily confused with a zero.

- *Fifth*—The Categories are arranged, to the extent possible, in order of scope (meaning involvement or overlap with respect to other Categories). Litigation, for example, may involve itself with all of the other Categories; it is also the most pervasive topic for the profession. *Any* matter can end up in litigation, and for lawyers, it usually does; so it is at the top. Probate (which includes Estate Planning) may involve all of the other topics below it, since from item 3 on down, some type of human property right may be affected. Administrative agencies are worlds unto themselves; so they bring up the rear.

Throughout much of the remainder of this book, the discussions will be framed in reference to the Nine Major Categories. It is therefore important to know what types of matters are handled within each:

1.
* * * *Litigation* * * *

As the name suggests, litigation pertains to civil and criminal court cases. As a general rule, if a matter involves any State or Federal Court, it would fall within this particular Category. *This* rule generally prevails even though the issues may overlap one or more of the other Major Categories. For example, a breach of contract lawsuit for Specific Performance may involve Real Estate (Category 4). Nevertheless, Category 1 retains jurisdiction.

I give Litigation a Black Label, because it is the most common color for labels. Mnemonically, Litigation is often associated with the darker aspects of human relationships.

2.
* * * *Probate* * * *

This element covers a topic that is a bit broader than the name suggests. We use the term "Probate" in its widest sense; it pertains, not only to Testamentary matters, but also Inter Vivos Transfers (Latin for "between the living"). Moreover, matters such as Gifts, Transfers, Living Trusts, Testamentary Instruments, and Estate Administration, would all fall within this particular Category.

Estate administration pertains not only to decedents, but also to minors, mental incompetents, physical incompetents, and even simple name changes. All of these matters are covered in the broad Category of "Probate." Unlike eviction lawsuits, or tax refund litigation, there is no concurrent jurisdiction with the civil court system. Probate, or surrogate courts, have limited, well-defined jurisdictions; that is why Estate Administration "battles" do *not* go into Category 1.

A Red Label stands out; Probate is a very important topic, and therefore deserves the color. Associate red with probate in any way you choose. Mnemonically, the Category involves life, death, *blood*-lines, etc.

3.
* * * *Corporate and Business* * * *

The scope of this particular Category is *extremely* broad; it covers matters that pertain not only to Corporations, but to all other business entities such as Partnerships, Limited Partnerships, Joint Ventures, and Sole Proprietorships. In addition, all matters pertaining to the Uniform Commercial Code and business contracts, in general, belong to this Category. It therefore involves the types of instruments that businesses normally use, such as releases, promissory notes, and an endless variety of agreements. If a lawsuit involves the breach of a contract, such litigation matters would fall within the scope of Category 1; other matters pertaining to the contract itself, however, would fall within this Category 3.

We suggest a Green Label. No one should have any problem associating that color with the world of Corporations and Business.

4.
* * * *Real Estate* * * *

This is one of the best-ordered and most discrete Categories. There is little doubt with respect to items that pertain to Real Estate. Lawyers and Paralegals know them to include Fee Simple Estates, Land Contracts, Concurrent Estates, Divisible Estates, Easements, Servitudes, Leases, Mortgages, and Liens. Any matters concerning Deeds would, of course, also fall within the scope of this particular Category.

The color of all Real Estate, at the deepest level, must be Brown. Such is the color of its label.

5.
* * * *Tax* * * *

This topic pertains to all types of Taxation, Federal, State, and Local. It also covers all types of taxes, such as Income, Real Estate, Ad Valorem, Sales, or Intangible Taxes.

For the color Yellow, you can associate Tax in any way you choose. Perhaps it is the way most clients feel when confronted by the IRS.

6.
* * * *Workers' Rights* * * *

But for a desire to keep the first letter of each major Category distinct, this one would have been titled ''Labor,'' instead of ''Workers' Rights.'' But Litigation already claimed the ''L.''

Labor law is one of the most important, far-reaching, and complex areas of the law. Even the Internal Revenue Code, with all of its complexity, pales when compared to the myriad of Federal, State, and Local Statutes, Agencies, and Bureaucracies, all attempting to govern and control the Employer-Employee Relationship. Collective Bargaining, Unfair Labor Practices, Wage and Hour disputes, and Discrimination problems (sex, age, race) cover only a few of the most prevalent concerns.

Though the term includes matters pertaining to guilds and craft unions, Labor generally refers to, or is thought of, as a ''blue'' collar matter. So it is assigned a like color.

7.
* * * *Motor Vehicle* * * *

This is the ''most minor'' Category of them all; it pertains only to those forms and procedures involved with respect to the operation or ownership of a motor vehicle, such as an automobile, boat, aircraft, or Hovercraft. The topic would be of greatest interest to those who deal frequently with the office of Secretary of State.

Purple is a somewhat unique color. And in the scheme of things, so is this Category.

8.
* * * *Administrative Agency* * * *

This category covers all of the many Administrative Agencies, both Federal and State, situated throughout the country. For example, it covers such Agencies as the Social Security Administration, the Bureau of Patents and Copyrights, the Federal Trade Commission, the State Bureau of Workers' Compensation, Etc.

Orange is the only common color that is left. So this last, but nevertheless important, Category will receive an Orange Label.

9.
* * * *Et Al.* * * *

This is a title that every structure must possess. For, no matter how perfectly a system may be planned, there will always be something that does not fit into one of the pigeon-holes. As of this date, we know of no other ''Other''; at least at this point in time, everything fits into the preceding eight. But the law is known for its propensity to move into new, often unanticipated realms.

If you ever find a matter that fits into this Category, please assign a color of your choice. But do not use a pure white label; it should be reserved for General Office Forms, yet to be discussed.

LABELING CONVENTIONS

The list of the Nine Major Categories that you have just memorized will be used to form decimal numbers for use in *all* of your office operations. It is perhaps one of our system's greatest assets that all of those functions can now be interconnected and unified. So equipment and storage media can come, go, change form, upgrade, or downgrade, but you need never change the basic System, nor should it ever be necessary to *undo* any prior arrangements or labels.

The recommended labels will be similar to the one set forth in this figure:

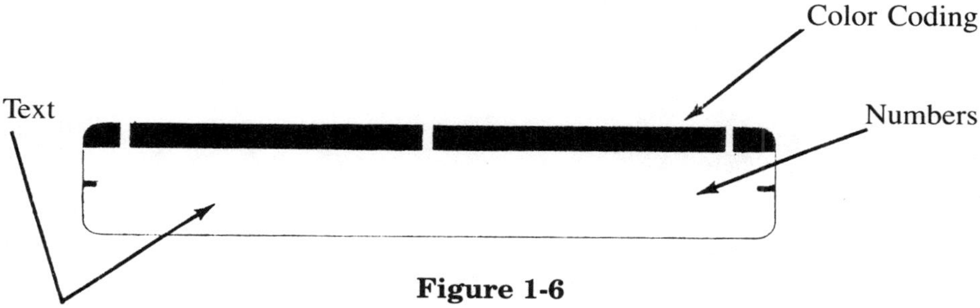

Figure 1-6

Notice that only a portion of the label is colored; the typed material can therefore be set against a white background, making it more legible. The recommended nine colors (per Figure 1-2) are: Black, Red, Green, Brown, Yellow, Blue, Purple, Orange, and Gold. A tenth label (Pure White) might be kept for continuously used office forms. If you can't find as many colored labels, or the exact colors, no serious problems will result. Your own mnemonic scheme will probably be no stranger than mine.

2

Constructing and Labeling the Client's Files

How to Assign File Numbers
How to Prepare Labels and File Folders
Your Automatically Created Closed File System
Integration with Your Old Systems

- **Existing Numeric Systems**
- **Existing Alphabetic Systems**

Index Card Systems
Complex Category Overlaps
The Care and Handling of Client Files

For want of the tab, the page was lost; for want of the page, the motion was lost, and for want of the motion the case was lost. Exaggeration? Not at all! At one time or another, we have all fumbled through disorganized files for crucial information at a critical point of some proceeding. So the "want" should be for a better system.

We can't guarantee that you will never have to search again. But we *can* provide a logic-based system that will speed up the process, and keep your files neat and organized. Here is all that you need.

Required Materials:

- Color-coded labels (9 Colors)
- Standard size (9 × 14-3/4) manila file folders
- Brown expandable wallet envelopes
- Index card file
- File cabinets

The listed materials are not particularly exotic; they can be found as standard issue in most law firms, or at any local office supply store. Though rudimentary, they are nevertheless very important.

An *over*-supply should be kept on hand at all times. I use the term "over" instead of "sufficient," with good cause. The items listed are so inexpensive that to permit delays in the construction or maintenance of your Client File System, would not be cost effective. The systems that you are preparing to set up can be created expeditiously, and operated rapidly; so it would be foolish to interrupt the process, at *any point,* just to await the next office supply delivery.

The recommended labels are discussed in Chapter 1 (See Figure 1-6). They should not be difficult to locate. Remember to purchase an adequate distribution of colors—nine, if possible.

The manila file folders are nothing other than the standard 9″ × 14-3/4″ tabbed cardboard folders used by most law firms. The brown expandable wallet envelopes come in a variety of depths; however, the length-width dimensions should be fixed so as to permit easy insertion of the manila file folders. I recommend that you do *not* use wallets that come with built-in dividers.

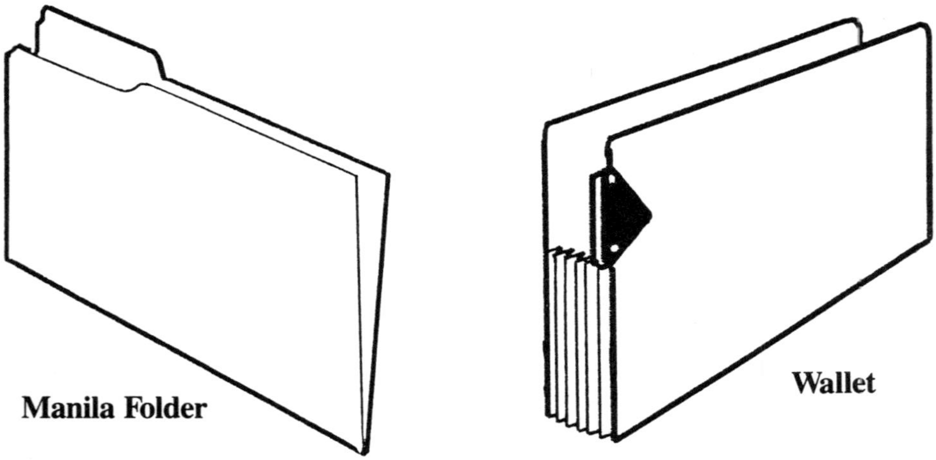

Figure 2-1

Manila Folder and Expandable Envelope

Index cards and their accompanying tabbed alphabetic dividers come in a variety of shapes, sizes, and forms. Most will serve the purpose; but make certain that any set you buy, is constructed so that cards can be *instantly* removed or added.

File cabinets are a matter of personal preference. Any that your office has, or intends to purchase, should be able to accommodate the manila folders and expandable envelopes. Personally, I prefer *drawer* cabinets, instead of lateral filers. The movable back-ends help keep the files upright and compact.

HOW TO ASSIGN FILE NUMBERS

To each new client file that is opened, we will assign a single, simple, six-digit number; for those law firms that may have occasion to open 1,000 or more files per year for any single Major Category, a seven-digit number would be more practical. In no event should you need eight digits (unless your law firm happens to be the U.S. Department of Justice). In any event, the simple rules for number assignment remain the same.

Once the files are numbered according to the simple rules that follow, you need only place them in numerical order into your file cabinet. This will *automatically* cause the folders to "file themselves" into a very nice, logical pattern, *first* categorically *then* chronologically within each Category. I recommend that you keep your cabinet drawers separated *by* Major Category (i.e., files with different Category designations should not be placed in the same drawer). This will allow you to more quickly zero-in on a client file by going *only* to the pertinent drawers containing the correct "Category" of clientele.

The rules of number assignment for each client file are as follows:

Number Structure

CDY,QXX

1. The first digit (C) represents one of the Nine Major Categories (see Figure 2-2).
2. The next two digits (second and third) represent the year that the file was opened. ("D" for decade, "Y" for year.)
3. The fourth digit (Q) represents the quarter that the file was opened (the only possible numbers are 1, 2, 3, or 4). If you ever anticipate opening more than 99 files for *any* one Category in *any* one quarter, but less than 1,000 per year (in any one Category)—you should eliminate the Q designation and use all three remaining digits for consecutive numbering (i.e., adopt structure CDY,XXX). Of course, if you think that you will open more than 999 total files in any one Category during any year, you should consider using seven

digits. The first quarter comprises January 1 through March 31; the second represents April 1 through June 30; the third includes July 1 through September 30; and the last quarter takes you from October 1 through December 31.

4. The remaining digits (the Xs) represent the chronological order in which the file was opened.

Example 1

Assume that on April 1st, 1986, your firm was retained by the personal representative of Harold Hughs to defend probate proceedings launched against his estate. The following Red Label should be used (assuming that the case was your *first Probate* matter opened in April):

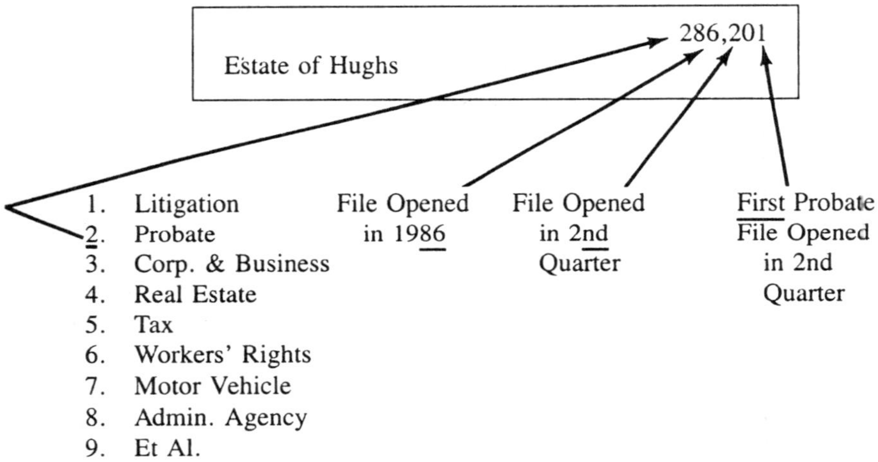

Figure 2-2

Example 2

Your firm represents Swindlecorp. Assume that you set up that Corporation during the latter part of 1975 (Corporate file number—375,429). On January 19, 1987, the Chairman of the Board informs you that his corporation is being sued for fraud by an angry Freddy Jones. Figure 2-3 shows the label for the new matter.

Notice that we have set up a completely separate Litigation label and folder, instead of combining it with the existing corporate file. This is a critical point; the matters should be kept *separate*.

Continue the example by assuming that one month later, both the Chairman of Swindlecorp (Harry Hustler) and the corporation itself are named

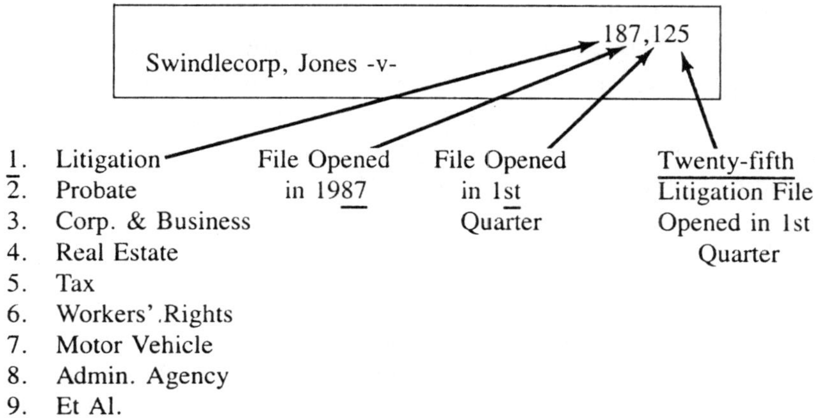

Figure 2-3

in a single indictment arising from activities pertaining to the fraud (assume that during that past month, you opened up three new litigation files for unrelated clients). Assuming further that there is no conflict of interest with respect to your firm's representation of both entities, you should then set up *yet* another file with a label similar to *one* of these, but not both:

Swindlecorp, People -v- 187,129

or

Hustler, People -v- 187,129

Figure 2-4

Notice that the last two digits (29) are greater than those of the civil litigation (Figure 2-3), by four. This is due to the intervention of three unrelated litigation matters, which would have presumably "taken up" numbers 187,126 through 187,128.

As indicated, you should select one of the above two labels, but *not* both. There *is a need* to maintain *separate* files for the Civil and Criminal Litigation. But there is *no apparent need,* at least initially, to further split the criminal matters, just because two separate entities are involved. It would appear that both matters are to be prosecuted and defended jointly. Strategy, if not convenience, would dictate that those matters be kept in a single file for ready ''joint'' availability, with cross-references to the civil and corporate files.

Note, that if Swindlecorp survives its not-so-good year, and wants you to set up some Employee Benefit Plans, you would *not* set up a new file; rather, you would expand existing Corporate file 375,429.

Example 3

His union's health and welfare trust fund has denied Henry Piker certain benefits that he may (or may not) be entitled to, by reason of a partial disability (resulting from an on-the-job injury). Your firm has been retained, on April 1, 1986, to represent Henry with respect to his intra-union appellate rights. Consider this:

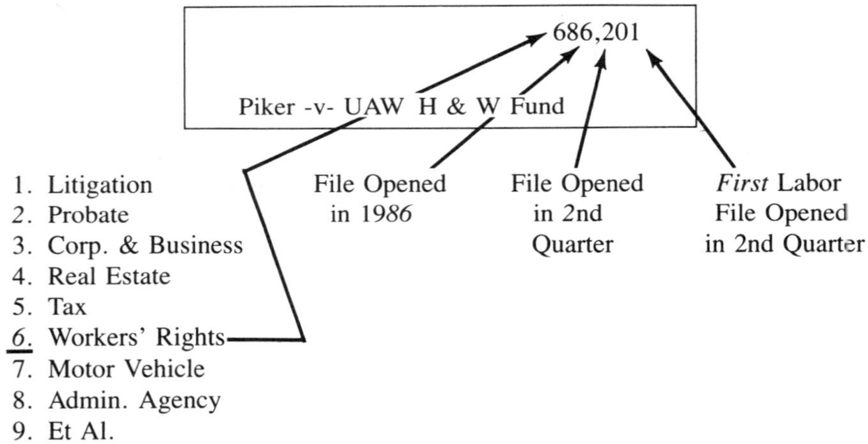

Figure 2-5

If later, you decide to commence Workers' Compensation proceedings due to a loss of work, the new file label might look like this:

886,305

Piker, Henry -v- Ford (W.C.)

Figure 2-6

As simple as it may seem, this system causes the file arrangement to exhibit some very beneficial properties. By numbering all firm files in this simple manner, and then placing them in their natural numerical order, a logic-based system is automatically created. Consider its:

Advantages

- *FIRST,* the files are separated and pigeonholed according to MAJOR CATEGORY (and Area of Practice). This makes sense, and should provide a natural division that corresponds to the manner in which most law firms are already constructed. Litigation files, for example, are different from Probate or Corporate files; they not only look different, but they are structured differently, as are the lawyers who service them.

  Let's consider a situation involving *separate* matters that should be treated *together.* Attorneys who handle Probate matters, for example, normally involve themselves in Estate Planning; so both of those topics fall within the scope of Category 2.

  In fairly large firms, where file rooms are separated, the system provides an excellent method for division according to the firm's areas of specialization. Such a segregation would, for example, permit the Corporate files to be close to their Corporate attorneys. A purely alphabetic system would not produce such a result.

- *SECOND,* by knowing the MAJOR CATEGORY, and the approximate time that the file was opened, any attorney or secretary could go to the general location of the file, *without* referring to an index. Most secretaries seem to develop a knack for knowing a file's number, once the general whereabouts have been suggested. This is particularly true where secretaries and files have been with the firm for a period in excess of one year. Of course, you may wish to construct an index as a backup. However, in many cases, if not most, files can be located without reference to an index.

- *THIRD,* the files are arranged so that the oldest ones will be toward the front of the file cabinet; the newest files will be located at the rear. Knowing this can often be helpful.

  The newest files in a firm normally receive, or should receive, immediate and repeated attention. This means that for a brand-new file, an attorney or a secretary can go directly to the rear of the correct Category drawer, and know that the file will be in that vicinity.

  Since the oldest files are toward the front of the drawer, they would receive first attention during a *visual review.* Drawers should be routinely examined for closed files; the arrangement would assist that effort. This brings us to our next subject.

- *FOURTH,* a closed file system is *automatically* constructed. As files are pulled from the active drawer and placed into your closed file cabinet drawers (perhaps somewhere in the basement), each would automatically fall into its appropriate categorical and chronological order. This would occur as a result of files being kept in simple numerical order in the closed file drawers. The file clerk could simply handwrite the letter "c" before the first digit of the file number on the file label, so as to mark it "closed." Closed files would be as easy to locate as active ones; the same rules would pertain. There would, therefore, be no need whatsoever for renumbering, relettering, or recreating a separate system for closed files. And for older closed files, the chronological arrangement would prove to be particularly helpful during the weeding-out processes.

- *FIFTH,* confusing problems created by clients with multiple matters would be avoided. Alphabetical filing systems tend to group, and confuse, different matters involving a single client. Under our system, there would be no such confusion.

  If, for example, a client had both a Corporate matter and a Litigation problem, there would be no confusion as to which file was which. The litigation file would always bear a Black Label and its number would have a "1" as its first digit. The Corporate matter, on the other hand, would bear a Green Label, with a "3" as *its* first digit. There would be no need for confusing designations such as "Jones pre-nuptual agreement," "Jones divorce," and "Jones bankruptcy" to distinguish the different matters.

Questions

How Does the System Mesh with Billing and Timekeeping Systems?

It will work just as other filing systems do, *but better.* Like other systems, our files have names or labels to be used for status sheets, billing sheets, calendar entries, and docket control devices. Our single, six-digit number can be written more quickly than any single name. It takes up very little space on calendars; and it can be quickly keyed into a computer. Thus, the short number specifically, quickly, efficiently, and precisely identifies its file. Since it is a number instead of a bulky verbal description, it is capable of being ordered, listed, sorted, and processed more efficiently.

Wouldn't the Separation of Files by Category Make It Difficult to Pull All of a Given Client's Files at Once?

Why would anyone want more than one or two specific client files at any given time? It's often difficult enough to handle one file properly. When *work* is to be performed, it's the *type* of work that concerns the lawyer, not the *history* of the client. Where, however, the *client* is the focus of inquiry, billing sheets, status sheets, or computerized client data can provide a better comprehensive picture than one would otherwise obtain by fumbling through pounds of paper.

What Is the Purpose of Separating the Client Files in the Same Manner as the Form Files if the Two Systems Are Different?

Both systems separate files according to their respective Categories; but that is their *only* common bond (at this point). It makes sense to keep Probate forms close to Probate files, for example. Even if the forms and client files are physically separated, the labels and first digits will provide a *visible* common-link, indicating that they are in the same Category. These markings suggest companion use.

HOW TO PREPARE LABELS AND FILE FOLDERS

All clients are not created equal; nor are their files. Some are thick; some are thin. Interior arrangements also vary. Some papers are stored in chronological order; others are ordered according to topic, and still others may be arranged according to a combination of the two. So there is no sense in attempting to use a single arrangement for all Categories of clientele; reality will not conform. However, notwithstanding their differences in arrangement, all of the Categories will make use of the same ingredients (the manila folder and expandable wallet; see Figure 2-1). But the recipes will vary.

The following internal structures are set forth for purposes of suggestion only. If you have an internal file structure that works, then continue to use it. Such use should not interfere, in any manner, with our basic numbering schemes. However, do consider our suggestions carefully.

1.
* * * *Litigation* * * *

Classically, litigation documents have always been arranged in some type of chronological order *by* date of receipt or preparation—that is, of course, until discovery proceedings (and the accompanying document demands) start. After that, it is anyone's guess as to the shape of expansion that a file will assume. Perhaps one of the most frustrating experiences (and we have all been through it) involves attempts to locate important papers or pleadings from among tons of potentially irrelevant exhibits and materials. In a nutshell, it becomes exceedingly difficult to find "the important stuff" among all of the junk.

Quite common is the ploy known as "litigation by burial." It is a very effective tool used by litigation attorneys, particularly those defending complex cases. The strategy is simple; it calls for a bombardment of the enemy attorney, with as much irrelevant paper as possible. Briefs are as thick as possible, and copies of prior exhibits and pleadings are always attached. This adds to the volume of the paper and, of course, increases the difficulty in attempting to locate any given pleading or document.

A closely associated problem involves files that become large through time, use, or complexity. In such cases, it often becomes difficult to locate the most recent, or current, matters and pleadings. An instruction to a secretary to "put the Murphy file on my desk" could result in one of two responses — a collapse of the desk, or an inquiry as to "which" portion of the file is desired.

We have all grown up under one of two systems, neither quite adequate. The first method suggested that we use *only* manila file folders. This system would keep the folders uniform in appearance, and in one location, though several separate folders might be required for a single case. But with this uniformity comes a mess. And that mess is not content to *just "bulk up" the file;* rather, it will only be satisfied when it fouls up the entire file *cabinet.* So our otherwise neat folders are crammed with exhibits, deposition transcripts, and pounds of extra copies and attachments. Removing a large file, with all of its accompanying folders, usually involves a collapse of other files (into the void), often requiring a complete rearrangement of the entire cabinet.

A second system, which attempted to correct the first and bring together the loose ends, involved the use of the expandable wallets. In particular *all* of the manila folders, exhibits, transcripts, and papers would be stuffed into one or more expandable wallets, thereby keeping the case "together." This method made it easier to assemble and retrieve an entire file, but it didn't solve the problems encountered with respect to the drawer "mess." And worse, it made finding the *most current* matters difficult, if not impossible. In the cabinet, a skinny little manila file might be hidden by a wallet, or stuffed into the wrong wallet quite accidentally, never to be heard from or seen again. Moreover, the classic mix of manila folders and expandable wallets did not provide a neat, uniform arrangement.

Proposed Solution:

I have *always* had an extremely strong preference for keeping things unified and "in one place"; but here an exception is warranted. Litigation drawers should be divided into two sets; one set of drawers contains, what I refer to as the "Current" files. The others are referred to as the "Exhibit" files. The Current File Cabinet Drawers will contain *only one* neat single manila folder for *each* case; this folder will house the most recent pleadings and materials. This means that the Current Drawers will contain only neat manila file folders cleanly lined up for quick location. These drawers will *not* contain any expandable wallets.

The Exhibit Drawers, on the other hand, will be used to keep the masses of discovered materials, previously received pleadings, and duplicated materials. They will contain *only* expandable wallets, which may in turn contain several manila folders.

All manila folders, and expandable wallets, will bear the same client file number; however, the Current Manila Folders will also pick up an additional marking as they become full. More particularly, as the first Current File becomes full, it will be given the designation "E1" (which will be noted on its label) and then transferred to the Exhibit Drawer. A new Current Folder will then be opened, and placed in the Current File Drawer, ready to receive the new pleadings. As this second current folder becomes full, it will be given the designation "E2" and then take its place behind E1 in an expandable wallet in the Exhibit Drawer. Collateral exhibits, such as discovered materials, transcripts, or duplicate materials, can be specifically labeled as such and placed in the expandable wallets. The files (expandable wallets) in the Exhibit Drawers will, of course, be placed in simple numerical order.

The Current File Folder will contain all of the most recent information and pleadings. Also, on the left inside flap should appear a very large label with an indication as to those files that are in the Exhibit Drawer along with a very brief description of the contents. I suggest the use of a bright red label, which, by its size and color, will stand out as a readily identifiable guide to the Exhibit Drawer portion of the file. Contents of prior files can be typed on the label. The addition of collateral papers or transcripts can be handwritten on the label, as those items are later added to the Exhibit Drawer wallets.

SEE EXHIBIT FILE

E1 – Complaint, Answer & Attachments

E2 – Medical Reports

E3 – Deposition Transcripts (Treating Dr.)

E4 – Psychiatric Reports

Figure 2-7

THE ADVANTAGES of this Proposed Solution (for Litigation client files) are several. *FIRST,* current litigation files can be located very quickly from among fewer drawers; the separation prevents very large files from "clogging up the cabinets.'' I am sure that we have all experienced situations where a single case would take up several drawers. Where, however, each case is limited to a single manila folder, the person seeking any given litigation file can thumb quickly past the others in a matter of seconds to arrive at the right one, without wasted time.

SECOND, when a lawyer calls for a given file, the secretary or legal assistant will automatically *know* to bring the Current File, and only that file. Nine out of ten times, he or she will want the most recent material filed or received in a given case, and *only that* material. As previously suggested, an oversized label, clearly visible on the left side of the folder, will provide a quick directory as to the contents of the more voluminous files situated in the Exhibit Drawer (see Figure 2-7). So, if one of *those* files is needed, an intelligent examination can first be conducted, before going to the Exhibit Drawer and wading through the voluminous materials. Of course, this method should be preferable to having pounds of files dumped upon the lawyer's desk, and then attempting to determine which ones are *not* needed.

THIRD, the Current File Drawers can be kept in a neat, organized manner. All of the ''junk''—extra copies, oversized copies, maps, diagrams, blueprints, etc.—can be specially labeled and placed in the expandable brown wallets situated in the Exhibit Drawer, so these types of documents will not interfere with the remainder of your chronological track of important paper as it fills the series of ''current'' files (E1, E2, etc.).

FOURTH, the system avoids clumsy combinations whereby some cases have expandable wallets, while others only have manila envelopes. You can thus avoid situations where single manila folders are lost behind expandable wallets, or worse, accidentally placed inside of expandable wallets for the wrong files. With the suggested system, the Current File Drawers will contain *only* manila folders; and the Exhibit Drawers will contain *only* expandable wallets (which include manila folders) along with transcripts, extra copies, etc. Therefore, there will never be a need to mix the clumsy, large expandable wallets with the neat, crisp manila folders in the Current Drawer.

A solution to the problems, *which does not work,* is the use of expandable wallets for *all* litigation matters. The reason this does not work is simple—In litigation, many cases may involve simple, or small, matters for which *only* a single manila envelope is needed. Therefore, many litigation matters may never need more than one manila folder. But it is impossible to know when, if ever, a file will become large or merely *settle.*

FIFTH, our method provides flexibility; for, at the start of litigation, it may be difficult to predict whether or not a file may require more than one folder. If a single manila folder is sufficient, then that folder will be found in the current file drawer. If, however, additional files are added at a later date, a large label on the current file folder can clearly indicate the existence of files in the Exhibit Drawer. Therefore, there will never be a need to mix the clumsy, large expandable wallets with the neat, crisp manila folders in the Current Drawer.

2.
 * * * *Probate* * * *

As indicated in our earlier chapters, the term ''Probate'' is used in a very generic sense. It includes not only Estate Administration, but also Estate Planning (wills and trusts). Sometimes, of course, an attorney may perform both functions on behalf of a once-living, now-deceased client. In either event, the file folders are given a red label, and the file numbers, of course, commence with the designation ''2.''

Files fitting into Major Category 2 seem to be ideally suited to using an expandable wallet (with included Manila Folders) *from* the outset. For Estate Planning, more often than not, the documents themselves are thick. Multiple copies of wills, trusts, and related instruments are commonplace. Normally, these will never fit into a single manila folder. Also, the materials to be received and drafted are quite predictable. So manila folders can be advance-labeled and stored in an expandable wallet.

While it is true that, in many respects, Estate Administration is similar to Litigation, there are some significant departures. For example, it often happens that a Litigation file may be opened and never require more than one manila folder. The case may be settled before coming to trial, as most are. However, Estate Administration is another matter. Even the simplest estate normally requires the practitioner to follow each of the procedures carefully outlined in the applicable probate code until the estate is officially ''closed.'' There is no opportunity for ''calling an end to the case'' or settling the proceedings in mid-stream.

Proposed Solution:

For Estate Planning and Probate matters, or a combination of the two, a single set of file drawers is recommended. Every file should be set up with an expandable wallet.

3.
 * * * *Corporate and Business* * * *

As a rule, Corporate or Business Matters will involve voluminous amounts of materials. Such matters are particularly suited to the expandable wallets, which are, therefore, recommended for Category 3. Minute books, in addition to other corporate documents, normally fit comfortably within the dimensional confines of those wallets. This means that every Corporate file would have at least one Expandable Wallet. Free-Standing Manila folders (i.e., folders without expandable wallets) will *not* be used.

4.
* * * *Real Estate* * * *

Real Estate matters, like lawsuits, can range widely, in terms of file size. For those firms whose Real Estate cases are limited to simple closings, or other "singular" proceedings, simple manila folders may suffice. If a "simple" matter becomes complex, an Expandable Wallet might be added. This means that you may be required to suffer that unholy alliance of wallets and folders, sharing the same file drawers. I don't like that mixture, but, on the other hand, I do not recommend a Litigation configuration (with separate Exhibit drawers), *unless* the firm does *extensive* Real Estate work. And even then, I would prefer that *all* Real Estate matters be given an Expandable Wallet for uniformity's sake.

5.
* * * *Tax* * * *

This particular category can encompass a wide variety of matters. Normally, the firm that handles Corporate, Business, and Real Estate problems, will also be involved in some type of Category 5 representation. If the firm's Tax matters involve items more complex than tax return preparation, the expandable wallets should be set up in a manner similar to Corporate files. If not, free-standing manila folders may suffice.

6.
* * * *Workers' Rights* * * *

Labor law can be a complicated matter; it seems to involve itself, in one way or another, with many of the other Major Categories. It is a complex arena, to be sure, and one that involves great numbers of overlapping federal and state statutes. Labor lawyers tend toward extensive involvement with Litigation, but other matters pertaining to Business (particularly Employee Benefit Plans) may also surface.

To make matters a bit more complicated, Labor often involves "one-shot" singular proceedings known as Labor Arbitrations. Labor lawyers engage heavily in these types of proceedings. The Arbitrations often involve single folders or files that may be provided by a company (if one represents companies) or by a labor union (for union lawyers). In many cases, labor arbitrations may be settled shortly after the attorney receives the file or "pouch" from the company or union. But even for those arbitration cases that are protracted, files rarely remain open for a period in excess of several months.

Proposed Solution:

For non-arbitration matters, files should be set up in the same manner as Litigation with *Current Files* and *Exhibit Files* separated; but this structure should apply *only* to those firms that specialize, or do extensive work in Labor Law. Others should consider setting up Expandable Wallet configurations similar to Corporate files.

Labor attorneys, who may be struggling with a method for integrating Arbitration files (provided by an outside source) into the Workers' Rights structure, might be relieved to know that there is really no need to do so. It is too simple a matter to merely set up a separate file cabinet or drawer for storing these discrete files.

7.
** * * Motor Vehicle * * **

This Category is so minor that very little discussion is warranted. The files will concern matters such as automobile or airplane licensing.

For those law firms that do an extensive amount of work involving Motor Vehicle License Restorations, this might remain a substantial Category. Some Litigation firms, that handle drunk driving cases, for example, may wish to utilize this particular Category for such matters, thereby carving out a narrow exception from Major Category 1. In such a case, a file folder structure similar to that suggested for Litigation should suffice.

8.
** * * Administrative Agency * * **

For firms that handle matters involving particular Administrative Agencies, their degree of specialization will normally be quite intense. One would not, for example, expect a general practice firm to handle matters involving the Federal Communications Commission or Securities and Exchange Commission proceedings. Moreover, any firm handling such matters will probably do so extensively. In such a case, such administrative matters will overlap and reach out into the other categories.

For example, if a firm handles a great deal of FCC matters, it will probably also handle matters pertaining to FCC litigation, FCC Corporate and Business matters, and perhaps even Real Estate. Such will probably be true of other firms handling matters involving Securities and Exchange Commission problems or FTC problems. In any event, structures similar to those set up for Litigation matters would seem most practical.

YOUR AUTOMATICALLY CREATED CLOSED FILE SYSTEM

Years ago, I worked for a law firm that provided an interesting "maze" for locating closed files. First, you would go to an alphabetical index and attempt to locate the file by referring to the name of the client; if *successful,* a card index would provide a "number-letter" combination, which would then lead to another index that had cards arranged in a different "number-letter" format, designed to distinguish a particular case or file, from other matters involving that client. If you were able to locate that card, you would be presented with yet another card that would provide yet another "number-letter" combination, which was used to cross-reference the active file number to the closed file number.

As ridiculous as that system was for the user, try to imagine how much time was wasted by the secretaries who were required to perform the otherwise simple operation of "closing a file." At one time or another, we have all seen such systems—more or less ridiculous.

Our suggested methods require *no additional work whatsoever* for the construction of a separate Closed File System. As a matter of fact, the Closed File setup is almost "self-executing." The steps are simple:

1. When a file is to be closed, a simple "c" is handwritten on the label preceding the file number.
2. The file is then physically placed into a separate closed file drawer, in simple numerical order.
3. A "c" is then placed on the index card, which is removed from the open file tub and placed into the closed file tub.
4. *Optionally,* the year in which the file is closed may also be noted on the label, although the files will not be arranged according to that date.

Wilson -v- Ford	C182,309

Figure 2-8

Notice that there are no new additional numbering systems required, and no new or additional cards to be created. The system could not be simpler. Notice also that the closed file system will fall into a very neat and logical order, precisely identical to your open file system.

By placing the closed files in their natural numeric order, they, like their active-file counterparts, will be grouped *first* according to Major Category, and next according to the year and quarter that the file was opened. This arrangement will occur automatically. Anyone who can put files in a simple numeric order can construct this system.

When searching for a closed file, the grouping by "year" (within each Category) becomes very important. For old, dead files, personnel can generally remember the approximate year that the file was opened. Of course, the "Category" will be obvious. This allows retrieval without reference to an index, in most instances.

INTEGRATION WITH YOUR OLD SYSTEM

To implement your "New" and "Closed" file systems, there is no need to bring present operations to a halt, or engage in an extensive rearrangement and relocation of existing client files. This system can be integrated gradually, partially, or all at once, for those willing to exert only minimal effort. There is, however, one critical REQUIREMENT—Files should be rearranged and divided according to the MAJOR CATEGORIES. Once put in that particular arrangement, the new system can easily be superimposed upon virtually any existing office "confusion."

Existing Numeric Systems

If your files are presently arranged according to some numeric order, those numbers should not interfere with the suggested system. As previously indicated, there will be a need to separate the files according to the MAJOR CATEGORIES; however, those files may retain their basic order, subject only to that division.

As a rule, the numbers that we are using in our System are very large numbers, far larger than the actual number of files that your firm would open. Such is a characteristic of most decimal systems. In all probability, the *new* files that you set up as part of your *new* system will therefore automatically fall into their respective places to the *rear* of the file drawer, where they belong. Therefore, the basic order and structure of the system will be maintained. In particular, once you have rearranged the files by Major Category, the chronological portion of the system should take care of itself. The suggestions pertaining to the manila folders vs. the wallet envelopes remain optional. Time will eventually weed out your old files, leaving you with your new "pure" system.

To assure that the numbers will not interfere or cause an intermingling, the number of digits to be used for the new file labels should be at least "one digit greater" than the largest number on any of your existing old files. But, as previously indicated, our use of the decimal system will probably guarantee this. Nor should you encounter any insurmountable problems if you have a strange number-letter combination. Just see to it that the new files fall to the rear of the existing ones for each separate Category.

Existing Alphabetic Systems

There is no room in today's world for alphabet-based systems. They tend to be random and illogical; files are extremely difficult to find, unless the user happens to have memorized the precise alphabetic spelling and title of each client. But fortunately, alphabetic systems are the *easiest* to convert.

Once again, the first step involves a separation of files according to the MAJOR CATEGORIES. After that is accomplished, the newly opened files can merely be placed to the rear of the existing files without any interference or confusion.

There is no need to number the existing alphabetized files; however, if one wished to do so, each of those *old* files could be assigned digits of the *prior* year. The first digit would, as always, correspond to the ''Category.'' The next two digits would represent the preceding year. For example, if your filing system were set up in 1989, the second two digits for *all* of the pre-existing files could be labeled as 88s. More specificity could be utilized, if one wished to go back through the files to determine the year that each was opened. But there is no need. You will automatically know by the number ''88'' that the file *predates* your new system.

INDEX CARD SYSTEMS

Depending upon the size of your office, it may be possible to locate most client files without an index. However, this *does not mean* that an alphabetical index tray should *not* be used. Some consider them to be ''low tech''; and I would agree to dispense with them, *but only* if a computer terminal is located at the cabinet, or on everyone's desk. If not, as each new file is set up, index cards should also be set up. The alphabet does have location assistance properties, even though it should never form the *basis* for your arrangements.

To have a truly efficient system for which a file can always be located quickly, it may be necessary to utilize more than one index *card* for a given file. For, it may often be the case that files are referred to, or thought of, by names other than those of the client. On many occasions, a single large client may have many files. In such a case, each file should have some other, or different, form of reference. The alphabetical index cards should reflect this.

COMPLEX CATEGORY OVERLAPS

The fact that a *single* client may have *several* different matters in the office at the same time, should not create any major problems, although it often does. In this section, we are going to consider some complicated problems involving matters that overlap several Categories. Consider these:

Example 4

On January 1, 1987, a new client by the name of John Smith retains your office to represent him with respect to the purchase of a large block of commercial real estate; a Brown label (Category 4) is assigned, with a first digit number of "4." A single manila folder is used, since the closing appears, at first blush, to be quite simple. But the closing is delayed.

Six months down the road, the sellers refuse to close; Mr. Smith instructs your firm to start a lawsuit for Specific Performance, to force the Sellers to sell. At this juncture, a separate Black-labeled Litigation File is opened (Category 1).

Problem—What documents go in each file?

The litigation materials *should not* be placed in the existing Real Estate file. On the contrary, the Litigation material should be placed in the litigation folder to receive the attention and daily review that litigation requires.

The next problem involves the selection of materials that should be shifted from the Real Estate File to the Litigation File. One solution may involve merely removing the Real Estate File from the real estate drawer, opening up a Litigation exhibit file, and placing it in there. But, you shouldn't be hasty to merge the two. The litigation may eventually settle and result in a closing after all.

A better solution, therefore, would be to remove (or preferably photocopy) *just those* "one or two" documents that would pertain directly to the Litigation. For example, the preliminary closing statements, title reports, and appraisals would *not* be of immediate concern to the litigants. The offer to purchase *would* be, and that document could merely be photocopied, so that the Real Estate file remains intact.

> *NOTE!* Duplicating documents unnecessarily is wasteful and inefficient. Only primary crossover documents should be duplicated. Think of the two files as two intersecting lines; they only have a *single* point in common. Keep the duplication to an absolute minimum, a "single point," if possible.

A large label, or indicator, on the left flap of the current Litigation File Folder, could be used to indicate the corresponding number of the Real Estate file and the information that it contains. Likewise, a corresponding label can be placed in the Real Estate file, as a cross-reference to the Litigation folder.

For Closing Papers See 185,332

Figure 2-9

It is to be noted, that, as each Litigation manila folder becomes full, and takes its place in the exhibit drawer, the newer manila file would have a label on the left side indicating the "newly increased" contents of the exhibit drawer. It is important to note that this label would be cumulative in nature; and, as each new file went into the exhibit drawer, the exhibit labels would accumulate and indicate the contents of each. Cross-references to other Categories can also be included on those labels.

Consider a second example. This particular one, involves the most graphic illustration of overlap, and is one of the most common.

Example 5

A wrongful death action comes into the office. From the outset, two proceedings are going to be needed, an Estate Administrative proceeding and, of course, a lawsuit against some negligent defendant. Mixing the two matters together in a single client file can result in a disastrous mess, which you may have already experienced. If ever there were an argument for dividing separate matters into two separate files, this is it.

The administration of the estate involves its own *separate* chronology of proceedings; many of the stages are totally unrelated to the wrongful death litigation. Likewise, the wrongful death lawsuit involves proceedings that are of only passing concern to the estate. There is overlap, to be sure; however, more than mere convenience dictates that the matters be set up in two separate files.

Those documents or pleadings that are ''common to both'' should be duplicated, with one copy placed in *each* file. Such documents should be very few in number, the most common of which would be the settlement agreement, if any, which normally requires the approval of the probate court.

Failure to keep the matters separate will *assure* that at least one serious foulup or missed deadline will occur in each proceeding. You wouldn't mix two separate litigation files together; mixing a Wrongful Death action and an Estate Administration matter is almost as dangerous.

THE CARE AND HANDLING OF CLIENT FILES

It seems that everyone has her or his own method of madness when it comes to handling client files. Some are ''neat freaks''; others cannot possibly function unless perpetually buried under a pile of rubble. Those who fall into the latter category would probably resent a lengthy ''preach'' urging change. There are, nevertheless, a few brief points that must be mentioned as a prelude to some simple, but very important rules.

First, the quantity of lawyer malpractice cases has been skyrocketing; but failure to ''know the law'' accounts for less than 10% of all claims. The overwhelming majority of problems are due to clerical or ministerial errors.

Second, frustrations that are attributable to time spent on wasteful ''search and duplication'' missions, often cause us to delay and forget important matters. We will put a case aside or have our train of thought irreparably interrupted because we simply *can't find something*. And we don't ever seem to appreciate the resulting vast amount of wasted effort. For it is difficult to recognize just how much time is wasted until the "waste" has ceased.

Third, like the other systems presented in this book, the simple rules set forth hereunder, are logic based, and, if followed, will surely cut down significantly on the above problems. If you cannot cope with *all* of the rules, there is, however, no cause for alarm. As with our other methods, partial compliance helps.

Rule 1
Set Up File Immediately

During the initial stages of the attorney-client representation, it is not the "big case" or the "major matter" that is likely to run afoul of this rule. Rather, it is the marginal case, or the one that is being handled for someone's brother-in-law, without pay. It is this type of file for which delays cause problems. So, a simple rule-of-thumb suggests that once *any* pleadings, papers, or documents are generated or received, a file should be set up *immediately;* if not, you might rest assured that something important to someone will be lost or forgotten.

Rule 2
Avoid Taking Originals

If you do not take possession of original documents, then you cannot properly be accused of losing them. Make copies; *let the client keep the originals*, unless there is some issue with respect to authenticity. The originals can be obtained at a later date; and even if the client loses them, you will have copies. It is true that "The Best Evidence Rule" requires *original* documents for introduction into evidence during trial. However, I have yet to see that rule restrict the admissibility of a photocopy into evidence. Most courts have very liberal rules permitting such admissions.

For example, Rule 1003 of the Federal Rules of Evidence provides that: "a duplicate is admissible to the same extent as an original unless (1) a genuine question is raised as to the authenticity of the original or (2) under the circumstances it would be unfair to admit the duplicate in lieu of the original."

Rule 3
Pull File with Mail

Mail and hand-delivered envelopes should be opened by the secretarial staff; attorneys should keep "hands off." The *current* file should be pulled immediately by the secretary; the new papers should be placed loosely *inside* the folder, not on top. The file should then be placed on the desk of the responsible attorney.

The loose papers should signal the responsible attorney that they have yet to be examined and processed. An important corollary suggests that all papers should be clipped into the file, *after* they have been processed or examined by an attorney. If these procedures are followed, one will always know whether or not the papers have been examined. This method should also avoid lost loose papers, if the next rule is followed.

Rule 4
Attorneys Should Be Encouraged to Examine Papers and Respond Simultaneously

To be able to process all of your papers *immediately* upon receipt would be a nice goal to attain, particularly for litigation firms. However, this is not always possible. A very dangerous tendency of litigation lawyers is to examine incoming mail, groan a bit, and then put off the response, until some court-imposed or statutory deadline approaches. This means that the lawyer has to "re-think" the thoughts originally sparked by the initial review. The strategic force of those strong first reactions may be lost forever.

Rule 5
Do Not Tolerate Loose Papers Scattered Around the Office

More often than not, *loose* papers, outside of files, translate into *lost* papers. Exhibits should be neatly positioned in their appropriate exhibit folders. Papers, pleadings, and other documents should be clipped into the Current File. Newly received papers should be placed inside their appropriate files, per Rule 3.

I recognize that this is one of the most difficult rules to follow, and it is one of those habits that takes time to develop. It is worth the effort, however, when you consider that one of the principal causes for lost pleadings or documents is "*misfiling.*" Consider that it is nearly impossible for a document to get placed into a wrong file, if there are no loose papers or multiple files stacked upon the desks, tables, or floors of the office.

Rule 6
Keep the Client Files in the Client File Drawers Whenever Possible

Closely associated with the preceding rule, this one suggests that office personnel should work on as few files at a time as is practical. Personally, I prefer to work on one file at a time. As long as there is only one file on my desk at a given time, it will not be possible for its papers to get placed into the wrong file, nor are they likely to be lost.

Violations of this rule cover a wide range. I have known attorneys who keep files at home, in the trunks of cars, in briefcases, and lockers. Attorneys who engage in such conduct, can be absolutely assured of wasting as much time as possible searching for files and information. There is much efficiency and time savings to be gained by merely *knowing* that all files (except those very few that are in process) are in the file cabinet, where they belong.

Rule 7
Keep a Complete Paper Track with the Client

Failure to obtain written client consents is a significant cause of malpractice litigation. Failure to keep clients posted is also a major cause of attorney-client troubles. There is no need for either problem; clients should *always* be informed as to what their law firm is doing for them. Other than the simple, and relatively inexpensive, letters that the firm should periodically send to them, clients generally have no idea about the time, effort, or preparation that is being performed on their behalf. Keeping the client informed should *not* take a backseat to your other procedures. *All* documents prepared or filed on behalf of a client should be "copied to that client."

Rule 8
Keep Neat

Neatness helps, and helps greatly. We deal with many complex matters on a regular, continuous, and often stressful basis. Keeping neat makes the work less hectic and far more efficient.

3

Instant Form Location with the Direct Reference System

Some Unprecedented Benefits
An Index-Free System
Litigation (Category 1.) As a Base Pattern
Alphabetical Indexes
Recapping Important Structural Points
Creating Identifiers
Office Administration Forms (Category 0.)
Developing the Major Categories

1. Litigation
2. Probate
3. Corporate and Business
4. Real Estate
5. Tax
6. Workers' Rights
7. Motor Vehicle
8. Administrative Agency
9. Et al.

SOME UNPRECEDENTED BENEFITS

The Direct Reference Form System is the first of its kind; it is truly unique. Unlike conventional arrangements, it allows an attorney, paralegal, or secretary to rapidly locate any one of thousands of forms, *without* knowing the name of the form and *without reference to any index*. Alphabetization, and the classic inexactitudes that accompany it, can ''almost'' be rendered obsolete.

The System can be used with or without a computer; either way, since the methods presented slash retrieval time, your bank of forms and stored ''text'' can be expanded well beyond current conventional use. The System provides the requisite basics and details for such expansion. Correspondingly, the quality of forms can be greatly augmented since the increased numbers allow for greater variation, flexibility, and ''tailoring,'' not to mention enhanced ease in updating and revising.

A person wishing to locate any particular form, need only know the use or *purpose* of the form—the System takes over from there. The forms are arranged in ''logical groupings,'' by function, instead of by alphabetization, thereby eliminating the ambiguities that are prevalent in all alphabetical systems. Related forms are located close to one another for inspection and companion use.

For example, assume that you wanted to commence garnishment proceedings. With a typical alphabetical filing system, the ***A***ffidavit for the Writ of Garnishment and the ***W***rit itself would be separated by 21 letters of the alphabet; so even though the two forms are *always* used in tandem, they would be at opposite ends of the filing system. This makes no sense. Moreover, after mentally debating the whereabouts of the form (Is it under ''A'' or ''W''?), you would probably look under the letter ''G'' and not find *either* form.

Your next step might involve reference to a form file index, which would either be arranged similarly in alphabetical order, or some other haphazard grouping. An index might then, perhaps, assign numbers which would also have to be located within the filing system. In any event, if you could not remember the *exact title* of the form, it might *never* be found either in the index or in the file drawer.

Let's assume that you finally found your fill-in-the-blank garnishment forms, and then wanted to refer to a completed set of garnishment pleadings (as a sample); you would very likely encounter yet another entirely different procedure. Most often, you would resort to the apex of inefficiency—the random search through old client files.

The solutions that we propose involve a topical grouping system that avoids all of the problems encountered in our example. Under the System, the Writ and the Affidavit of Garnishment would be side by side; and moreover, all related checklists, completed forms, samples, briefs, and other relevant documents concerning garnishments would be grouped together. The System thus cuts across the traditional lines of separation between standard printed forms, constructed forms, interview sheets, checklists, prototype pleadings, and sample pleadings. All of these different law office aids, and more, are brought together by topic, under "one roof," thereby keeping research and finger-walking time to an absolute minimum. In essence, the System causes the forms to be grouped in accordance with the manner in which a lawyer, paralegal, or secretary should think, and *not* by the random manner in which the title of the form is alphabetized.

By constructing a single Master Book for all Forms (Chapter 5), your System will *also* cut across equipment barriers. For example, your pre-printed garnishment forms will, of course, remain in your file cabinet along with all of your other LEVEL I forms (see Chapter 1 for "LEVEL" definitions). A brief, with case law required to "defend" the garnishment from attack, may be stored on your computer (LEVEL III). Nevertheless, *all* entries in the Master Book that pertain, in any way, to garnishments, will be located *together* even though your computer and file cabinets may be "floors apart."

The time that you spend learning the System, will also provide some unique fringe benefits. Since the System is ordered according to law's "natural structure," the user will automatically learn how each document fits into the overall scheme of things. Moreover, it should provide some insight into the complex inner workings of the document production process. The system also has many other advantages that will become apparent as we proceed.

AN INDEX-FREE SYSTEM

Each form is assigned a six-digit number, with a traditional comma between the third and fourth digits. Six-digit numbers, in general, seem to be easy to vocalize, and thus relatively easy to remember. The first digit from the left denotes one of the Nine Major Law Practice Categories, first mentioned in Chapter 1. The second digit denotes an element of the Major Group that comprises the Category. The third digit denotes an element of a Subgroup of the Major Group, etc.

This may sound complicated; it really isn't. If you are patient enough to follow through our examples, the simplicity and practicality of the system will become apparent. Above all, do not let the length of this Chapter scare you. It is a rare person indeed who will need to know the detailed substructures of more than a few Major Categories.

The most important division involves the Nine Major Categories encompassed by the first digit. "All of Law" is divided first according to these Categories. Because of their importance, I want to list the elements again:

CATEGORIES

1. Litigation (Black)
2. Probate (Red)
3. Corporate and Business (Green)
4. Real Estate (Brown)
5. Tax (Yellow)
6. Workers' Rights (Blue)
7. Motor Vehicle (Purple)
8. Administrative (Orange)
9. Other (Gold)

Figure 3-1

LITIGATION (CATEGORY 1.) AS A BASE PATTERN

First Digit

Because of the nature of Litigation and the fact that it often overlaps other office matters, it is positioned as the *First* Major Category. This means that all of the *Litigation* forms that we are about to consider, will have numbers that start with ''1'' as the left-most digit.

Ordinarily, I do not recommend jumping ahead. But if you want to get some idea of where all of this is headed, you might take a look at Figures 3-2 and 3-3; but then come back. We have to discuss the remaining digits of our form number.

Second Digit

The second digit of our six-digit number will correspond to an element in the Litigation hierarchy (pecking order of elements). As with our eight other Major Categories, for Litigation there exists a natural, ''*memorable*'' pecking order. Litigation's hierarchy happens to be the Federal-State Court system. The Litigation Category elements best conform to this Country's Court Structure; no matter which state you work in, the structure is basically the same.

Per the Supremacy Clause (Art. VI, U.S. Constitution), we will list the *Federal* Courts first. They form the top five elements on our list, with the U.S. Supreme Court leading the pack. Next, it is safe to assume that every state has a single ''highest'' court (in position six), followed by some intervening court of appeals (position seven). In the next position (eighth) is a hot item commonly referred to as the State Court of Original or "General" Jurisdiction. Normally, it is not limited as to dollar amount or subject matter. The name of this Court may vary from state to state, but its ranking (Number eight) is always the same. It is a very important slot because *all* state court forms that are *not* tied to any particular court (i.e., Notice of Hearing, Notice of Deposition, Motion to Strike a Vague Pleading) are, by convention, put into the position represented by this court. Next follow the inferior Village, Municipal, and Local Courts, to bring up the rear (position nine).

I would be willing to bet that those of you with some experience in Litigation, are probably *already* quite familiar with this "pecking order" and could memorize the list of nine courts, in order, in a matter of minutes. But as we shall see, *memorization* is *not* as important as basic familiarity:

1. United States Supreme Court
2. U.S. Circuit Court of Appeals
3. Federal District Court
4. Federal Court of Claims
5. Tax Court
6. California Supreme Court*
7. California Court of Appeals
8. California Superior Court
9. California Municipal Court
0. Other

The California Court system has been selected to serve as our example; for like the other state judicial systems, it possesses a court of general jurisdiction (Superior Court), two appellate courts, and one or more courts of inferior

---

*Consider Michigan's typical state court configuration:

6. Michigan Supreme Court
7. Michigan Court of Appeals
8. Michigan Circuit Court
9. Michigan District Court

or New York's *not-so-typical* arrangement:

6. New York Court of Appeals
7. New York Supreme Court, Appellate Division
8. New York Supreme Court (Civil Part, Criminal Part, Etc.)
9. New York Supreme Court (Inferior Parts)

jurisdiction. It should also be noted (with respect to Group three) that Federal District Court includes Bankruptcy Court.

Observe that an alphabetical system would not distinguish between Michigan's State District Court and its Federal District Court. Both use "District Court" pleadings; and while those pleadings may be vastly different, their titles are the same. As a result, I have seen unabashed secretaries use Michigan District Court Summons' for Federal Cases. Our System would hardly permit such an error, because forms are arranged by use—not by title.

Third Digit

The Subgrouping, represented by the third digit, designates the *stage* of the proceeding for the litigation process; it *also* has a natural order (chronological in nature), which can best be represented as follows (the parenthesized forms are common examples of each stage):

1. Commencement (Complaint, Summons)
2. Response (Answer, Affirmative Defenses)
3. Discovery (Interrogatories, Notice of Deposition)
4. Pre-Trial (Motion in Limine, Motion to Strike Jury)
5. Trial (Motion for Mistrial, Pattern Jury Charges)
6. Judgment (Judgment, Order of Dismissal)
7. Execution (Execution, Garnishment)
8. Appeal (Claim of Appeal, Notice of Appeal)
9. Substantive Law (Sample Briefs, Stored Text)

The nine elements are best suited to the Courts of Original Jurisdiction (Federal District Court, California Superior Court, etc.); however, for simplicity, they should be left intact and used in conjunction with each of the nine Courts. For example, the fact that there may not be any pre-trials conducted in the California Supreme Court, creates no major problems for our arrangement; it just means that there will be no forms with the numerical structure "164,XXX" (refer to chart in Figure 3-3).

Before we go into more detail, let's take a moment to consider how much can be accomplished by using nothing more than the few structures already discussed. If, for example, you were to divide all of your Litigation forms up and arrange them, *first* according to Major Category, you will have "segregated out" all of the other unrelated matters (Wills, Corporate Minutes, etc.). Next, by grouping the forms according to Court, and then subgrouping them by "stage of proceeding" (as we have), one should be able to find virtually any Litigation form or get "darn close." And, remember, when thumbing through forms, "*close counts*"; for you will *want* to see and examine the proximate forms for companion or alternate use. Here are some additional examples:

Example 1

Consider the prior discussions about the aggravating search for garnishment forms; only this time pretend that you must find them *without* your index and *without* your alphabet. In their place is the Direct Reference System that you have created. You might not be conversant with all nine of the Major Categories, but you would certainly be familiar with the subgroups pertaining to *your* particular field (i.e., Litigation). Of course, you would know the Court in which you intended to file the garnishment (8. California Superior Court), and it is hoped that you will know whether or not the garnishment is being filed at the "commencement" of the lawsuit or after judgment (Execution Stage—7); assume the latter. Having no more facts at your fingertips than those indicated, you will know that the form is circa 187,000:

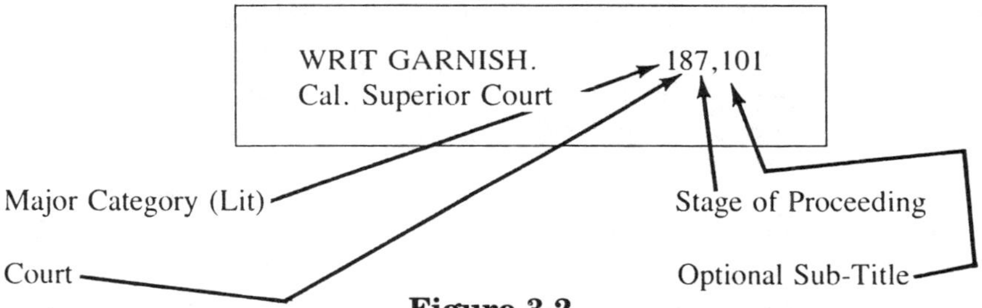

Figure 3-2

The fourth digit could be used, as indicated, to denote a further Division, that would pertain only to the execution phase of the proceeding. An example of such a denotation could look like this:

1. Garnishment Forms
2. Execution Forms
3. Post-Judgment Debtor Proceedings

To be consistent, if the Writ of Garnishment were given the designation 187,101, then the Affidavit in Support of the Writ of Garnishment might be given the number 187,102, etc. Sample garnishments or "filled in" forms pertaining to garnishments should be circa 187,105, or perhaps 187,110 (to "free up" the last digit).

Example 2

Assume that you wish to commence litigation in Federal District Court. You would have a hunch that a Summons might be required; and, although you might not know the exact title of the document (i.e. District Court Summons, Federal Court Summons, Summons, etc.), you would certainly know that you are dealing with a Court of General Federal Jurisdiction (group element three). Thus, quickly you would be led to those forms circa 131,000. To find the documents that would accompany the filing of your suit, you need only glance at the adjacent form file labels to see such ''accompanying'' titles as a ''Marshall's Service form,'' ''Federal Court Face Sheet,'' and other documents that may be required by local court rules. The fact that the forms are located *close together* and grouped according to ''purpose,'' should jog your memory as to what is necessary for the particular procedure under consideration.

It is therefore important, once again, to emphasize the fact that the person wishing to find the form *does not* have to know the exact form number; the person need only be ''close.'' It takes but a few seconds to flip through folders that are ''close together.'' The finger flipping will always be kept to a minimum because of the ''topical grouping'' structure. At the outset, perhaps as many as 90% of the firm's irrelevant forms will be eliminated totally from consideration, by merely glancing at the colors of the labels.

The following charted example (Figure 3-3) should present a clearer picture of how the numbering system works, but first *a word of warning—*

> WHAT YOU ARE ABOUT TO SEE LOOKS COMPLICATED; BUT REMEMBER THAT IT IS *NOT NECESSARY* TO CARRY THE SYSTEM ALL THE WAY TO THE FOURTH DIGIT (AS THE CHART DOES); TWO OR THREE DIGITS WILL OFTEN DO THE JOB—*CLOSE COUNTS!*

Additional divisions for the Litigation Category later in this chapter and *hundreds* of additional examples covering all of the Categories are provided in Appendix A. Shortly we will provide structures and examples for the remaining Major Categories.

At this point however, I want to draw your attention to the structure of the form number. Notice how it is composed.

By following this pattern, each form will be assigned its own *special identifying number*. And that number will, in turn, provide the characteristics of the form that it represents. Then, the forms need only be placed in simple numerical order.

ALPHABETICAL INDEXES

It is not absolutely essential that *every* user learn the system; diehard alphabetizers can peacefully co-exist. Once the forms are organized in the

Numbering Structure for Litigation

INTERROGS.BREACH/CONTRACT 183,310
Cal. Superior Court

MAJOR CATEGORY

1. *Litigation*
2. Probate
3. Corporate and Business
4. Real Estate
5. Tax
6. Labor
7. Motor Vehicle
8. Administrative
9. Other

LITIGATION GROUP (G)

1. U.S. Supreme Court
2. U.S. Cir. Ct. of App.
3. Federal District Court
4. Fed. Court of Claims
5. Tax Court
6. Cal. Supreme Court
7. Cal. Court of Appeals
8. *Cal. Superior Court*
9. Cal. Municipal Court
0. Other

Litigation Subgroup (S)

1. Commencement
2. Response
3. *Discovery*
4. Pre-Trial
5. Trial
6. Judgment
7. Execution
8. Appeal
9. Substantive Law

Optional
Further Division (D)

1. Interrog Face Sheets
2. Interrog (general)
3. *Interrog (contract)*
4. Interrog (tort)
5. Interrog (prod. liab.)
6. Deposition Notices
7. Motion to Compel
8. Recent Decisions

Figure 3-3

required fashion, an alphabetical index can be prepared as a backup location device. Moreover, several different indexes could be prepared and tailored to individual preference.

One such index could contain a breakdown corresponding to the Nine Major Categories with alphabetical sublistings; another could consist of a simple numerical list (which, of course, would *per se* fall into the topical patterns). It's your choice. The indexes would *only* serve as fail-safe devices, so as to guarantee that everyone should be able to locate any form within the System.

It is important to emphasize that, by using the number System, any person should be able to come very close to the required form, within a matter of

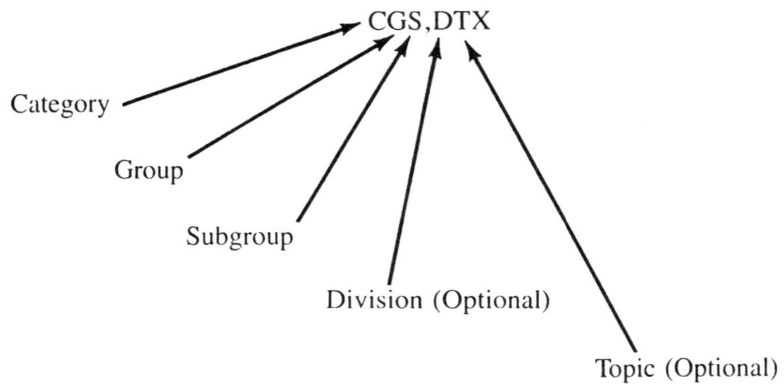

Figure 3-4

seconds. Adjacent forms could serve as location aides and reminders with respect to other related proceedings, forms, and sample documents.

The Master Form Book that we are going to create shortly (Chapter 5) will contain a Master Index page (or pages) for each Major Category, which will, in turn, provide lists of *all* drafting aids; related forms can be seen at a glance. Thus, an alphabetical index *should not* be necessary.

RECAPPING IMPORTANT STRUCTURAL POINTS

Notice that forms related by *subject matter* will be physically close to one another. Groupings by name, title, or appearance do *not* occur. This makes sense; if, for example, you have located, and intend to use, printed fill-in-the-blank Execution forms, which would you rather see as the *next* form in the drawer—a *prototype* execution form (all filled-in) or other *blank forms* unrelated to executions? In summary, there is simply no need to keep all of your *blank* forms together. You will never want to see *all* of your firm's blank forms at one time. But you *may* very well want to see all of the Execution forms at once.

The arrangement also makes it easy to eyeball closely positioned forms for possible alternative use. In a supermarket, for example, you would never find products grouped according to the alphabetical order of the manufacturer's name. All of the milk is normally positioned in one place, *close* to the cream. This trait of proximity is perhaps the most important characteristic of a logic-based system. It mirrors the proposition that logically related items should be proximately positioned. Such is the predicate for our System. Consider a recap of some other beneficial characteristics:

- A simple number is assigned to each form;
- The form's number may be proximately determined without reference to any index;

- Forms may be located *without* knowing their names;
- Forms that are *used together,* or are otherwise related, are *close together;*
- The System works for *all* offices, regardless of size, specialty, equipment, or software;
- Numbers can quickly be assigned to forms by using the charts and indexes of your Master Form Book (Chapter 5);
- The single Master Book will tell you, at a glance, about every form in your office—what it is, where it is, and what physical shape it assumes;
- The System will bring all of your forms and drafting aids together under "one roof," even though some may be in the file cabinet, and others may be on various computer discs, or even in your closed client file drawer (see Chapter 5 for details);
- The user will gain insight into the structure of his or her area of practice;
- Errors involving form selection will be reduced;
- The time required to search for forms will be cut;
- Far more forms can be created and used efficiently, because numerical arrangements allow storage for far more elements without causing alphabetical confusion.

CREATING IDENTIFIERS

When you create your forms, as previously indicated, you must assign an official File Number for the label of the folder that will house each form (per Figure 3-3). This number will become a *file name* for the form if and when it is ever stored "on computer" (per Chapter 4). However, even though our System allows retrieval without knowing the form's name or title, you will, nevertheless, want to assign an Identifier (name), which will serve an important dual purpose.

First, the Identifier will allow you to provide verbal descriptions (though abbreviated) to be assembled and used for the index of your Master Book (Chapter 5), so that you will be able to see your forms listed, at a glance. Next, the same Identifier can be typed on the label of the folder that will house a copy of the form (in your file cabinet).

To assist in assigning an Identifier, consider this rule:

To create Identifiers, always start with a noun, never an adjective. (Unless the adjective happens to be so integrated with the noun that separation would result in two ambiguous concepts; such as—"closing statement.") Then assign adjectives, in order of declining generality; i.e., go from the general to the specific.

Good Examples	*Bad Examples*
Complaint. Libel. Media	Libel Complaint against Media
Interrog.Prod Liab. Plaint.	Plaintiff's Interrogs. Prod. Liability
Will.Simple.Male Sing.	Simple Single Male Will
Closing Statement. Buyer.C-21	Buyers Closing Statement for Century 21
Bank.Proof of Claim	Proof of Claim—Bankruptcy
Brief.Fed.Juris D. Div.	Brief—Requirements for Diversity Jurisdiction
Copyright.Tx	Form TX—Copyrights.

Using the ''Good Examples'' and Rule above, will result in a logical grouping, and a *better* index, *even* if you decide to Alphabetize. A Century 21 Closing Statement, for example, would *not* be separated from a Lawyer's Title Company Statement by nine letters of the alphabet under the above rules. And it is far more likely that, for a given closing, you would greatly prefer to peruse related closing statements than unrelated forms that happen to start with the same letters.

OFFICE ADMINISTRATION FORMS (CATEGORY 0.)

For those ''general office forms'' that seem to cut across all of our established Categories, the first digit should be designated ''0.'' Such forms would include: Time Sheets, Retainer Agreements, Billing Sheets, and forms relating to intra-office matters. The ''0'' designation will *automatically* cause these forms to appear *first* in the file cabinet drawer, which makes sense since they are most commonly used. I suggest a pure white label for the file folders that will house these often-used forms.

DEVELOPING THE MAJOR CATEGORIES

Numbering systems for all of the remaining major groupings will be constructed in the same manner as Litigation. First, a hierarchy or natural order will be created that encompasses *all* of the forms for the subject Category. Second, for each element of *this* ''natural order,'' a subgroup is developed. Thereafter (beyond the third digit) substructuring is optional.

Once the structure for Litigation is soundly grasped, the other Major Categories should not be difficult to fathom. And, to better ''grasp'' Litigation before moving on, we will consider a few of its most difficult problems. Thereafter, as each Category is considered, we will first present some comments, followed by that Category's own ''NUMBERING STRUCTURE'' chart, and then some examples. Whenever assigning numbers, this chart should be kept handy.

Because Litigation has already been developed, we will go right to its chart (Figure 3-5). You may notice, that it is essentially the same as Figure 3-3, but with some Divisions (fourth digit items) added:

1.
* * * Litigation * * *

Most number assignments should be easy to determine by referring to the Chart (Figure 3-5). But some numbers may not be quite so obvious; a little thought might be required for peculiar cases. For example, assume that you wish to locate a set of sample or form Interrogatories for a Products Liability Case. Applying what you know about Subject Matter Jurisdiction, you may remember that such a case can be tried in a Federal District Court, a State Court of general jurisdiction, or a State Court of inferior jurisdiction. Which do you choose? The rule is simple: If the case arises only under Federal Law, choose Group Element 3 (Federal District Court); if it does not, then apply the Rule of *Erie v. Thompkins**, and look to the State Court system. Products Liability Cases do *not* arise under Federal Law; so you must select a State Court.

Next, you know that several State Courts may share jurisdiction over a Products Liability Case. Or maybe you're just not sure; so once again apply a simple rule: *Choose the Court of General Jurisdiction* (Court Number 8) regardless of the amount in controversy. The form number would, therefore, be circa 183,510 (see also Element 4, of Optional Division, Figure 3-3). In most cases, if in doubt, a *lawyer should be able to direct you to the appropriate Court.*

Example 3

Another area where thinking might be required concerns Appeals. Forms circa 188,000 would pertain *only* to those appeal forms to be filed in the Superior Court (for example, a Motion to Stay Proceedings Pending Appeal to The Court of Appeals). The Claim of Appeal would normally be the first document filed in the State Court of Appeals. Even though a copy of it might

---

* The U.S. Supreme Court held that in Federal Courts, for cases that are based upon Diversity of Citizenship (or otherwise do *not* arise under some Federal Statute or Law), the substantive law of the State applies.

NUMBERING STRUCTURE

DIGIT STRUCTURE: 1GS,DXX

MAJOR CATEGORY

1. Litigation
2. Probate
3. Corporate & Business
4. Real Estate
5. Tax
6. Labor
7. Motor Vehicle
8. Administrative
9. Other

LITIGATION GROUP (G)

1. U.S. Supreme Court
2. U.S. Cir. Court of App.
3. Federal District Court
4. Federal Court of Claims
5. Tax Court
6. Cal. Supreme Court
7. Cal. Court of Appeals
8. Cal. Superior Court
9. Cal. Municipal Court
0. Other

LITIGATION SUBGROUP (S)

1. Commencement
2. Response
3. Discovery
4. Pre-Trial
5. Trial
6. Judgment
7. Execution
8. Appeal
9. Substantive Law

DISCOVERY DIVISION (D)

1. Interrog Face Sheets
2. Interrog (general)
3. Interrog (contract)
4. Interrog (tort)
5. Interrog (prod. liab.)
6. Deposition Notices
7. Motion to Compel
8. Recent Decisions

TRIAL DIVISION (D)

1. Opening Statements
2. Exhibit Entry
3. Evidence
4. Mid-trial Amendments
5. Mid-trial Motions
6. Closing Statement
7. Jury Charges
8. Other

SUBSTANTIVE LAW DIVISION (D)

1. Criminal
2. Domestic Relations
3. Contracts
4. Torts
5. Personal Property
6. Statutes
7. Constitutions
8. Other

Figure 3-5

be served upon the Superior Court, the forms concerning the actual Claim of Appeal would be found circa 171,001. (See Figure 3-6.)

Example 4

Figure 3-7 is a form containing citations of law, text, or actual Jury Charges that might be required during trial.

Claim.Appeal.Right 171,010

MAJOR CATEGORY

1. *Litigation*
2. Probate
3. Corporate & Business
4. Real Estate
5. Tax
6. Labor
7. Motor Vehicle
8. Administrative
9. Other

LITIGATION GROUP (G)

1. U.S. Supreme Court
2. U.S. Cir. Court of App.
3. Federal District Court
4. Federal Court of Claims
5. Tax Court
6. Cal. Supreme Court
7. *Cal. Court of Appeals*
8. Cal. Superior Court
9. Cal. Municipal Court
0. Other

LITIGATION SUBGROUP (S)

1. *Commencement*
2. Response
3. Discovery
4. Pre-Trial
5. Trial
6. Judgment
7. Execution
8. Appeal
9. Substantive Law

Figure 3-6

Example 5

Substantive law is the last slot of the Litigation Subgroup. It is designed to store frequently used briefs and citations. As opposed to ''procedural'' text, ''substantive'' law involves cases that decide the final outcome of a given type of Litigation. For example, case law to support the dismissal of a case for failure to answer Interrogatories, would be *procedural* (*not* substantive) and, therefore, fall into The Discovery Subgroup (Subgroup 3). But a sample brief indicating that ''Breach of Promise to Marry'' no longer exists as a cause of action, would be *Substantive.* Before leaving Litigation, consider one more substantive brief label as provided by Figure 3-8.

2.
* * * Probate * * *

For System purposes, the term ''Probate'' is much broader than the legal definition implies. Notice that the natural order of elements of the Probate

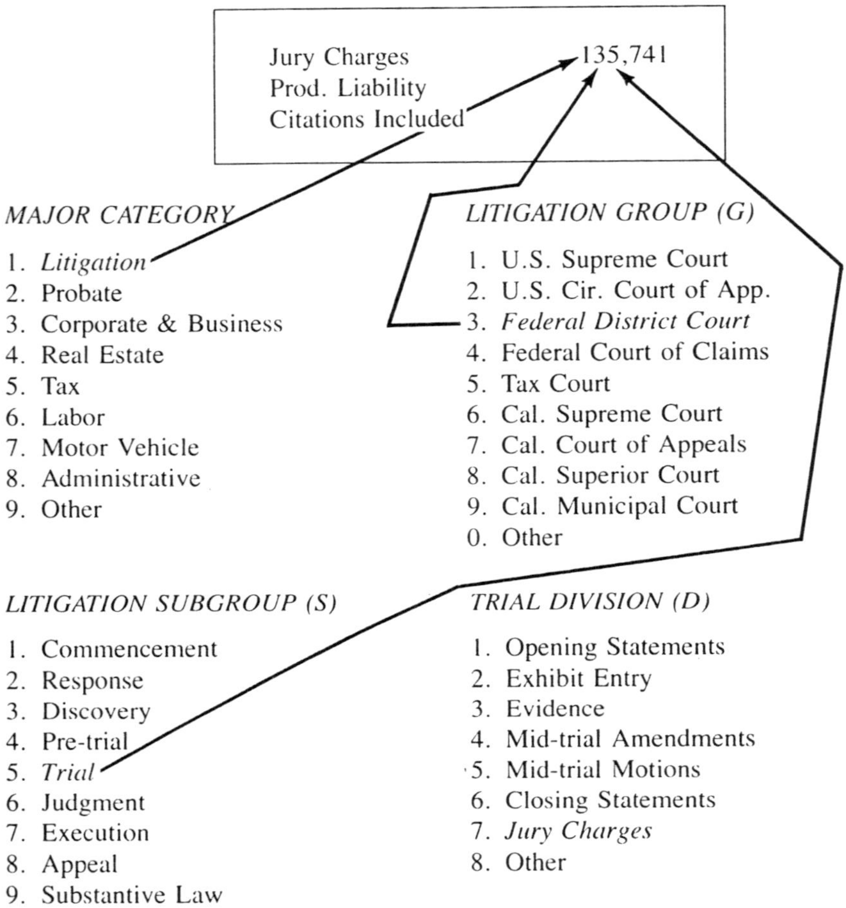

Figure 3-7

Group (Figure 3-9) corresponds to a person's corporeal or "bodily" status. Group 1 covers Inter-Vivos (living) Transfers; Group 2 provides a framework for Testamentary Instruments. And Groups 3 through 7, all pertain to Surrogate (substitute) Administration.

This particular Category provides an excellent vehicle for distributing forms among all four Levels of Technology. Pre-printed petitions, Notices of Hearing, Inventories, and other similar forms are heavily relied upon by Probate and Surrogate courts. These forms (Level I) will, therefore, be used frequently for Items 3–7 of the Probate Groups. However, for Estate Planning forms, particularly Wills and Trusts, levels II and III are well-suited, since heavy use can be made of standardized text. At our Fourth Level, an excellent opportunity is provided to allow the computer to

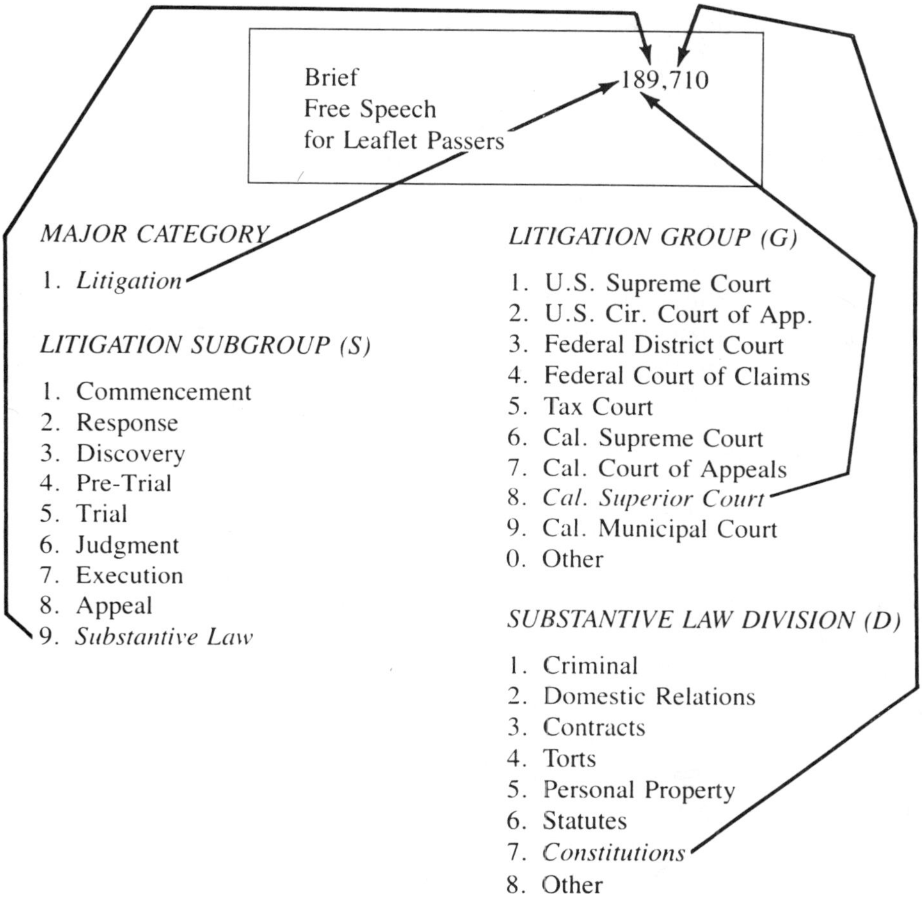

Figure 3-8

prepare Wills and Trusts due to the highly structured language often contained in those writings.

Perhaps more so than any group of documents, testamentary instruments are highly segmented and standardized. In other words, Wills and Trusts have certain specific provisions that are common from state to state; many phrases are universally recognized and utilized. For example, we would expect *every* Will to have a clause or two pertaining to Appointments (actually "Nominations of Fiduciaries"), and a lengthy "Powers clause," followed by some Specific, Demonstrative, or Residuary bequests. At the tail end would come the usual Signature and Attestation clauses. Trusts likewise operate according to some fairly well-defined structures, not identical to Wills but similar.

The arrangements for Wills and Trusts are quite uniform and do not involve as much creativity or originality as the instruments pertaining to the other Major Categories. This means that common clauses are similar. It is also notable that most of the clauses contained in a given instrument follow a predictable format and order, as indicated above.

Because of their predictable structures, testamentary instruments fit very well into our logic-based structure. As a matter of fact, not only is it easy to classify the instruments, but we can *also assign specific recognizable numbers to each of the clauses contained within those instruments.* This will later allow us to piece together clauses, by referring only to the assigned numbers, thereby creating entire instruments, in seconds. You will find that it is much easier to "piece together" the parts of a puzzle than it is to *create* one from scratch.

The first digit for any form falling within this Major Category (Probate), will of course be a "2." The Probate Group determines the second digit; notice that there are essentially three different types of matters listed in the groups: Inter Vivos Transfers, Testamentary Matters, and Estate Administration.

The four different types of Estate Administration (minors, mental incompetents, physical incompetents, and decedents) will normally involve a single state tribunal; it will usually be referred to as a "Probate" or "Surrogate" Court. The forms for the four different types of administrations may be quite similar, if not identical. In other words, it is not unusual that a given state Probate Court will procedurally treat the administration of an estate for a mental incompetent, the same as that of a decedent. The procedural steps, and perhaps even the court rules, may be identical. And so will the forms.

The Inter Vivos Subgroup pertains to inter vivos transfers, and applies *only* to item 1 of The Probate Group. Likewise, the *Testamentary Subgroup* pertains only to the second element of the Probate Group (i.e., "Testamentary"). But the Estate Administration *Subgroup* is to be used for *all* of the Estate Administration elements (in particular, items 3 through 7 of The Probate Group). It is almost litigation-like in its structure.

The Testamentary Subgroup is divided into ten different types of Wills. This is one of those rare situations where we have used all ten digits for a breakdown. Normally, I like to avoid the "0," since it often leaves the user guessing as to whether it precedes the 1 or follows the 9. However, as you can see from the list, it took all ten slots to properly cover the various combinations and possibilities.

The process is continued as *each* Will is broken down into individual clauses, by the WILL DIVISION. That Division is further split into Bequest Topics (fifth digit). This carries the process as far as it should go, down to the fifth digit, leaving only one digit for random assignments. In effect, this allows up to ten different types of provisions for each type of Bequest, for each Will.

NUMBER STRUCTURE FOR PROBATE

DIGIT STRUCTURE: 2GS,DTX

MAJOR CATEGORY:

2. Probate

INTER VIVOS SUBGROUP (S)

1. Gifts
2. Powers of Attorney
3. Private Annuities
4. Revocable Living Trust
5. Revocable Life Ins. Trust
6. Irrevocable Living Trust
7. Irrevocable Life Ins. Trust
8. Charitable Trusts

ESTATE ADMIN. SUBGROUP (S)

1. Pre-Admin.
2. Appt. of Fiduciary
3. Marshaling Assets
4. Claims
5. General Admin.
6. Accounting
7. Distribution & Discharge
8. Appeal
9. Other

PROBATE GROUP (G)

1. Inter Vivos
2. Testamentary
3. Estate Admin. (minors)
4. Estate Admin. (mental inc.)
5. Estate Admin. (phy. inc.)
6. Estate Admin. (decedents)
7. Post Estate Trust Admin.
8. Other

TESTAMENTARY SUBGROUP (S)

0. Will.Simple.Male.Sing.
1. Will.Simple.Female.Sing.
2. Will.Pourover.Male.Sing.
3. Will.Pourover.Female.Sing.
4. Will with Test Trust.Male.Sing
5. Will with Test.Trust.Fem.Sing.
6. Will.Pourover.Male.Married
7. Will.Pourover.Female.Married
8. Will with Test Trust.Male.Marr.
9. Will with Test Trust.Fem.Marr.

TRUSTS DIVISION (D)

1. Headings & Intros
2. Transfer of Prop.
3. Distrib. Lifetime
4. Distrib.Sub.Death
5. Trustee Powers
6. Revocation
7. Administrative
8. Sign. & Schedules
9. Letters

BEQUEST TOPIC (T)

1. Nothing
2. Gen. Personal
3. Specific
4. Demonstrative
5. General
6. Residuary

WILL DIVISION (D)

1. Headings & Intros
2. Appointments
3. Debt Payments
4. Powers
5. Bequests
6. Special Provisions
7. Sig. and Attest.
8. Letters

Figure 3-9

Notice that Wills and trusts each have their own particular Division. As with Wills, the structure of the Trust Division is predicated on the notion that some elements are common to all of them, regardless of type, duration, or state. But please do not confuse Wills and Trusts. Trusts are basically Inter Vivos instruments (Group Element 1); they can normally be altered and changed by the creator (Settlor) by way of a simple amendment. Wills, on the other hand, are strictly testamentary (Group Element 2); to change *them,* all of the formalities of Will execution are required. Some Wills may contain a Trust within their "four corners." Such "testamentary trusts" are nonetheless "testamentary" (Group Element 2).

As we create labels for this Category, or any other, it is always important to keep in mind that we will *only* use those Subgroups and Divisions that apply to the form that is being used to create the label. Notice therefore, that in Figure 3-10 there is no reason to refer to the Estate Administration subgroup. We only use those structures that pertain to the Inter Vivos Group Element.

It is important to state, and repeat, that *initially,* while you are setting up your system, *do not* fret and worry over numbers beyond the first three digits. As a matter of fact, if you get the first two digits correct, you should not have any trouble whatsoever locating the form in your Master Index. However, for those who wish to take the time, it would certainly be worth your while to study the entire chart very carefully; for, *all* of *your* forms pertaining to this particular Category should fit nicely into the pigeonholes that we have constructed.

At this point, some examples are in order:

Example 6

One form of Inter Vivos transfer involves a Durable Power of Attorney. This particular form provides us with a good opportunity to present an "informal" sub-subheading. In particular, notice from the chart that all Powers of Attorney should start with the first three digits "212." After that, it would normally be anyone's guess as to the numbers to be assigned to the different Powers of Attorney that you might have. As your own optional "fourth-digit division," consider the three types of Powers in conjunction with Figure 3-10:

1. Limited or Special,
2. General, and
3. Durable.

Example 7

Figure 3-11 provides our first example of breaking a form, or more properly—"a piece of text," down, not only by type, but by *individual*

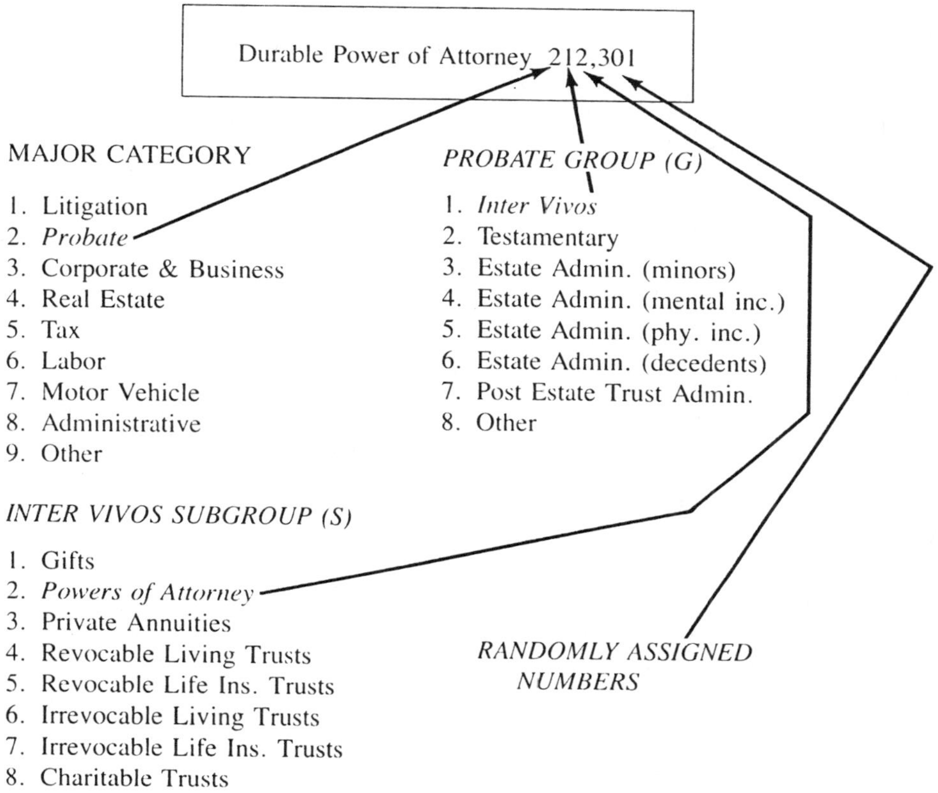

Figure 3-10

paragraph. In particular, notice that the Will Division has a structure that lists each and every separate item in a Will.

As our structures indicate, creating a thorough, complete, and well-organized bank of forms to fill this Category, should be quite simple. It has one of the most well-defined structures of the System. Perhaps this is attributable to the fact that the forms have had a recognized existence for hundreds of years.

Things will, of course, change. And your System should quickly be able to adapt. For example, if you refer to the Inter Vivos Subgroup (Figure 3-10), you will notice that there are eight elements. When first developed, the System had an additional element at position nine titled "Irrevocable Short Term Trusts." Now, however, because of changes in Federal Tax Laws, this particular type of trust has been rendered all but obsolete. Like any form system, there must be some fluidity and flexibility to allow for such changes. We would, however, expect changes to occur at *no* greater point than the third digit from the left.

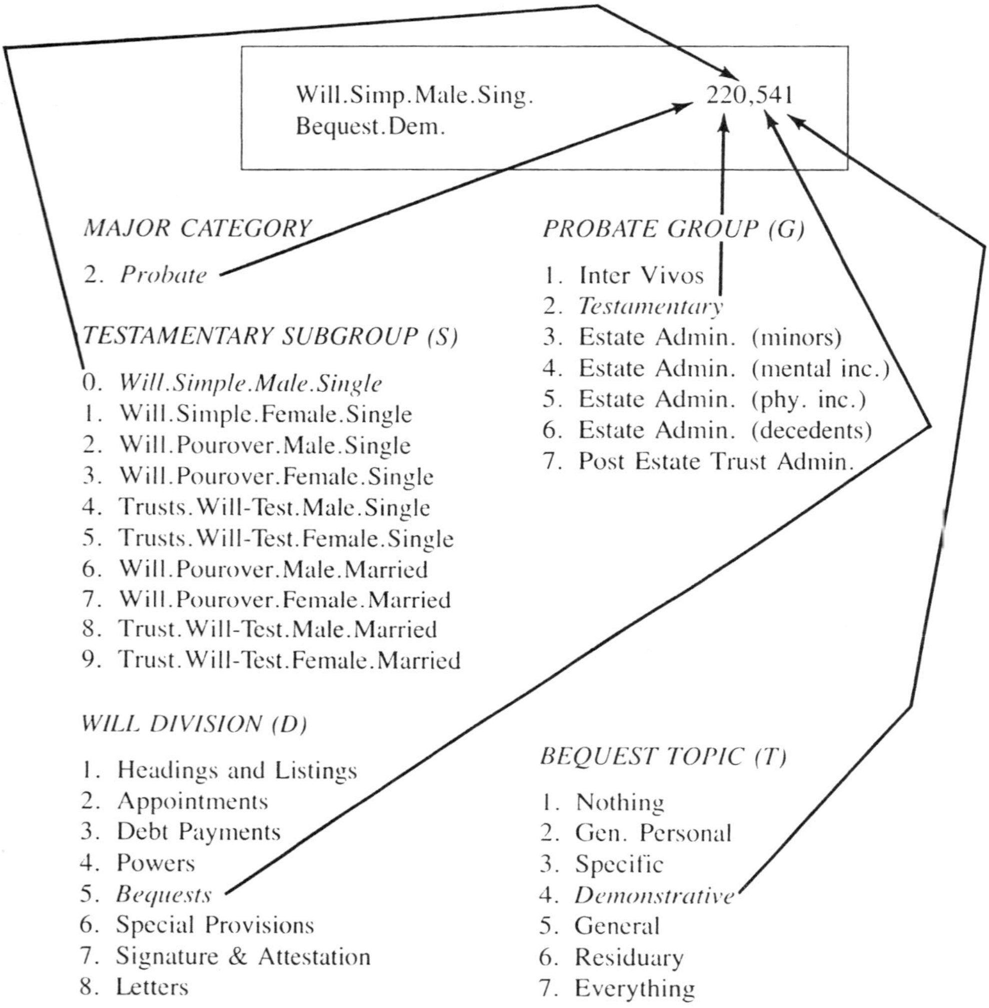

Figure 3-11

3.
* * * Corporate and Business * * *

Responsible for much of the world's paper, this particular Category has a relatively comprehensible structure. It is a bit more complex than some of our simpler categorical arrangements; but, nevertheless, if your firm practices in this particular area, the structures, and the elements that compose them, should be quickly recognizable.

The Category involves a relatively broad range of documents, consisting of Contracts, Notes, Minutes, Articles, and Multi-Part U.C.C. Forms. As might be expected, all of the first four Levels (I, II, III, and IV) are involved. From what you know about the System thus far, see if, from Figure 3-12 alone, you can determine the number that we should assign to the Form officially titled "UCC-1"; it is a "financing" statement form used to *secure* a debt or transaction. Refer to the chart, but do not attempt to handle the number all at once. Take it digit by digit, starting from the left. If the answer does not become apparent, look at Example 10 (Figure 3-15). Remember, close counts; so if your choice for the first three digits is correct, *you're* correct.

Notice that the Group elements for this particular Category consist of a hierarchy of entities, starting with Corporations (requiring the greatest sophistication, and the most amount of paperwork). The arrangement then works its way down to the simple Sole Proprietorship. Items 6 and 7, admittedly do not fall within any rank or order in this particular hierarchy. But they are nevertheless too important to omit.

By far, the greatest number of business forms pertain either to Corporations or to Uniform Commercial Code matters. Partnerships, Joint Ventures, and Sole Proprietorships account for relatively few forms (that pertain *exclusively* to those entities). Of necessity, there will be some overlap. But this is inescapable.

The Corporations Subgroup follows a general chronological scheme, that you may recognize if you have ever prepared Corporate documents. The two Corporation Divisions are somewhat self-explanatory.

The "Contracts" Group (7) would, for example, include sample agreements pertaining to the purchase and sale of businesses and commercial properties; it could also encompass any type of written arrangement, "deal," or contract. And those of you who are fans of the Uniform Commercial Code will notice that the U.C.C. Subgroup numbers conform to the Official Chapters of the Uniform Commercial Code *both* in title and in number. We have, therefore, taken the liberty of referring to the U.C.C. components as "Chapters" instead of elements of a Subgroup.

Notice that the Employee Benefit Plan Division (Figure 3-12), has the effect of dissecting a single document. Employee Benefit Plans include certain classic lengthy documents such as Employees' Pension Trusts, Profit Sharing Plans, and Keogh Plans. Their respective paragraphs are well-ordered and well-defined, similar to our "wills and trusts."

Example 8

For corporations, an official, state-issued form (Level I) known as "Articles of Incorporation" must be filed at inception (see Figure 3-13).

Example 9

Retirement Plans are lengthy documents. But due to heavy federal regulation per ERISA (Employee's Retirement Income Security Act), many

NUMBER STRUCTURE:

DIGIT STRUCTURE: 3GS, DTX

MAJOR CATEGORY

3. Corporate & Business

CORPORATE & BUSINESS GROUP (G)

1. Corporations
2. Limited Partnerships
3. Co-Partnerships
4. Joint Ventures
5. Sole Proprietorships
6. U.C.C. Matters
7. Contracts
8. Other

CORPORATIONS SUBGROUP (S)

1. Pre-Incorp. Agreement
2. Incorp. Documents
3. Minutes
4. Employee Benefit Plans
5. Employee Agreements
6. Shareholder Agreements
7. Mergers, Reorganizations and Dissolutions
8. Other

U.C.C. CHAPTER (S)

1. General
2. Sales
3. Commercial Paper
4. Bank Deposits
5. Letters of Credit
6. Bulk Transfers
7. Warehouse Receipts
8. Investment Securities
9. Secured Transactions

INCORPORATION DOCUMENTS DIVISION (D)

1. Profit Corporation
2. Professional Corporation
3. Non-Profit Corporation
4. Ecclesiastical Corp.
5. Municipal Corporation

EMPLOYEE BENEFIT PLANS DIVISION (D)

1. Titles and Intros
2. Purposes and Definitions
3. Eligibility and Vesting
4. Contrib. and Allocations
5. Retirement and Payment
6. Powers, Rights, Duties
7. Other
8. Recitals
9. Letters, Schedules, Other

Figure 3-12

provisions are standardized. There may, for example, be different methods for distributing or paying out benefits from a Qualified Pension or Profit Sharing Plan; but those methods will be *well-defined* and *limited* in number. (See Figure 3-14.)

Example 10

Study Figure 3-15.

Articles of Incorp. 312,301
Non-Profit Corp.

MAJOR CATEGORY

1. Litigation
2. Probate
3. *Corporate & Business*
4. Real Estate
5. Tax
6. Labor
7. Motor Vehicle
8. Administrative
9. Other

CORPORATE AND BUSINESS GROUP (G)

1. *Corporations*
2. Limited Partnerships
3. Co-Partnerships
4. Joint Ventures
5. Sole Proprietorships
6. U.C.C. Matters
7. Contracts
8. Other

CORPORATIONS SUBGROUP (S)

1. Pre-Incorp. Agreements
2. *Incorp. Documents*
3. Minutes
4. Employee Benefit Plans
5. Employee Agreements
6. Shareholder Agreements
7. Mergers, Reorganizations, and Dissolutions
8. Other

INCORPORATION DOCUMENTS DIVISION (D)

1. Profit Corporation
2. Professional Corporation
3. *Non-Profit Corporation*
4. Ecclesiastical Corp.
5. Municipal Corporation

Figure 3-13

4.
* * * Real Estate * * *

Of all of the hierarchies, Real Estate forms one of the nicest and most natural orders. This is because interests in Real Estate form a very precise and recognizable pecking order, commencing with the most superior form of title, the Fee Simple Absolute (referred to as a ''Fee Simple Estate''); most likely, this best describes the form of title to the house that you last purchased. From there, the list works its way down to Land Contracts, which also normally involve the *purchase* of a Fee Simple Estate; however, when land contracts are involved, the conveyance of title is normally delayed.

Concurrent Estates involve Joint Ownership, and Tenancies in Common. Divisible Estates involve Future Interests, and those that are otherwise limited by time. From there, we proceed down to the four non-possessory interests. From this list, you can see how commonly used real estate terms, such as ''Mortgage'' and ''Lien,'' fit into the overall semantic scheme.

Ret Plan.Dist. 314,501
Distribution (Method 1)

MAJOR CATEGORY

1. Litigation
2. Probate
3. *Corporate & Business*
4. Real Estate
5. Tax
6. Labor
7. Motor Vehicle
8. Administrative
9. Other

CORPORATE AND BUSINESS GROUP (G)

1. *Corporations*
2. Limited Partnerships
3. Co-Partnerships
4. Joint Ventures
5. Sole Proprietorships
6. U.C.C. Matters
7. Contracts
8. Other

CORPORATIONS SUBGROUP (S)

1. Pre-Incorp. Agreements
2. Incorp. Documents
3. Minutes
4. *Employee Benefit Plans*
5. Employee Agreements
6. Shareholder Agreements
7. Mergers, Reorganizations, and Dissolutions
8. Other

EMPLOYEE BENEFIT PLAN DIVISION (D)

1. Titles and Intros
2. Purposes and Definitions
3. Eligibility and Vesting
4. Contrib. and Allocations
5. *Retirement and Payment*
6. Powers, Rights, Duties
7. Other
8. Recitals
9. Letters, Schedules, Other

Figure 3-14

As might be expected, this particular Category will make heavy use of pre-printed (Level I) forms, such as Deeds, Leases, and Closing statements. However, in addition, there may be riders or clauses that you may wish to place in your file cabinet (Level II), or on your hard disk (Level III), to be used in conjunction with those printed forms. For example, you may have a printed form for a Commercial Real Estate Lease, that you would, of course, store in your file cabinet (Level I). But, by the same token, you may have some "special language" that you regularly attach as addendums to those leases; you may wish to store those on your computer (Level III). Such a situation will involve a case where a single form will be physically separated from itself. But this should not cause any great concern, since *all components* will come together in your Master Form Book index. (See Figure 3-16.)

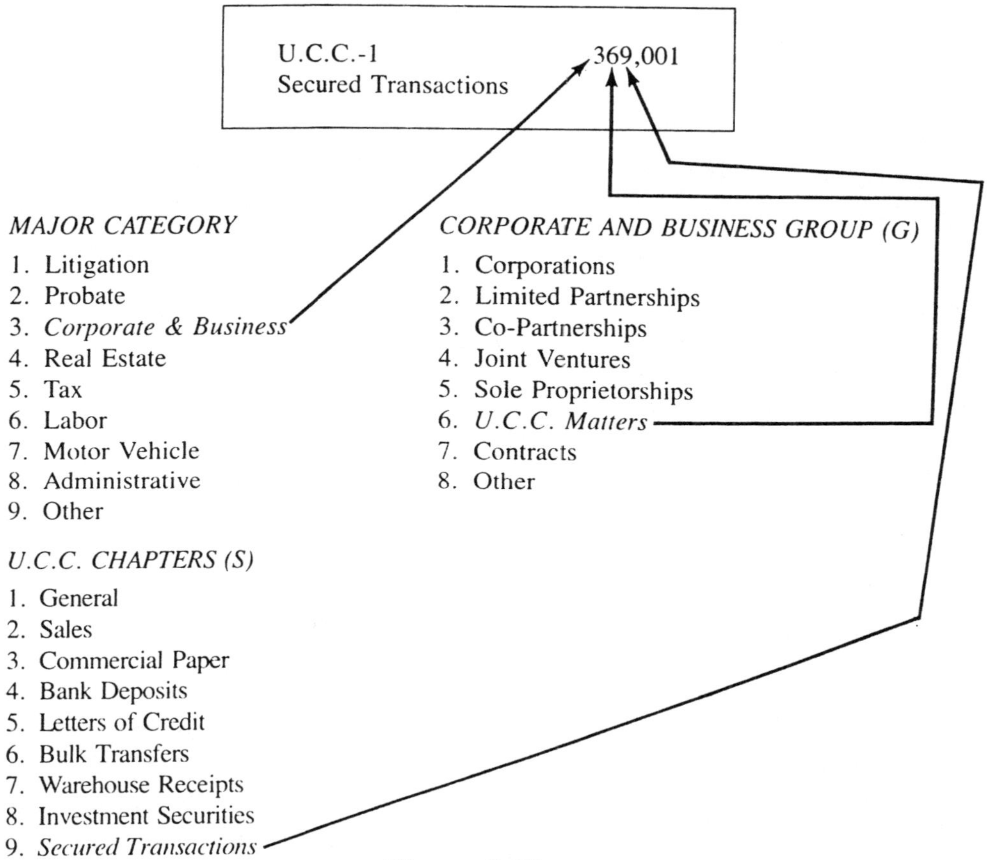

Figure 3-15

In accordance with our pattern, the first digit for any form falling within the scope of this Major Category (Real Estate) will be a "4." The Real Estate Group determines the second digit. Notice the very distinct, and recognizable, pecking order of these estates. The first four estates list the higher level possessory interests in Real Estate; the last four are non-possessory. The nine elements listed in the "Fee Simple Subgroup" could easily pertain, not only to Fee Simple Estates, but *to any of the first four group elements,* since, as previously indicated, each involves a possessory interest in Real Estate.

The items listed in the Deeds Division should be quite recognizable. The last item (7 pertaining to "corrections"), involves the topic of "Correction Deeds," which are used for the specific purpose of rectifying some defect in title.

The "Use Division," as its heading indicates, covers the normal "uses" that one would make of Real Estate. Notice, however, that buying and selling

NUMBERING STRUCTURE FOR REAL ESTATE

DIGIT STRUCTURE: 4GS,DTX

MAJOR CATEGORY

4. Real Estate

REAL ESTATE GROUP (G)

1. Fee Simple Estates
2. Land Contracts
3. Concurrent Estates
4. Divisible Estates
5. Easements and Serv.
6. Leases
7. Mortgages
8. Liens
9. Other

FEE SIMPLE SUBGROUP (S)

1. Options to Purchase
2. Offers to Purchase
3. Brokerage Forms
4. Disclosure Forms
5. Lending Institution Forms
6. Closing Statement
7. Escrow Forms
8. Deeds
9. Use

DEEDS DIVISION (D)

1. Warranty.Individual
2. Warranty.Partnership
3. Warranty.Corporation
4. Quit Claim.Individual
5. Quit Claim.Partnership
6. Quit Claim.Corporation
7. Corrections

USE DIVISION (D)

1. Development
2. Construction
3. Zoning Compliance
4. Management
5. Exchange

Figure 3-16

are not included within that Division; those matters are taken care of completely by the ''Fee Simple Subgroup.''

Example 11

A quit claim deed is a very common item for this category (see Figure 3-17).

Example 12

A Joint Purchase of Real Estate simply involves a purchase by more than one individual. If title is taken by the purchasers, Jointly or as Tenants in Common, a Concurrent Estate will be formed. (See Figure 3-18.) Notice that we can make use of the Fee Simple Subgroup for this particular estate. In essence, the fact that more than one individual may be purchasing the property does not change its ''Fee Simple'' status.

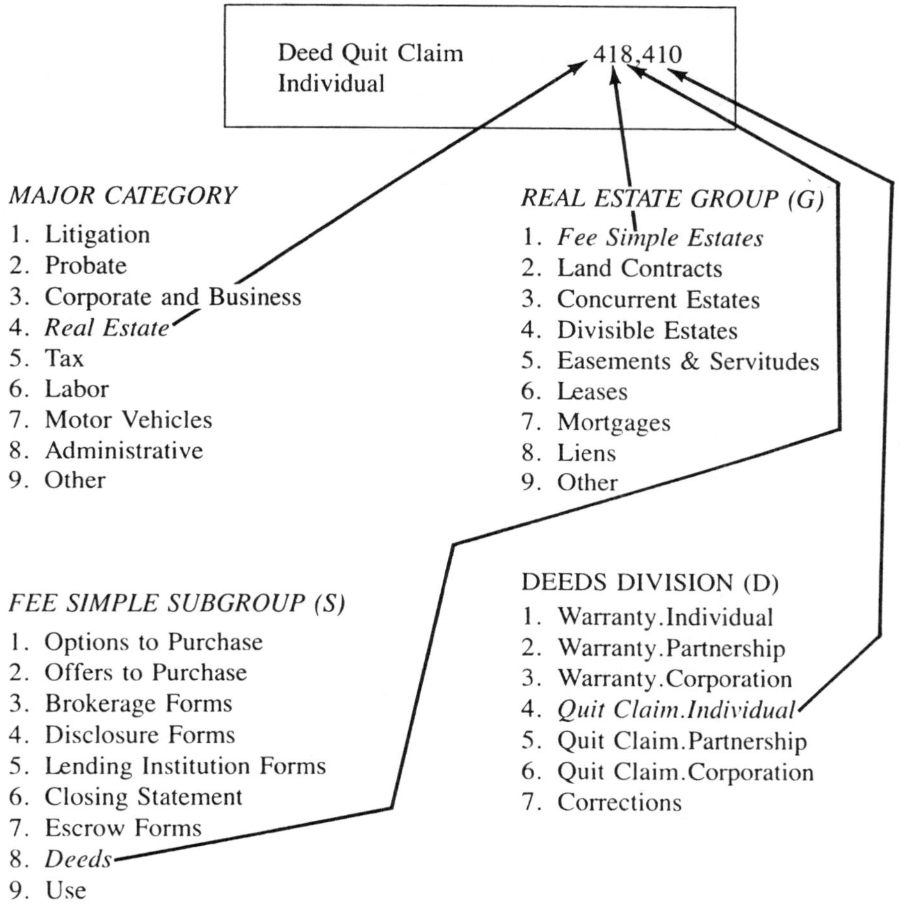

Figure 3-17

Example 13

There are limited uses to which Real Estate can be put, *after* it has been purchased. Those uses are set forth as elements of our "Use Division" (Figure 3-19). The first element, "Development," is designed as a "catchall." Item number two of that particular Division will most likely involve construction contracts. You may wish to break down your construction contracts to reflect your firm's favorite clauses, in much the same fashion that we subdivided our wills and trusts.

If there is ever any doubt as to which major group will include a given contract, you should treat item one (Fee Simple Estates) as your catchall. A long-established rule of Conveyance Law states that when in doubt, "Fee Title" is always preferred.

Offer to Pur.Joint 432,101

MAJOR CATEGORY

1. Litigation
2. Probate
3. Corporate and Business
4. *Real Estate*
5. Tax
6. Labor
7. Motor Vehicles
8. Administrative
9. Other

REAL ESTATE GROUP (G)

1. Fee Simple Estates
2. Land Contracts
3. *Concurrent Estates*
4. Divisible Estates
5. Easements & Servitudes
6. Leases
7. Mortgages
8. Liens
9. Other

FEE SIMPLE SUBGROUP (S)

1. Options to Purchase
2. *Offers to Purchase*
3. Brokerage Forms
4. Disclosure Forms
5. Lending Institution Forms
6. Closing Statement
7. Escrow Forms
8. Deeds
9. Use

Figure 3-18

As previously indicated, our mix of Real Estate printed forms and office-created Masters will rely upon the tandem use of Levels I and III. If you are not computerized, the hybridization could come together in the form of Level II. In particular, you may wish to store multiple copies of your form leases or construction contracts (*together* with pull pages for your addenda) together in your file cabinet. But do not be confused; copies of printed forms are ''technically'' Level I. Anything that *you* create with your photocopier becomes Level II. The distinctions, however, should not create any problems; Levels I and II always go in file cabinet folders, in any event.

5.
* * * Tax * * *

Tax practitioners speak, think, and communicate with numbers; they even greet one another by their social security numbers instead of names. Those of

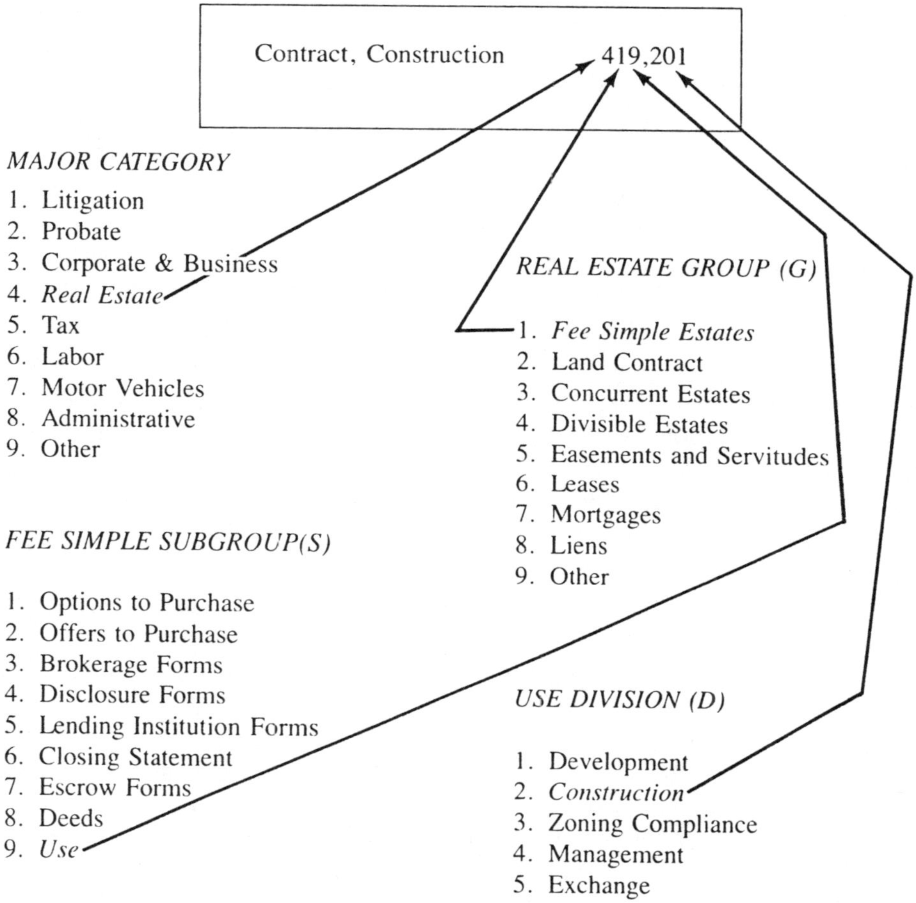

Figure 3-19

you who are not tax specialists, will nevertheless recall that whenever you had any communication whatsoever involving the Internal Revenue Service, it always consisted of a series of numbers.

To The IRS, you do not even exist unless you have an Employer Identification *number* or Social Security *number*. Any written correspondence must be assigned a Document Locator *number*. Of course, all Returns have their own *numbers;* and every return must be identified by the number representing the end of the subject tax period.

Before casting stones, I am, however, quick to acknowledge the fact that the system structures of this book are all predicated upon numbers, and when it comes to forms and client files, I *do* recommend that you begin to think in terms of these critical numbers. However, I would like to think that *our* numbering structures have some logic or order about them. This is not so with respect to our taxing systems. For all of us are aware of the fact that when it comes to The IRS, or the Internal Revenue Code, there is no logic, or semblance of order whatsoever. But, be these facts as they may, practitioners and non-practitioners alike have become accustomed to certain numbers that represent an endless variety of forms, returns, and schedules. It would therefore be a sacrilege to reassign numbers to tax forms that *do not* correspond to their common, well-recognized titles.

Essentially we will create our normal decimal structure for the first two digits only, but after that we will merely plug in the Official Return Number. Thus, there will be very little to remember, other than the actual number that is assigned to the form. For example, once the two major digits are given their decimal positions, you should be able to locate the form merely by flipping to the number of the Return. All returns will be in simple numerical order. For example, your standard annual Federal Income Tax Return for Individuals would be found under the ''Federal Returns'' group at position 1040. As might be expected, most, if not all, of your form bank for this particular Category will consist of pre-printed tax return forms, which will of course, fall squarely into Level I.

We should distinguish the forms of *this* particular Category from those of Group 5 (Tax Court) of the *Litigation* Category. We can best do so with this suggestion—keep all forms, checklists, and papers that pertain to the processing or the filing of tax returns within *this* Category 5. However, once any tax matter has reached the ''court level,'' then it will fall within the jurisdiction of either the United States Tax Court (15X,XXX) or a United States Federal District Court (13X,XXX); both of these matters, of course, fall within the Litigation Category. (See Figure 3-20).

For our Tax Category structure, the rules are going to be the same as for our other Categories, but the results may come out a little bit different. In particular, the first digit of this Category will always be a ''5,'' as might be expected. And, to be perfectly consistent with the structure of our other categories, the second digit will denote a Tax Group Element. As might be expected, most of the forms within this particular Category will have a ''51'' as their first two digits. From there, we will use our *four remaining digits* to *represent* the *official name* of the Return (recall, that most tax returns *already* use numbers as names).

The official forms, recognized as such by the Department of the Treasury, exceed 300 in number, and are all named on the Official Treasury List of Forms and Returns, which is itself an official form (Form 701). All such forms consist of numbers, or number-letter combinations. Some have letters preceding the numbers (p.e., Form SS-4), and others have letters following

NUMBERING STRUCTURE FOR TAX

DIGIT STRUCTURE: 5G,XXXX

MAJOR CATEGORY:

5. Tax

CORRESPONDENCE SUBGROUP (S)

1. General Letters
2. Enclosure Letters
3. Protest Letters
4. Request for Rulings
5. Other

RETURNS SUBGROUP (XXXX)

The last four digits
of the form number are
determined by the numbers
appearing in the tax return;
letters are ignored
(See examples that follow.)

TAX GROUP (G)

1. Federal Returns
2. State Returns
3. Local Returns
4. Federal Correspondence
5. State Correspondence
6. Local Correspondence
7. Other Federal
8. Other State
9. Other Local

Figure 3-20

them (p.e., Form 1040-C, sometimes referred to only as "Schedule C"). For our purposes, we will initially *ignore* the letters, regardless of whether they precede or follow the numbers. We will label the last four digits so as to correspond to the official form number. For example, Tax Form 941 would be assigned a label number 51,0941. Likewise, Form 1040 would receive label number 51,1040.

Notice that we have tampered slightly with some of the rules that we were taught in arithmetic. In particular, it is normal that the comma should follow each *3* digits. And, to keep things perfectly "normal," we have followed this rule throughout our *other* Categories. However, just because we have been putting the comma after every three digits since the Second Grade, does not mean that there is a law against moving it. And, in this particular case, it pays to do so. Thus, by moving the comma one digit to the left, we can keep the four digits that represent the official form number all together. This will make looking for the form much easier on the eyes.

Another slight variation from our own prior rules may involve mixing letters with numbers. In other words, you may wish to create separate folders for schedules or forms with different letters. For most firms, this should *not* be necessary, and I recommend against it; however, if you choose to do so, you may, without causing any confusion. *I prefer* that all letter variations with respect to a given tax return number merely be placed in the same file folder as other letter variations.

For example, Schedules A, B, C, and D are quite common; officially, all of these are "Form 1040" Schedules. In essence, Schedule C is officially "Form 1040-C." Thus, all of the "1040" schedules, together with Form 1040 itself, could go into a single folder. Recall, that we are dealing only with folders; almost all of the forms in this particular Category *will fall* within the scope of Level I. Therefore, it is simply a matter of putting all of the schedules that go *with* a given return in the same folder as *that return*. However, if your firm specializes in Tax matters, and you are required to keep numerous schedules on hand, and for varying years, *then* you may wish to set up a separate folder for each schedule. A label might read "51,1040-D." Or, it might read "51,0004-SS" (for form SS-4). But in any event, it would still be filed in *strict numerical order* even though the label contains letters. (See Example 1.)

State forms should present no major problem with respect to our structure, since they will all have a "2" for the second digit. Some practitioners actually mix the state and federal returns together. This would occur quite naturally, in a state that utilizes form names that correspond strictly to those of their federal counterparts. Michigan, for example, has a form called "MI-1040," which is used for reporting Michigan's Income Tax. I prefer to keep state and federal returns separate, as does our System.

As might be anticipated, the elements of this particular Category are somewhat fluid, though not quite as erratic as you might expect. For, although the tax laws change on a regular basis (as do the forms and returns), the names, nevertheless, seem to remain somewhat stable. Although it may change every single year, the Federal Income Tax Return for the individual, for example, has *always* been called the "1040."

Another variation with respect to the stored forms, may be the *year* of the return. Again, those firms that engage in extensive tax work, may find it necessary to save returns and schedules for several years, particularly those that represent serious delinquents. In such a case, I recommend that the returns nevertheless *not* be separated by year. In other words, a single folder could contain several years of a given return, depending, of course, upon the quantity that must be maintained.

Look at the samples that follow. For most of us, Figure 3-21 will suffice. For those who are serious practitioners, additional labels, such as those presented in Figure 3-22, might be required. And for the truly large and specialized tax firms, one might expect the configuration presented by Figure 3-23.

In addition to the preceding breakdowns, for those who may prepare returns on an interstate basis, things could get a bit complex. They may wish to break down the forms and their folders, not only by letter and by year, but also by state. In that case, I would recommend once again that the number *govern first.* Then the arrangement could be in alphabetical order by schedule, and each schedule would next be arranged by year.

The simplest method suggested, would apply for most of us. In particular, for the "1040," and *all variations* of *letters, schedules,* and *years,* we would use this one folder label:

Indiv. Return	51,1040

Figure 3-21

Figure 3-22's configuration provides a separate folder for *each separate schedule.* The folders are first filed in numerical order, and then alphabetically.

For those specialized tax practitioners, who need to divide the folders up, not only by schedule, but by year, Figure 3–23's configuration is suggested.

Example 14

The folder for the label in Figure 3-24 would contain not only the ubiquitous Form 941, but also the Schedules listed in the lower portion of the label.

Example 15

Figure 3-25 represents an official publication issued by The IRS (referred to as "IRS Publication No. 5"), which provides instructions for the preparation of Protests; it also provides information about Appeals.

Example 16

Figure 3-26's format is used for a State Income Tax Return for Individuals. It assumes, of course, that the State uses the same numbering system as the IRS. If that is *not* the case, then the state's official form number should be used to determine the label number. The same rules with respect to letters and years should apply.

6.
* * * Workers' Rights * * *

Labor law is a very complex matter, with arms reaching into virtually every other Major Category on the list. And thus it is a topic that could have

Indiv. Return	51,1040
Schedules A & B	51,1040 AB
Schedule	51,1040 C
⋮	⋮
Amendment	51,1040 X

Figure 3-22

been swallowed up by those other Major Categories (most notably, Categories 1 and 8), instead of receiving its own separate treatment. Because of its importance, we have excised the topic from the remaining Categories; it is far too important to be denied its own.

There are some distinctions that we must keep in mind to avoid unnecessary overlap. First, we should be reminded by its label color, that Labor involves *blue* collar workers; if, on the other hand, we were dealing with the problems of non-union employees, then *green* would probably be the more appropriate color (per Category 3).

Perhaps the key attribute of Category 6 is the fact that it will involve, or touch upon, the National Labor Relations Act. So, if unions are involved, the matter properly belongs within this Category 6, *even though* the practice of

Indiv. Return	51,1040 (85)
Indiv. Return	51,1040 (86)
Indiv. Return	51,1040 (87)
Indiv. Return	51,1040 (88)
Schedules A & B	51,1040 AB (85)
Schedules A & B	51,1040 AB (86)

.
.
.
.

Figure 3-23

Labor Law may involve several Administrative Agencies (Category 8) in addition to the NLRB.

The Labor Group is tailored to fit labor proceedings only. This fact should always be kept in mind when dealing with Labor Group 5 (Court). Perhaps the

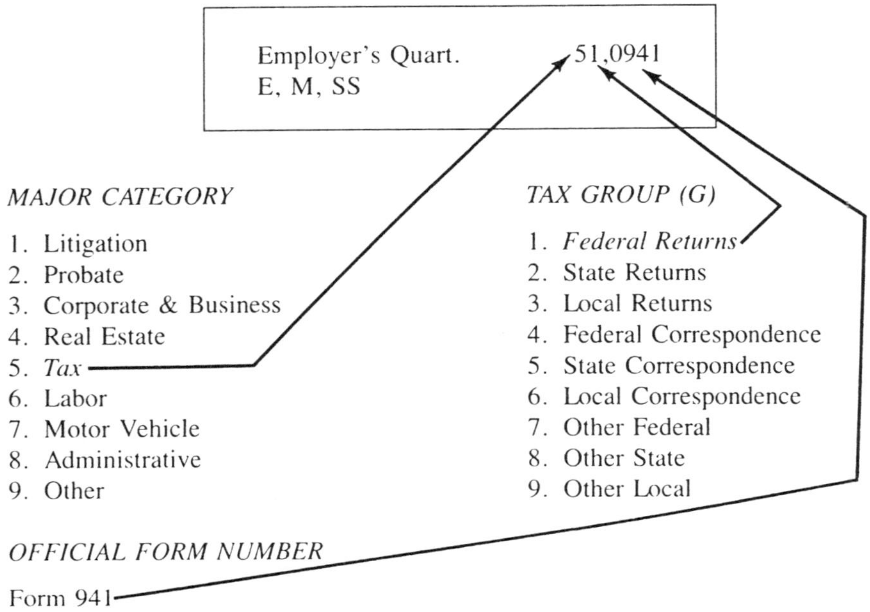

Figure 3-24

best way to avoid confusion would be to consider placing *only* those pleadings and briefs pertaining *directly* to Labor, within Category 6; most others would be placed in Category 1. If your firm practices Labor Law, you will probably have no problems whatsoever identifying the particular forms that would fall within this particular group. For example, a Petition for Removal of an action from State to Federal Court, which is predicated upon Section 301 of the Labor Management Relations Act (Breach of Duty of Fair Representation), would provide a commonly used pleading that pertains *solely* to Labor. Any Removal Petitions not based upon the LMRA would fall within Category 1.

Though tenuously related, labor practitioners consider Workers' Compensation matters to be outside of their sphere. Such matters more appropriately, therefore, fall within Group Element 6 (State Bureau of Workers' Compensation) of Category 8 (Administrative Agency). Workers' Compensation matters will be treated as an area of practice, separate from Labor Law.

Category 8 involves Administrative Agencies of all sorts. However, if you will examine the groups contained within that particular Category, you will notice that the National Labor Relations Board is specifically omitted. This, of course, is to permit such matters to fall exclusively within Major Category 6.

Perhaps, wherever a problem involves ''overlap,'' it is best to follow a simple rule—always let the specific govern over the general. If there is a

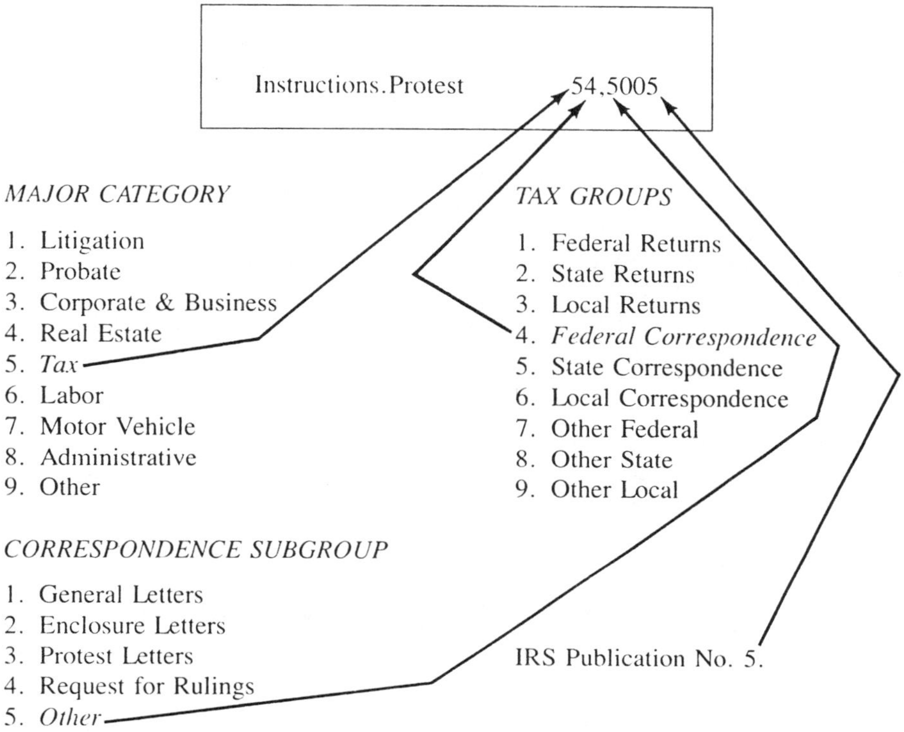

Figure 3-25

specific Category, or group, or even subgroup that deals with a particular named matter, then that specific item should ''catch the form'' in question.

Much of what Labor lawyers do is related directly to the handling and processing of employee grievances (see Figure 3-27). Indeed, for many labor lawyers, grievance arbitrations and the matters relating to them constitute a very large portion of the practice. Mediation, the fourth item in the Group, usually involves contract negotiations. The remaining items in the Group (5 through 9) are either self-explanatory, or are further developed by the elements listed in the applicable Subgroup.

The Arbitration Subgroup, perhaps the most important, is divided into nine Divisions, which should encompass virtually any type of dispute or argument that would arise in conjunction with the management or enforcement of a Collective Bargaining Contract. Arbitration Subgroup elements 5, 6, and 7, comprise more than 95% of the matters raised during most arbitration proceedings.

Of all arbitration proceedings, perhaps 60% to 70% pertain directly to discipline. The Discipline Division (which is an element of the Arbitration Group) is divided into nine separate Topics, represented by the fourth digit.

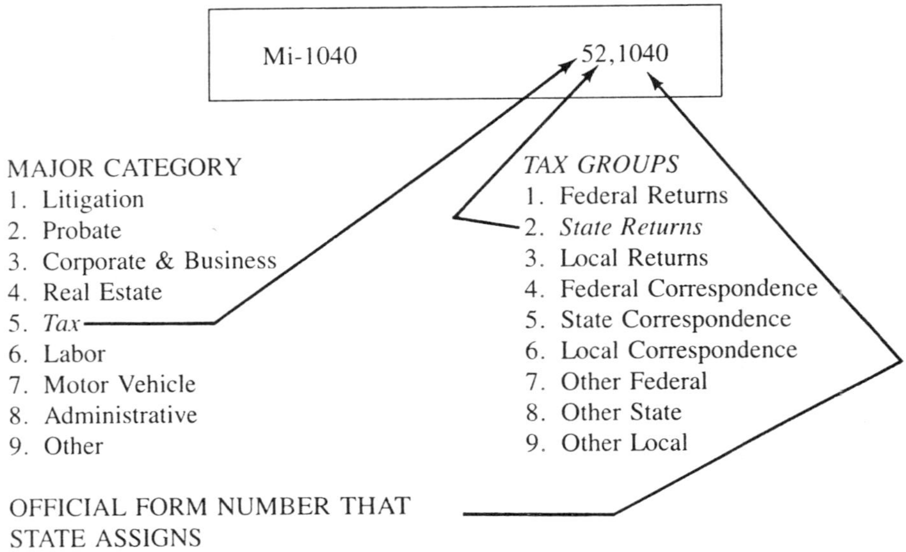

Figure 3-26

With respect to Group 5, which is simply titled "Court," there are some very specific types of matters listed. Only those that pertain directly to Labor, such as items listed under the Group heading, would fall within this Major Category. Others would possibly fall within Category 1.

The NLRB Group is comprised of the most common elements that fall within the jurisdiction of the National Labor Relations Board. For the most part, such matters involve Union Certifications, Decertifications, and Unfair Labor Practices (commonly termed ULPs).

Example 17

Tardiness is a very typical issue for which briefs would be prepared and submitted to the arbitrator appointed to decide it. Figure 3–28 provides a label for such a brief.

Example 18

Look at Figure 3-29. We used a "3" at the fourth position somewhat randomly. But this need not be the case. As a matter of fact, you may refer back to your LITIGATION SUBGROUP (Figure 3-5), which lists a hierarchy of *proceedings*. You may follow that order if you wish.

Most printed forms are issued *by* the National Labor Relations Board. There are exceptions. Those that are lawyer-prepared would fall within the scope of Levels II or III.

Once again, be careful so as not to cause undue confusion between your "normal" litigation forms and those used exclusively for labor matters. The

NUMBERING STRUCTURE FOR WORKERS' RIGHTS

DIGIT STRUCTURE: 6GS, DTX

MAJOR CATEGORY (6)

6. Labor

ARBITRATION SUBGROUP (S)

1. Subpoena Power
2. Jurisdiction
3. Arbitrability
4. Successorship
5. Discipline
6. Seniority Issues
7. Wage Issues
8. Other CBC* Issues
9. Enforcement

COURT SUBGROUP (S)

1. Unfair Representation
2. Strikes
3. Anti-Trust
4. Labor-Erisa Matters
5. Inter-Union Disputes
6. Other

SENIORITY DIVISION (D)

1. Temporaries
2. Vesting
3. Posting
4. Bidding
5. Bumping
6. Accepting
7. Super Seniority
8. Losing
9. Other

LABOR GROUP (G)

1. Grievance Stage
2. Panel or Board Hearing Stage
3. Arbitration
4. Mediation
5. Court
6. NLRB
7. Wage and Hour
8. State Unemployment Agency
9. Other

NLRB SUBGROUP (S)

1. Representation Elections
2. Refusal to Bargain (Unf.Lab.Pract).
3. Other ULP—Employer
4. Other ULP—Union
5. Jurisdictional Issues
6. Decertifications
7. Other

DISCIPLINE DIVISION (D)

1. Strike-Slowdown
2. Drugs-Alcohol
3. Theft-Dishonesty
4. Insubordination-Fighting
5. Destruction-Negligence
6. Absence-Tardiness
7. Sleeping-Laziness
8. Poor Performance
9. Other

WAGE ISSUES DIVISION (D)

1. Straight Pay
2. Overtime Pay
3. Holiday Pay
4. Sick Pay
5. Retro-Pay
6. Bereavement Pay
7. Other Fringes
8. Other

* Collective Bargaining Contract

Figure 3-27

Tardiness, Sample Brief 635,601

MAJOR CATEGORY (6)

1. Litigation
2. Probate
3. Corporate & Business
4. Real Estate
5. Tax
6. *Labor*
7. Motor Vehicle
8. Administrative

LABOR GROUP (G)

1. Grievance Stage
2. Panel or Board Hearing Stage
3. *Arbitration*
4. Mediation
5. Court
6. NLRB
7. Wage and Hour
8. State Unemployment Agency
9. State Civil Rights Agency
0. Other

ARBITRATION SUBGROUP (S)

1. Subpoena Power
2. Jurisdiction
3. Arbitrability
4. Successorship
5. *Discipline*
6. Seniority Issues
7. Wage Issues
8. Other CBC Issues
9. Enforcement

DISCIPLINE DIVISION (D)

1. Strike-Slowdown
2. Drugs-Alcohol
3. Theft-Dishonesty
4. Insubordination-Fighting
5. Destruction-Negligence
6. *Absence-Tardiness*
7. Sleeping-Laziness
8. Poor Performance
9. Other

Figure 3-28

interrogatories presented in Figure 3-29 provide a good example of the latter. They are directed *specifically* to issues that are *only* present in the type of litigation that involves the Labor Category.

Interrogatories 651,301
Duty of Fair Rep.
Base Set to Pf.

MAJOR CATEGORY

1. Litigation
2. Probate
3. Corporate & Business
4. Real Estate
5. Tax
6. *Labor*
7. Motor Vehicle
8. Administrative

LABOR GROUP (G)

1. Grievance Stage
2. Panel or Board Hearing Stage
3. Arbitration
4. Mediation
5. *Court*
6. NLRB
7. Wage and Hour
8. State Unemployment Agency
9. State Civil Rights Agency
0. Other

COURT SUBGROUP (S)

1. *Unfair Representation*
2. Injunction-Strike
3. Anti-Trust
4. Labor-Erisa Matters
5. Other

Figure 3-29

7.
* * * Motor Vehicle * * *

This Category can be somewhat vague and esoteric, even though its elements are quite well-defined. Motor vehicles come in all shapes and sizes as do the models that comprise those vehicles. But perhaps more significant, is the fact that the vehicles, depending upon size, construction, or location may be subject to a variety of jurisdictions.

Most of us will be familiar with the private automobile, and the relatively simple processes by which those items are licensed and regulated by the several states. The Federal Government normally does not become involved, unless, of course, Federal vehicles become the focus. For aircraft, however, Federal Regulation is extensive, and for space craft it is exclusive.

For most practitioners, this Category will be relatively benign, and its inclusion in your numbering system will serve the cause of "completeness" more than anything else. It is designed primarily to fill the need, however small, to take care of those vehicular forms that do not fit any of the other categories. In any event, most of the forms will fall within the scope of Level I (pre-printed forms and applications).

NUMBERING STRUCTURE FOR MOTOR VEHICLE

DIGIT STRUCTURE: 7GS, DTX

MAJOR CATEGORY:

7. Motor Vehicle

OWNERSHIP SUBGROUPS (S)

1. Private
2. Commercial
3. Governmental
4. Foreign

MOTOR VEHICLE GROUP (G)

1. Automobile
2. Truck
3. Motorcycle
4. Offroad Vehicle (ORV)
5. Watercraft
6. Aircraft
7. Hovercraft
8. Spacecraft

Figure 3-30

Most of the forms and applications that concern us, would relate to automobile licensing. For example, an application for a driver's license, or reinstatement of a revoked license, would fall within Group 1 (Automobiles). As a matter of fact, the items encompassed by the first four groups would probably involve forms that are all readily obtainable from the State Office of the Secretary of State.

Group 5 could uniquely depend upon the location of the watercraft (boat), if jurisdiction were in issue. For example, if the boat involves activities on navigable waterways, it may very well fall within the scope of federal jurisdiction. If, however, it happens to leave its harbor in downtown Detroit and wander out into Lake St. Clair, and cross the Canadian border, it may find itself within a totally different sphere of jurisdiction.

The subject of ''Admiralty Law'' is *extremely* specialized, and might make good use of Group 5. This area of practice can be quite complex. To make matters even more problematical, it could involve one of those rare causes of action over which the United States Supreme Court actually has *Original* (as opposed to Appellate) jurisdiction.

Aircraft and hovercraft, can fall within the scope of *both* state and federal jurisdictions. And with respect to spacecraft, the Federal Government exclusively regulates such matters, assuming that there is origination within the confines of the United States.

Example 19

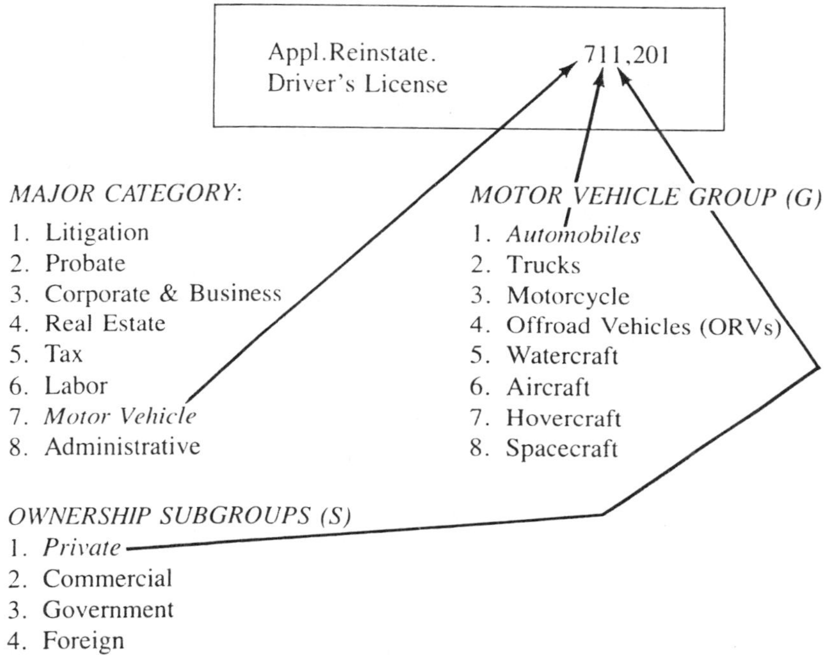

Figure 3-31

Example 20

Figure 3-32 provides an example of a label that might be used for an application for a commercial pilot's license.

8.
* * * Administrative Agency * * *

Administrative Agencies, it is said, are little worlds unto themselves. With respect to jurisdictional domain, a single agency may act as a licensing board, policing entity, rule-maker, judge, jury, and executioner. There are countless state and federal administrative agencies throughout the country, often with overlapping powers and jurisdictions. Normally, their decisions are subject to review by the court system. When that level is reached, Category 1 may come into play.

Each agency will often have its own jargon, and, of course, its own special set of forms and procedures. We could, of course, write an entire book

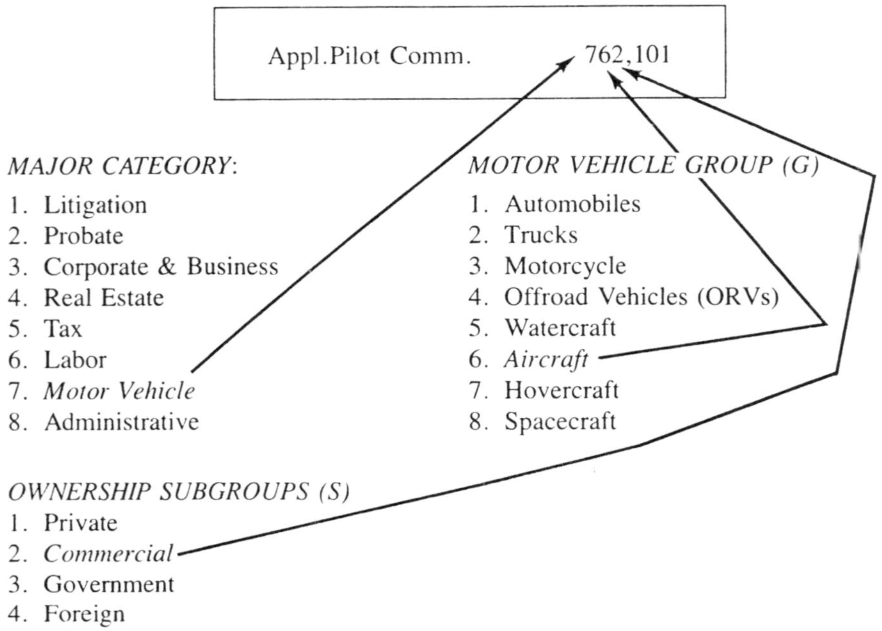

Figure 3-32

on each Major Agency, or perhaps set up a detailed structure with respect to every one. Most of us, however, will rarely, if ever, require such detail.

We are going to provide a skeletal structure for the Major Agencies. With the framework that we will set up, those of you who are specialists should have no trouble filling in the missing pieces to suit your own special need. For us to cover all of the forms encompassed by those agencies would not be terribly productive at this juncture.

This particular Category is structured in such a manner that each Subgroup can apply to each one of the eight Major Group Elements; each such element consists of a Major Agency (see Figure 3-33). Notice, therefore, that we may, in effect, divide *each* agency's jurisdiction into the six items listed in the ADMINISTRATIVE SUBGROUP.

We use the term "certification" in its broadest possible sense (Figure 3-33). For example, if we were dealing with the Bureau of Patents and Copyrights (Group 2), then the "certification" would take the shape of a Patent or a Copyright. For the Federal Trade Commission, such a "certification" may involve "Approval" or permission to market a given product. For the State Bureau of Workers' Compensation, Subgroup Elements 1 and 2 would serve no purpose or have no meaning; however, Element 6 would (Figure 3-36).

NUMBERING STRUCTURE FOR ADMINISTRATIVE AGENCY

DIGIT STRUCTURE: 8GS, DTX

MAJOR CATEGORY

8. Administrative Agency

ADMINISTRATIVE GROUP (G)

1. Social Security Admin.
2. Bureau of Patents and Copyrights
3. Federal Trade Commission
4. Federal Communications Commission
5. Securities and Exchange Comm.
6. State Bureau of Workers' Comp.
7. Other State Agency
8. Other Federal Agency

ADMINISTRATIVE SUBGROUP (S)

1. Certification
2. Licensing
3. Proceedings by AA Against Licensee
4. Proceedings by AA Against Third Party
5. Proceedings by Licensee for Relief
6. Proceedings by Third Party for Relief

PROCEEDINGS DIVISION (D)

1. Petition for Commencement
2. Response
3. Discovery
4. Pre-Hearing
5. Hearing
6. Ruling
7. Execution
8. Appeal
9. Other

Figure 3-33

We distinguish "licensing" from "certification," by using the former (Group Element 2) when a continuing relationship is involved. For example, an application for a broadcaster's license involves a continuing relationship with the Federal Communications Commission; whereas, an application for an SEC Offering would in effect be a "one-shot" deal, which would involve a "certification."

Example 21

Figure 3-34 presents an application to be used by anyone desiring a copyright for a nondramatic literary work (such as this book).

Appl. for Copyright 821,211
Form Tx

MAJOR CATEGORY

1. Litigation
2. Probate
3. Corporate & Business
4. Real Estate
5. Tax
6. Labor
7. Motor Vehicle
8. *Administrative Agency*
9. Other

ADMINISTRATIVE GROUP (G)

1. Social Security Admin.
2. *Bureau of Patents and Copyrights*
3. Federal Trade Commission
4. Federal Communications Commission
5. Securities and Exchange Comm.
6. State Bureau of Workers' Comp.
7. Other State Agency
8. Other Federal Agency

ADMINISTRATIVE SUBGROUP (D)

1. *Certification*
2. Licensing
3. Proceedings by AA Against Licensee
4. Proceedings by AA Against Third Party
5. Proceedings by Licensee for Relief
6. Proceedings by Third Party for Relief

Figure 3-34

Example 22

Figure 3-35 classifies a Petition to Deny a License to a Broadcasting Station, a complex matter.

Example 23

Figure 3-36 involves our previously discussed Worker's Compensation matter.

9.
* * * Et Al. * * *

The phrase ''Et Al.'' means ''and others'' in Latin. It is designed as a ''Catchall'' Category, in the event that a firm should ''take off'' in some new or unanticipated direction. Hopefully, however, our System has left no holes to be filled. For us the ''Catchall'' is a safety net, ''just in case.''

Pet.Deny.License	846,101

MAJOR CATEGORY

1. Litigation
2. Probate
3. Corporate & Business
4. Real Estate
5. Tax
6. Labor
7. Motor Vehicle
8. *Administrative Agency*
9. Other

ADMINISTRATIVE AGENCY GROUP (G)

1. Social Security Admin.
2. Bureau of Patents and Copyrights
3. Federal Trade Commission
4. *Federal Communications Commission*
5. Securities and Exchange Comm.
6. State Bureau of Workers' Comp.
7. Other State Agency
8. Other Federal Agency

ADMINISTRATIVE SUBGROUP (S)

1. Certification
2. Licensing
3. Proceedings by AA Against Licensee
4. Proceedings by AA Against Third Party
5. Proceedings by Licensee for Relief
6. *Proceedings by Third Party for Relief*

PROCEEDINGS DIVISION (D)

1. *Petition for Commencement*
2. Response
3. Discovery
4. Pre-Hearing
5. Hearing
6. Ruling
7. Execution
8. Appeal
9. Other

Figure 3-35

Petition for Hearing Workers' Comp.	866,101

MAJOR CATEGORY

1. Litigation
2. Probate
3. Corporate & Business
4. Real Estate
5. Tax
6. Labor
7. Motor Vehicle
8. *Administrative Agency*
9. Other

ADMINISTRATIVE GROUP (G)

1. Social Security Admin.
2. Bureau of Patents and Copyrights
3. Federal Trade Commission
4. Federal Communications Commission
5. Securities and Exchange Comm.
6. *State Bureau of Workers' Comp.*
7. Other State Agency
8. Other Federal Agency

ADMINISTRATIVE SUBGROUP (S)

1. Certification
2. Licensing
3. Proceedings by AA Against Licensee
4. Proceedings by AA Against Third Party
5. Proceedings by Licensee for Relief
6. *Proceedings by Third Party for Relief*

PROCEEDINGS DIVISION (D)

1. *Petition for Commencement*
2. Response
3. Discovery
4. Pre-Hearing
5. Hearing
6. Ruling
7. Execution
8. Appeal
9. Other

Figure 3-36

4

Computerized Document System

Storage of Masters and Working Files

Hard Disk Arrangements
Floppy Disk Storage
Added Digits and Extenders

Computerized form *storage* used in conjunction with word processing software provides one of the most powerful law office tools since the invention of the typewriter. We can now produce, generate, copy, and multiply data, faster than ever before. Interestingly, however, we have yet to take full advantage of this tool. Perhaps this is because much has been said about hardware and word processing software, but too little has been written about how to use these devices to properly construct, name, and place created forms on disk. Having thousands of useful forms is of little value if they are not properly designed or cannot be found.

As stressed in the last chapter, ''rapid storage and retrieval'' is the key to massive form development and efficient text storage. With a good system, and a *computer* in hand, our capabilities are truly unlimited. Luckily, the amount of money required for this technology is quite limited, when compared to the resulting benefits; here is your list of materials.

Required Materials:

- Computer
- Word Processing Program
- Sets of Floppy Disks or Micro-Floppies

The Direct Reference System (Chapter 3) will be used to number and label *all* of your Forms and Masters, *even* those that *are* computerized. So you do *not* have to learn a separate system. Rather, this chapter is designed to help you fine-tune that System for your particular hardware and software, by discussing computer *storage* methods. Once stored, your forms, or more accurately your Masters, are used to *create* ''working files,'' which in turn *produce* the final products.

Some of our focus may seem clerical. It is very important, nevertheless. For it is the attention to the *overlooked* details that count most.

DOCUMENT PRODUCTION COMPARISONS

Assuming that you are now familiar with the labeling and naming techniques presented in Chapter 3, try to visualize for a moment, that all of your copier-created forms are stored both in your computer and your file cabinet. As you know, our System allows immediate retrieval of forms from both storage places. In many instances, retrieval from your file cabinet may be faster than obtaining a hard copy from your computer. But the computer can perform some important post-retrieval functions that your photocopier cannot. To take maximum advantage of the computer's power, the user should be aware of these functions. And to become *fully* aware of them, we are going to consider an overly specific Example.

For those of you who worked for Litigation firms, at one time or another it was probably necessary to prepare a simple Motion to Compel Answers to Interrogatories; for those who did not, this is a common pleading that is used when the recipient of the Interrogatories (questions that must be answered under oath) either forgets or refuses to provide responses. Litigators will have repeated the Motion process dozens of times. It is a common one involving allegations that rarely change from case to case.

Let's back up for a moment, long enough to recall the process *without* any new methods or systems. Even if your office has performed it efficiently, the following steps were probably involved.

Someone—

1. Pulled the court rules and reviewed the sections pertaining to discovery sanctions;
2. Dictated a Motion, Supporting Affidavit, Notice of Hearing, and Brief (the basic allegations and legal principles were similar to the last Motion that was also dictated from scratch);
3. Turned the dictation over to a secretary, who typed the documents pursuant to instructions, and in addition prepared a Proof of Service and Enclosure Letters;
4. Proofread the pleadings and discovered at least one typographical or grammatical error;
5. Returned the documents to a secretary for revision and correction (which involved some retyping);
6. Redelivered the documents to the lawyer for a final review;
7. Returned the package to the secretary for mailing.

As you estimate the amount of time and effort expended by the sum of the above procedures, remember that we presented a rather conservative, and relatively efficient, view of the process. The example does not take into account form-finding time or "fumbling time," involving searches through the alphabetical indexes of court rule books and form files (that *never* seem to use words logically anticipated); and it does not consider second-and third-generation typos. Nor does it consider the time required to make certain that all supporting documents are included.

In any event, consider your physical operations if you used a computerized system:

1. A lawyer gives instructions to prepare a Motion to Compel Answers to Interrogatories; the names, dates, and required information are in the client file. (Total time 20 seconds.)
2. Both lawyer and secretary know that the motion obviously involves Litigation (Category 1), in a court of general jurisdiction (Group Element 8), and that discovery (Subgroup Element 3) proceedings are involved. So armed with that information alone, a glance at the Master Form Book Index (Chapter 5) will tell the secretary to retrieve file 183,701. (Total time 60 seconds.)
3. The secretary will then duplicate the applicable Master (60 seconds); the duplicate will become the Working Copy. To key in the names, dates, etc., and provide a final copy of all supporting documents ready for review, signature, and mailing, should take minutes, at most.

The differences between our two examples are subtle but critically significant. Intuitively, we know that time will be saved by using the computerized methods. But rarely do we appreciate the *full* extent of the savings. To assist the appreciation, here are some benefits that may not have been apparent:

- Attorney review time has been slashed.
- Research time has been cut or eliminated if the Master file's brief contains the required citations.
- It took less secretarial time to type a few fill-in portions on the computer keyboard than it did to type an entire set of documents from scratch on a typewriter.
- It is unlikely that any supporting documents will be omitted, particularly if they were all made part of the same computer file; less time, therefore will be required to assemble and check the supporting writings.
- For missed keys or errors that are spotted by the typist, it takes far less time to correct text "on the monitor" that has yet to be printed.
- Computer printers are faster than typewriters.
- Proofreading time will be cut substantially because the Masters will have already been proofed; added new text will be relatively minimal.
- If corrections or changes are needed, there will be a lesser likelihood of second-generation errors (these are "new" mistakes created as "otherwise" perfect text is retyped).
- Updating and revising Masters for "new" developments will be simpler because the person responsible will always have a well-defined base of existing text.

As with any new skill, speed and greater efficiency always come with practice. Your word processing operations may have seemed clumsy at first.

But with time, the movements became second nature. Likewise, your new systems should become almost reflexive, but not until they have been used for a while.

DEFINITIONS

As we approach your new endeavor, it is important to present some key definitions; eventually, these words should become second nature. In presenting our methods, computerese will be avoided; however, some terms are necessary to assist intra-firm communication and discussion. Please pay particular attention to the *first three* definitions; they are *extremely important* to the computerization of your Filing System:

1. *File*—A single unit of text that is stored on a disk (hard or floppy). A File can range in length from a few words to hundreds of pages. It should be thought of as a single item or element. Our definition, which is more *practical* than mathematical, suggests that ''things used together'' in practice should be kept in the same File.
2. *File Name*—The official ''Name'' that the computer will recognize and identify with a given file. This concept is much more important than it sounds, as it forms the basis for many of our methods. File Names are normally alphanumeric.
3. *Identifier*—A short, concise statement, written in abbreviated English, indicating the precise nature of the text contained in a given File. The Identifier is *not* part of the File Name (the concept of the ''identifier'' is developed in Chapter 3).
4. *Hard Disk*—A disc-shaped ''Storage Bin'' for your Files and File Names.
5. *Floppy Disk*—A Storage medium which serves the same function as a hard disk, except that you can touch and move it about; a single floppy disk will not have as much storage capacity as a hard disk.
6. *Micro-Floppy*—A smaller, heavier, more compact 3-1/2″ square disk; in truth, it does not bend or flop, but *does* hold more text and protects that text better than a standard floppy.
7. *Hard Copy*—A paper ''printout'' of all of the text contained in a given file.
8. *Final Copy*—As distinguished from a ''hard copy,'' a final, complete, formatted document, ready to be signed, sealed, and delivered.
9. *Format*—To provide the computer ''layout'' or arrangement for the print that appears on the pages of a given document.
10. *Formate*—A verb that we will coin for convenience, and use to mean ''creating a Master file from a pleading, form, or document, to be used repeatedly for the future creation of similar documents''; for example, to formate (the ''a'' is long) a Will or Trust.

11. *Working File*—A temporary file to be created in conjunction with one document, then erased after that document has been finalized and is no longer likely to be modified or needed.
12. *Database*—Fancy name for the "place" on your computer disks where you store text; your most important Database will consist of your Master Files.
13. *Master File* (or *Master*)—A file to be saved and used to create more than one document; one of our primary concerns will be to create, name, and store as many Master Files as we can.
14. *Download*—A transmission process whereby text is electronically sent from some Database, however distant, to your computer system.

With slight variations, most of the above definitions and terms are becoming universal. We will develop additional words later as the topics require.

FILE NAMES AND IDENTIFIERS

The extension of your file drawer form system to your computer's hard disk is probably the simplest act of computerization that any business could ever hope to perform. There is nothing to shut down, convert, or discard. The introduction of the computer to your existing form system involves nothing more than preparing to enter the Roman Number III in the Level Column (third) of your Master Index pages, as your forms gradually take their places on your disks (see Chapter 5 for construction of Index Pages). There is no retyping, refiling, reorganization, or re-anything. There are some very simple rules, however, necessary to cope with the transfer.

When creating *any* computer file (Master File or otherwise), you must assign an official alphanumeric File Name that your computer understands. The system for doing so will be thoroughly described shortly; however, *labeling* should first be considered, to avoid confusing it with file naming.

Even though the System allows retrieval without knowing the form's name or title, you will, as we discussed in Chapter 3, want to assign an *Identifier* (label written in abbreviated English), which will serve a dual purpose. *First,* the Identifier will be used for both the indexes and actual hardcopies of your Master Form Book (See Chapter 5). *Second,* the same Identifier can be typed on the label of the folder that will house any hard copies of the form that you may wish to keep in your file cabinet for immediate use or inspection.

You might think of a Will, for example, as a form to keep "on disk"; however, keeping a hard copy in your file cabinet (and in your Master Book) will greatly assist draftsmanship and location. You might think of a tax form as an item to permanently keep "in the cabinet"; however, eventually you may purchase software that fills in that form. You should give the same Identifier to the file cabinet form and its disk counterpart. They will probably be used together, if at all. Many more examples of Identifiers are provided in Appendix A.

Now it is time to assign an official *File Name* to the forms (Masters) that will be used with, and stored on, your computer. Those of you who are currently using The Direct Reference Filing System for your file cabinets will quickly understand the rationale of the proposed disk arrangement; for, it is nothing more than a natural *extension* of that System. For those of you who are not familiar with the System, please read Chapter 3. The rules for assigning File Names are basically the same ones that we used for the Direct Reference Filing System.

Recall from Chapter 3 that our form-naming system neither separates nor distinguishes Pre-printed Forms from Created Masters or Sample Documents. Nor does it even distinguish file cabinet forms from those stored on your computer disk. In effect, all types and manners of forms in your office are brought together under one ''roof'' or system. The shape of your roof may, however, vary slightly, depending upon your particular word processing software. That software will be the vehicle by which text is brought to, and stored on, your hard or floppy disk.

All major brands of word processors use some form of ''Alphanumeric'' base for assigning File Names. Some systems allow names consisting purely of numbers; others require at least one letter. Some allow only six characters; most allow eight or more. Some allow non-alphanumeric characters, others do not. We are now going to make the adjustments that may be required for your particular brand.

When assigning a formal file name to a computer master file, there are two possibilities:

[1]
Your Word Processor Allows Pure Numeric Names

If your particular brand of word processing software permits you to use *all* numbers for your file name, then you may use the exact numbering methods described in Chapter 3, *without variation.* It's that simple. You may, however be required to drop the commas after the third digit. Some word processors do not permit non-alphanumeric characters (such as commas) to be included in file names.

[2]
Your Word Processor Is "Strict Alphanumeric"

Some word processing programs require that the *first* letter of *every* file name be a letter; the remaining characters can be either alphabetic or numeric.

For such software, you must change the Category digit (the first) from its ''normal'' number to the first letter of the Category's English name. The remaining digits stay intact. Litigation, for example, would be changed from a ''1'' to an ''L.'' Each Labor file would have its first character changed from a ''6'' to a ''W'' (Worker's Rights), so as to distinguish it from Litigation.

In other words, your basic filing scheme remains intact, and the listings in your Master Book remain the same. Our ''pure number'' systems remain the same for file labels, hardcopies, and indexes. But to keep some word processors happy, the following substitutions occur for the first *digit* only, and for computer entry *only:*

Category	*First Character of File Name*	*Modified First Character for Strict Alphanumeric Software*
Litigation	1	L
Probate	2	P
Corporate & Business	3	C
Real Estate	4	R
Tax	5	T
Workers' Rights	6	W
Motor Vehicle	7	M
Administrative	8	A
Et al.	9	E

Figure 4-1

We have intentionally omitted the case of the word processor which allows *only* letters (i.e., strict alphabetic), because I know of *no* such software. It is unlikely that any commercial brands with such a restriction exist; and, if they do, I strongly urge against their purchase or use. The most common naming format is alphanumeric; so let's consider some additional examples at random:

SAMPLE INDEX ENTRIES	IDENTIFIER	NUMBER	FILE NAME
Motion to Compel Answers to Interrog.	Mot.Comp.Int.	133,701	L33701
Pleadings Removing Case from State to Federal Court	Removal Pack.	132,110	L32110
Simple Will for Single Female	Will.Simp.F. Sing.	221,000	P21000

Opening Corporate Minutes for Professional Corp.	Min.Op.P.C.	313,201	C13201
Construction Contract for Small Office Bldg.	Ct.Const.S.B.	419,201	R19201
Request for Private Ruling for ERISA Plan	Rule Request. ERISA	545,010	T44010
Arbitration Brief Theft Discharge	Brief.Arb. Theft	635,301	W35301

You might ask—If I have to use a letter to satisfy my computer, then why not use the same letter-number combination for the file cabinet? The answer is simple; we want our file drawers to consist of numerically ordered forms for fast filing and faster retrieval. Humans can find things *most* quickly when they are in simple numerical order. Letter-number combinations are clumsy for people, *but not* for computers, which have ‘‘random access’’ capability. The computer can locate a file by its File Name instantly, no matter where it is positioned or how it is named; a human being cannot.

Notwithstanding the fact that you have software that allows pure numbers, you may, *nevertheless,* wish to use the above lettering convention for your computer, particularly if staring at pure numbers on a monitor screen drives you buggy. After a while, the association between the few letters and their respective numbers should become second nature.

In summary, the *Computer File Name* is nothing more than a common Label Name with a minor change: the comma is dropped, and the first digit (representing The Major Category) is changed from a number to a letter (the first letter of the title of the Major Category). In general, regardless of your brand of word processor, the advantages of this System should quickly become apparent:

- *FIRST*—A single naming method (with a potentially slight variation for the first number) applies both to your computer and file cabinet—you may wish to check *both* places before using or modifying your forms. Or you may wish to create, change, or ‘‘fill in’’ documents on your computer and store extra copies in your file cabinet; photocopier toner is cheaper than printer ribbons or laser disk cartridges.
- *SECOND*—Even though a single Master may be located in separate media (i.e., computer and file cabinet), the Master Form Book Index (Chapter 5) provides a singular reference for rapid location.
- *THIRD*—You do not have to go through the aggravation of playing ‘‘guess the letter’’ as you would with an alphabetic system. You do not *need* an index, nor do you need to know the name of the form; you need only know its purpose.

- *FOURTH*—You do not need complex storage or database software to logically store your forms. Such software often involves learning an entire programming language just to store data. With the Direct Reference System, you learn *only* how your form is used, and how it fits into our legal system.
- *FIFTH*—The methods are designed to fit virtually any word processing software, so that your computer files are ''immediately ready'' for being accessed and processed.

BASIC RULES FOR CANDIDACY

A Master File could consist of a will, a pleading, some principles of law (with citations included), a complete brief, or an entire SEC Offering. When creating *any* Master File, carefully consider the following questions:

What Forms Should Remain in My File Drawer?

There are forms and pleadings that should be stored on disk, but there are also those which should remain exclusively in the file cabinet. Do not go crazy with your new toy; remember that for some repeatedly used forms, the human eye works faster than the laser printer-screen-menu-keyboard set of procedures. Forms such as time sheets, billing sheets, check lists, and documents that seldom change might best be left *in the file cabinet* (Level II).

Officially printed court forms (praecipes, subpoenas, etc.) and multi-part impression forms should obviously be left in your file drawer (Level I). Some documents, that can be computer-stored, have a proper place both on disk and in the file cabinet for quick reference.

Some consultants and software vendors like to use terms such as ''low tech'' to disparagingly describe the use of photocopiers to stock up on forms for your file cabinets. This is understandable since they are oriented toward selling and designing expensive microware, *not* inexpensive file cabinets or paper labels. They are generally computer technicians, *not* practicing lawyers. These people may very well be experts when it comes to the latest micro-advances. But those of us who have spent decades moving paper in and out of the law office know the best tools for that process. That is why methods designed to best use all of the office equipment will run circles around their best systems.

Each piece of equipment has its place and function. So, as we speak of the microprocessor and its truly incredible powers, don't lose sight of the fact that it is only one of our many tools. Even the old metal file cabinet is still extremely important. For cooking, the ''highest tech'' may be the microwave cooker. Many modern cooks have purchased them; but how many of those cooks threw away their stoves and ovens in the process?

How Large Should My Files Be?

For citations that are to be plugged into briefs, a file should be limited to a single often-used principle. A good rule-of-thumb suggests that a given *file* should stand for no more than one basic ''proposition'' of law; for it is much easier to string together several small files than to butcher-up, delete, and distribute part of one large file. Supporting a single proposition may, of course, take several pages, or it may only require a single sentence backed up by citations. In any event, the *subject matter* of the file, not its length, should determine its structure.

For pleadings other than briefs, the *opposite* principle prevails; files should be complete and comprehensive, containing all possible alternative provisions that a lawyer may want to see or consider. This type of file not only serves as a text generator, but it also provides a ''check list'' that assures the user that no key allegation or clause will be omitted. This general principle also applies to Wills, Trusts, Promissory Notes, and similar instruments.

What About Footnotes and Cross-References?

Avoid the use of footnotes for Master Files consisting of briefs, unless they are necessary (or unless you are a diehard footnote fanatic). If more than one Master File is used to create a document, the footnote numbers will rarely match up. It is much easier to create footnotes for your Working Files than for your Masters. Cross-references are allowable, but *only* between two items that are contained within the same Master File. Do not cite or refer to matter in another Master File. And be particularly cautious about citations that may refer to cases that were *initially* cited in a separate Master File:

Marbary -v-Madison, Id. 235
Wood -v-Lucy Lady Duff Gordon, supra.

The terms ''Id'' (meaning ''Identical'') and ''supra'' (meaning ''above'') are both Latin derivations that indicate to the reader that the full citation for the given case is located somewhere in a prior portion of the document. Under no circumstances should the designations be used unless *that* prior portion is also contained within the same Master File.

For My Brief Bank, How Much Law Should I Store?

Do not try to put your firm's entire law library on disk; there is no need. In deciding whether or not to create a Master File from a brief that you have obtained, use this simple test—if you anticipate that you will use the text at least one more time before it becomes obsolete, then save it to disk; if not, don't.

In most cases, your firm's particular area of specialization will dictate the type of substantive law that will be reused. I suggest that you make the decision to create this type of Master as you prepare to use it in the normal course of work.

THE ORIGINS OF YOUR DATA BANK

Now that you have your computer and your existing file naming system, what do you do? Where do your Masters come from? And how do you physically store them? The answers are relatively simple. But the questions are important, so we should consider them specifically.

For Levels I and II, your forms are simply named, labeled, and placed in a folder to be stored in your file drawers in simple numerical order. You can always see, feel, and grab them with unsophisticated manual movements. The computerized portion of your system, however, consists of tiny magnetic impulses, quite invisible. It is going to be our goal to take some of the mystique out of this data by arranging it.

We can't see the magnetic images on our videotapes, but we know how to find a particular movie if we have a decent arrangement and labeling scheme. For your computer database or bank, the need for arrangement is even greater; for unlike your file drawer or videotape library, your computer's data can come from several totally different species of physical matter. There are primarily four such species.

Manual Entry

Your goal, of course, is to start building up a bank of computer Master Files; the larger your bank, the more efficient your document production system will be. As technology marches on, the methods for getting text onto your computer's hard disk are expanding. The most common method still, however, involves straight typing.

You may, if you wish, start pulling forms out of your file drawer at random and begin creating Masters; you can be kept quite busy keying them all in. Or you could take some client files that contain good portions of master language, and then pick and choose from among the best pleadings, trusts, corporate minutes, and writings. But, even if you have that much extra time on your hands, neither of the above procedures would be too efficient.

I recommend a transactional approach. Don't stop what you are doing to try to figure out which forms will make good Masters; *rather,* let your day-to-day work make those decisions for you. When you sit down to type or hand-draft your *next* document, that is the time to ask: ''Is it likely that I will need a similar document at least once in the future before its basic content becomes obsolete?'' If so, *stop* and make the form. Your Masters will be easier to create and much more likely to ''fit'' the intended purpose if they are constructed in this manner. Masters created in a vacuum often fail under fire, regardless of the planning that went into them.

This suggested method means that your daily office work will be interrupted, but only momentarily. For the Master that you are going to take time to create will be used shortly thereafter as you complete the ''office work'' for your client.

The methods for following this procedure are new. So it might help to consider them step-by-step from the typist's point of view:

1. You are typing a document for a particular file and decide, midway through it, that several paragraphs should be made into a Master (i.e., Formated).
2. At that point, pull your Master Book and create a Master File number XXX,XXX; then give it an Identifier.
3. The object will be to structure your file so that you create the Master File and Working File almost simultaneously.
4. As the Master is completed, it should be separately hardcopied and put into the Master Form Book *immediately;* the index page containing the new form should then be modified to indicate the new inclusion. You can handwrite this entry and then reprint the changed index page at a later date.
5. Now polish up and personalize the Working File after the new Master has been saved to your disk for future use.

Caution: The ''seemingly'' most difficult thing in the world will be to ''worry about'' making a Master as your ''rush project'' is waiting to ''get into the mail.'' And it seems that *every* secretarial project is a ''rush.'' But if you don't take the extra seconds now, you won't be able to save hours later on.

If you study steps 1–5, you will notice that you did very little extra work in creating your Master. The time will have been well spent, as the next similar project should require much less drafting and work.

It is very important that the above steps be followed in the suggested order. For there will be an overwhelming temptation to create the Master and then immediately resume work on the Working File. Trust me when I say that you will be *engulfed* by that instinctive urge to get the current projects out, leaving the cataloguing of the Master for later. If you put off the naming and indexing, the Master's location and existence will be lost forever. The only lingering evidence of the Master will be those little electronic impulses stored on the disk; and they are quite invisible.

There are a couple of questions to be considered, at this point:

Which Comes First—Working File or Master?

Unlike the "chicken or the egg" controversy, the *answer* is not academic; it must be decided on an ad hoc basis.

Case 1:

If *most* of the document is to be reused, then merely continue it as you would any Working file, and after you are finished, copy it and create your Master.

Examples

Simple Wills, Standard Form Trusts, Powers of Attorney, Releases, Motions to Compel Answers to Interrogatories for Which No Answers Were Received.

Case 2:

If *only a part* of the document is to be reused, create the Master first, *then* go to work on your Working file; when you get to the appropriate spot, copy the Master into your working file.

Examples

Special clauses of complex Wills or Trusts, citations of law to be plugged into Briefs, standard rider language for Construction Contracts.

Often the choice between Cases 1 and 2 will involve a judgment call. If in doubt, make the Master first.

When feeling particularly lazy, I often allowed the Working files to merely serve as Masters until they could be polished. This was dangerous; for it seemed that no one ever got around to the polishing. As a result, when the Master was to be reused, it often contained some potentially embarrassing extraneous facts.

Where Are Good Places to Get Forms for Your Computer's Data Bank?

In the next chapter, we will cover form creation. But first, you need to know where to go to find the text that will be shaped, polished, and stored in your own data bank:

1. *Your Own Firm.* For areas of law in which your firm specializes (or specialized), your own "best" forms should be updated, polished, and made into Masters. For areas of non-specialization, the next choice may be best.
2. *Other Firms.* During the course of practice, you, or the lawyers in your firm, know what a quality document looks like. Often, the quality or reputation of

the firm will attest. In any event, all proposed text or completed forms should be checked by a responsible lawyer; nothing should be accepted through blind faith.

3. *Form Books.* Be careful; there are good books and bad books. For Federal matters, such books may be more reliable. For state matters, however, unless the book is for your particular state, the forms may not meet your court's requirements. Aside from state-to-state variations, time may also bring with it changes in statutes, laws, and court rules. Don't buy *old* form books. And be *extra* wary of secretarial manuals. Their forms are generally designed to teach general methods, not specifics.

Electronic Entry

Methods, other than typing, exist for getting text onto your hard disk. As you shall discover in Chapter 8, you can download text directly from some outside databases. This would, in effect, cause material stored elsewhere to be "plugged into" your hard disk. This means that you could assign your own personal file name to the obtained data; for, once the material is stored in your system, you can modify or name it at will.

The tool that permits transmission of text and data between attorneys or databases is a simple device commonly referred to as a "modem." Do not be misled by the apparent simplicity of the process. The text files that you have been creating and manipulating exist under the auspices of your word processing software. There are some steps required to convert other "incoming" text into that format (see Chapter 8).

Optical Entry

Some more exotic methods for obtaining data are being developed and refined at an accelerated pace. The Optical Scanner, for example, has the ability to "look at" some text and "copy it" directly into your computer's disk, much like a photocopier retains its visions for duplication purposes. "Digitizers" are optical scanning artists. They copy pictures and images into the computer, much as the scanner does text. There are presently some scanners that can look at handwritten notes and translate them into print (even those of doctors and lawyers).

Optical entry can be particularly useful for lengthy standard documents, such as trusts, pension plans, some recording contracts, and even portions of briefs containing lengthy citations. For such matters, tremendous amounts of typing time can be saved by using good standards or prototypes.

Acoustical Entry

The acoustical or "voice" input devices will serve as the ultimate method for processing text, at least until engineers figure out a way to get our brainwaves from head to paper, telepathically. Imagine giving dictation directly to your hard disk. The technology and equipment now exist; they are currently in the polishing stages.

The acoustical devices have the ability to "hear" and analyze words, and spell-check them. Soon they will grammatically perfect sentences such as: "Tell Mr. Bear to bear down and get to the bare bones of the project," notwithstanding the perplexities of distinguishing among synonyms.

WORKING FILES

In Chapter 2, you examined client files and the documents that comprise them. In Chapter 3 we considered the Forms and Masters that are used to service those Client Files. Until now, the lines of demarcation between those two sets were relatively clean. The computer has, however, helped to blur the otherwise nice distinction between Client Files and Masters; the confusion comes in the shape of the Working File (Figure 4-2), which is neither fish nor fowl. It is an intermediary item that is copied from a Master and used to produce a Final Copy.

Recall that Masters are not changed or modified when being used to create a Working File—rather the Master is copied, and that *copy* is then used to create the required document for the client. The Master can then remain intact for subsequent use. The copy becomes the *Working File;* it will be expanded, contracted, altered, or tailored as the client's individual circumstances require. But *then* what becomes of it?

Saving Working Files

There are good arguments for saving the Working Files; and there are equally good arguments for erasing them, but *never* before a Hard Copy has been obtained. Consider these positions:

In Favor of Preservation:

- They provide a copy of all prepared documents.
- If a document is lost, it can be reprinted quickly.
- If a document is to be modified or amended, time can be saved by merely changing the Working File.
- If a lengthy similar document is needed, the Working File can be altered and used to create it, thereby saving a lot of typing time.
- If the building burns to the ground, and the Working File disks are stored elsewhere, portions of Client Files can be rapidly reconstructed.

Opposing Preservation:

- If you store too much unnecessary text on your hard disk, the computer will operate more slowly and Masters could become more difficult to locate.

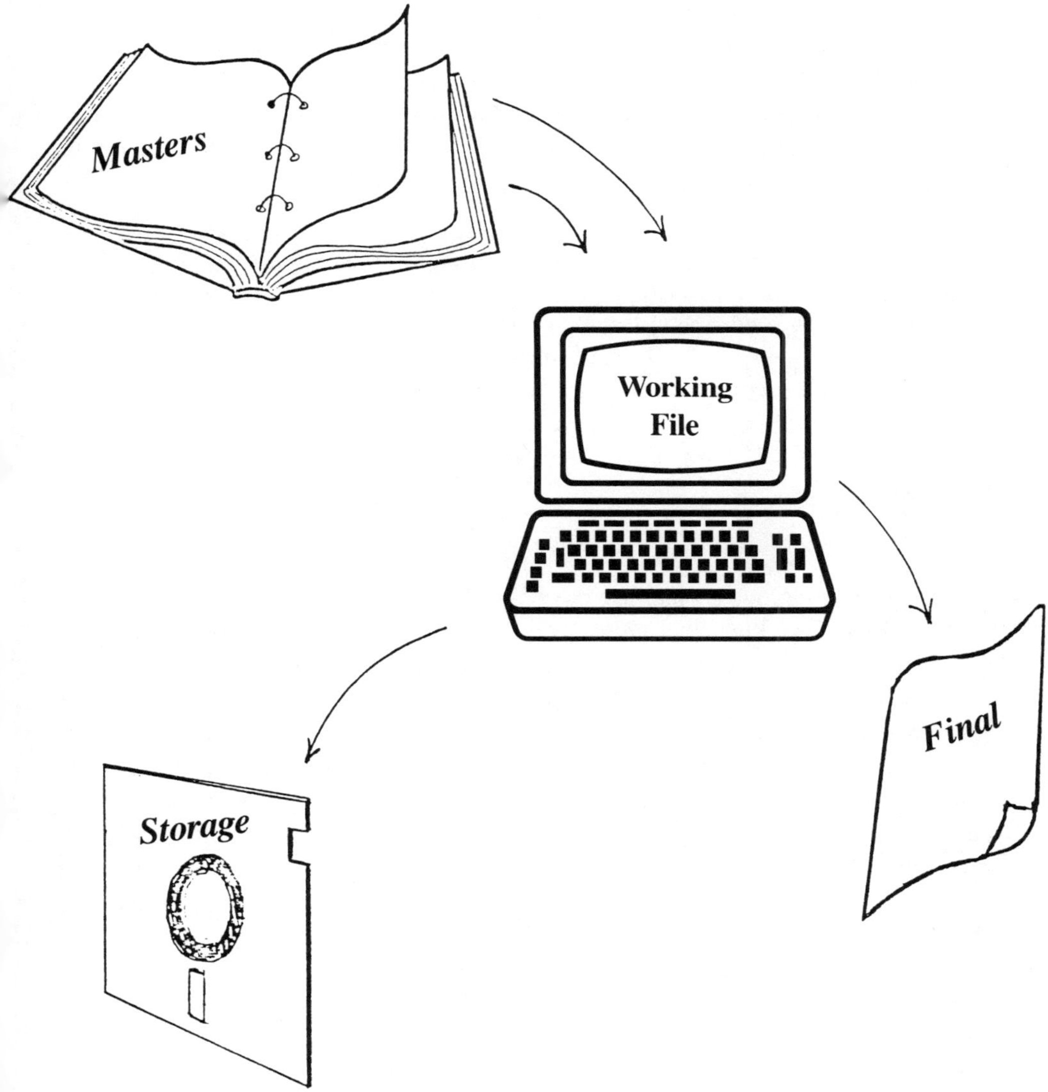

Figure 4-2

- There is little need to save the computer file after you get your hard copy; how often do you really lose those file copies? And for that rare case where a loss occurs, they can usually be obtained from other sources.
- With a good set of Master Files, there should not be any need to store Working Files; for the Masters should be able to reproduce any Working File with minimal effort.
- Confusion between Working Files and Master Files will be increased, unless the Working Files are erased. You may be increasingly tempted to use one client's Working File for another client (by changing names); this can lead to disaster.

In truth, neither set of arguments is presented for the purpose of deciding whether or not to save Working Files, but *rather* for the purpose of determining *how long* they should be saved; that is the crucial inquiry. Clearly, they should not be saved perpetually; there is no need. But under no circumstances should a Working File be erased until it has been hardcopied.

Perhaps the ideal time to erase a Working File is after the final copy has been "put to bed." Consider these points for determining when that has happened:

Example 1

Litigation—Once a pleading has been filed and mailed with a copy saved for the Client File, there is no real need to save it. If, however, an amendment may be required, the pleading should be saved until after the trial or conclusion of the case. Otherwise, if an extra copy is needed, it is probably cheaper to use your photocopier than your printer. There is, however, an important exception for lengthy documents that are to be reused with only slight modification. A lengthy Motion and Brief may, for example, only require slight modification before they are to be used for a subsequent appeal. They should definitely be saved until the litigation is concluded and all appeal periods have substantially expired. There may be lengthy fact arguments that would never be stored on your Masters. Saving the Working File could avoid a lot of retyping for repetitive facts and specific factual arguments.

Under no circumstances should Working Files be allowed to assume the status of Masters, unless they are tailored, proofed, polished, and assigned numbers. If one is careless in this regard, trust that sooner or later, some subsequent pleading with unrelated names and facts will show up to cause some rather extreme embarrassment.

Example 2

Probate—Once estate plans have been executed and mailed to the required recipients, there is no need to save the Working Files. Unlike

Litigation Masters, Estate Planning documents are suited to the creation of detailed, lengthy Masters. There is little use of truly original text. Confusion and potentially dangerous instrument mix-ups could result from an over-reliance upon Working Files.

When testamentary documents of any type are to be modified, normally the process involves the simple addition of text or language indicating the change or deletion (for example—Amendment to Trust, or Codicil to a Will). This is to be distinguished from modifications of Litigation pleadings which often involve redoing the entire instrument; in the latter situation, you must prepare a complete amend*ed* pleading instead of a mere amend*ment*. The amend*ed* pleading, unlike the latter, could make good use of an existing Working File. The amend*ment,* however, generally consists of material that is brand new.

For estate administration matters, it would seem that once the estate is closed, there should be no need to maintain the files. If, however, post-administration proceedings are going to occur, you may want to wait until *they* are concluded before erasing the Working Files.

Example 3

Corporate and Business—This category would seem to warrant the longest holding periods. For matters involving protracted negotiations, or long-term business relationships, certain documents should best be saved to floppy disk for storage. Unlike the documents considered in the prior examples, business relationships tend to be continuing, not discrete; and so are the instruments used during the course of those relationships.

Preservation of Working Files is particularly warranted for employee benefit plans because they are frequently subjected to modifications, updates, and revisions. Tax laws change every time that some Congressman gets an idea that will not work (a daily occurrence); and with those changes come revision requirements. So even after hard copies are obtained, it may pay to save the Working Files.

Example 4

Real Estate—Once the required conveyance has occurred, and all necessary papers have been executed, the Working File can be discarded. For most transactions, obedience to the Statute of Frauds (requiring that interests in Real Estate can *only* be conveyed by writings) will probably assure the existence of an adequate number of hard copies.

Example 5

Tax—For certain documents awaiting IRS approval, such as Retirement Plans (per ERISA), common sense would dictate that the Working File be maintained until approval has been issued. Modifications could be required at any point in the process.

Example 6

Workers' Rights documents would best adhere to the *preceding rules* pertaining to Litigation; in particular, the holding period would end when the subject document, case, or pleading becomes finalized. For Collective Bargaining Contracts, language should be stored in perpetuity, but as Masters, not as Working Files.

Motor Vehicle and Administration Agency documents will have holding periods that uniquely depend upon their types. For hearings and proceedings, for example, the Rules pertaining to Litigation would apply. For Agreements, the suggestions of Example 3 would pertain.

Naming Working Files

As we have already determined, Working Files are going to be somewhat ''temporary.'' So there may be a temptation to quickly assign some acronym or abbreviation that first pops into the typist's head. There are some dangers in this. As a matter of fact there are two evils to be avoided at all cost.

- *CAUTION 1*—Be careful that you *do not* assign a pre-existing file name, or you may erase that *entire* prior file.
- *CAUTION 2*—Be careful to assign a file name that you will remember.

With the foregoing in mind, I have a few suggestions that may help avoid the twin evils. No, we are not going to create another entirely new, logic-based structure to handle these temporary items; as a matter of fact, we can make use of our existing System. In particular, let your Client File Number be used to form the base.

Type 1—Pure Numeric Names Allowed:

If your word processor allows you to use a straight numeric file name, and you have elected to do so, then let the first digit switch to a letter (i.e., Litigation would use an ''L'' instead of ''1''; ''P'' for Probate instead of ''2''). Such letters will quickly signal a distinction between all of your Masters, and your Working Files. Next use a portion of your client file number, followed by some letters. The structure of such a ''number'' would best be shown by an example. Assume that your word processor allows at least eight alphanumeric characters for naming files (virtually all word processing programs allow at least eight characters). An Estate Plan for a particular client normally involves several instruments; some may have been prepared as multiple alternatives, with multiple drafts. Consider a Will Revision:

Example 7

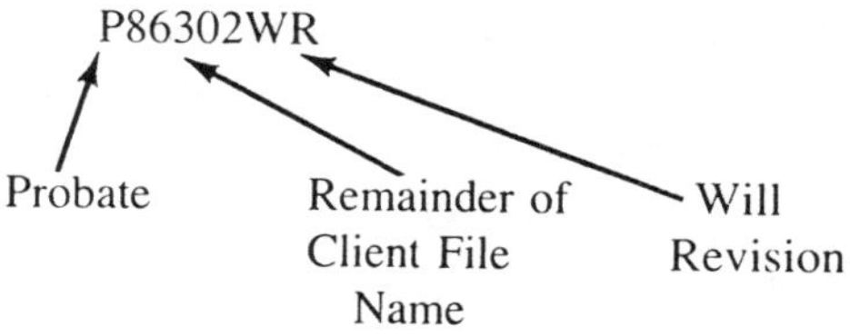

If your software permits, all files for client file number 286,302 should be kept together on the disk's menu of files. It might also help to keep a running list of Working File names on a red label somewhere on your client's folder. Let's consider some additional documents for the same client:

Explanatory Letter to Client	P86302EL
Pour-Over Trust	P86302PT
Amendment to Trust	P86302TA
Third Alternative Will	P86302W3

Example 8

You just filed a set of interrogatories for client file 186,302, and you want to save it. Assign number L86302IN. I am assuming that you are allowed eight alphanumeric characters for your file names. If not, you may wish to drop the decade or the decade-year combination. Most working files will not be saved for a year; and fewer will survive a decade.

So the file name might look like this:

L6302IN *or*

L302IN

The characters should allow you to find the file immediately. You will have the client's file in front of you and will, therefore, know the file number. The "two-letter" abbreviation should be more than adequate to locate the limited number of Working Files that you may wish to save for the given Client File.

If another pleading such as a Motion to Compel Answers to the Interrogatories is later prepared, that file can bear one of the following names:

L86302MC

L6302MC

L302MC

Type 2—Strict Alphanumeric Names Required:

If your word processing software requires a letter for the first character of your file names, then you will already be using a first letter for your Master File Names, regardless of your preferences. You may wish to place an ''X'' in front of all Working Files to distinguish them from Master Form Files. The purpose is to avoid confusion with (and potential erasure of) one of your Master Forms.

Example 9

According to the above suggestion, a Working File Number from our prior example might look like this:

XL6302MC

CAUTION: Use any configuration that will help identify the client file and document. Most of you may not need to waste a digit for the ''X''; the eight characters (instead of six), and the letters on the end may adequately distinguish your disposable Working Files from your precious Masters. If not, use the ''X'' as an *extra measure* of safety.

RECAP

At this point, there may be a lot of different number-letter structures floating around in your head, depending upon your particular brand of software. For the vast majority of you, we can simplify things greatly by saying that *most* popular word processing programs will be alphanumeric and allow at least eight characters for your file names. And thus, the following example should ''bring things together'':

Example 10

Sally Wells has a lawsuit because of some poisonous beer that caused her to become ill. Her client file number is 186,201. Interrogatories (using Master Form 133,510—see Figure 3-5) are to be used to send questions to the beer manufacturer. The Interrogatories Master is already stored on your hard disk as L33510.

- *Step 1*—Duplicate file L33510 with a simple ''copy function.''
- *Step 2*—The newly created file is named XL3510IR; this becomes the Working File.
- *Step 3*—The Master is tucked away; the Working File is used to prepare the Final Copy. It's that simple.

As an alternative, you can drop the ''X'' and use L33510IR, but *only* if there is no danger of confusing the Master Files with the Working Files. I might add that for most of you, the danger should not exist. If you use all of your eight alphanumeric characters for your Working File names, they should, as previously mentioned, be *clearly* distinguishable from your Masters, which consist of only six digits with *no* trailing letters.

Using Floppy Disks

You should strive to get the unnecessary data off of your hard disk as soon as possible. Even though your disk capacity may be large, you will want to fill it with usable Master Files, not text that you will never see again. So once the matters are completed, you should save potentially needed Working Files to floppy disk and then erase them from your hard disk.

It has been suggested that a separate floppy disk be set up for each separate "large" client. Depending upon your number of clients, this may not be a bad idea. Floppy disks are quite cheap, and their storage capacities are ever increasing. Labeling them is quite simple—Just assign the appropriate Client File Number, the same one that you assigned in accordance with the rules provided in Chapter 2. On the sleeve or envelope, you can affix a label that briefly tells of its contents.

Client—Trans Media Corp 382,401
Retirement Plans
Compensation Plans

Figure 4-3

STORAGE OF MASTERS AND WORKING FILES

Notwithstanding extensive standardization in recent years, word processing programs still possess their own peculiar quirks and personalities. Each has its own set of menus, instructions, and key strokes. In addition, programs may provide their own special methods for dividing up the masses of text (to be stored on the computer's hard disk) into separate parts, directories, or divisions.

As indicated throughout the preceding portions of this book, both the Direct Reference Form Filing System and the Computer Document System (which are essentially one in the same) can be used without regard to software or hardware. But some caution is urged with respect to the following discussions; unlike the earlier portions of this book, we are now going to consider some of the parts of your system that may be affected by your particular software. Therefore, if you have not already purchased a computer or word processing package, the person to ask about the following matters will be your prospective vendor.

Hard Disk Arrangements

Your computer's hard disk is a massive storage bin which will allow you to save, and obtain immediate access to, a very large number of forms, but not without some adjustment. The creation and use of a very large and voluminous form database should, by all means, be encouraged; for that is what will permit you to prepare documents and pleadings instantly and more accurately than ever before. Let us consider some potential "adjustments" that may prove helpful:

Directories and Subdirectories. Most word processing programs will not require you to keep one continuous listing of all of your files. That could indeed become obnoxious. Rather, most will permit methods by which you can divide or split your directory into sub-directories or sub-listings. If you are permitted to do so, I have the following suggestion:

> Set up at least one sub-directory for each Major Category; and name each according to its official Category name (i.e., Litigation, Probate, etc.); these sub-directories will house your Master Files.

You will, of course, be required to comply with the limitations and requirements provided by your particular software. However, today's word processing programs are becoming increasingly flexible and permissive. You should be able to set up your system in accordance with your own dictates. And remember that just because some special functions are allowed or permitted by the software, does not mean that you must use them. Not all word processing programs are specifically designed for the legal profession.

You must be aware of some of the structural limitations imposed. Only by recognizing the problems can you "get around them" and proceed to effectively create and use a massive storage system. A key limitation always involves storage capacity. The price that you must pay for *filling* your computer's hard disk can best be analyzed by considering the following:

1. *Defined Storage Limits*

In their justifiable eagerness to be *completely accurate,* software vendors, technicians, and "the people at the computer store" drive us crazy with numbers and equations when we ask very simple questions about the amount of text that we can store on our hard disks. So, if you will permit me to be a bit crude and allow me an inaccuracy range of plus or minus 10 percent, I will give you a very helpful and simple though slightly inaccurate rule-of-thumb.

If you have recently purchased a computer, your hard disk storage capacity should be at least 10 megabytes (hopefully 20 ''meg''). If you wish, you can think of a megabyte as a 1,000 kilobytes; 1 kilobyte (K) consists of 1,024 bytes. And 1 byte should be thought of as corresponding to a single character (i.e., letter, single digit integer, blank space, symbol).

Just because you have 20 megabytes of storage, however, does not mean that you are entitled to fill it up with Master Forms. Instead, some of those megabytes must be used for your computer's disk operating system, your word processing program, and other utilities that your computer needs, not to mention all of the miscellaneous letters, memos, and ''working files'' that you did not, or could not, take the time to erase or transfer to floppy disks. Therefore, when attempting to figure out how much space that you have for storage of your Masters, you should think in terms of ''available'' space. Consider ''available space'' as equaling the total capacity of your computer, minus the space required for the preceding items. Before we get bogged down any further, here is the quick answer that I promised:

> RULE-OF-THUMB: Think of 1 megabyte as permitting you to store approximately 700 pages of text; this assumes that you will use the normal 1-inch margins and double spacing, which will permit approximately 24 lines per page. I am also assuming that standard 8-1/2″ × 11″ paper is being used.

Assuming that you had 10 megabytes of storage available using the crude rule-of-thumb above, you would be able to store approximately 7,000 pages of text. If you are carefully designing and constructing your forms (Chapter 5), you should be able to store quite a few of them. However, if, for example, you are storing entire briefs instead of individual propositions of law (the latter being preferred), you could fill up the space quicker than you think.

Do not confuse the capacity of your hardware with that of your software. The size of your Files will be limited by both your hardware and word processing software.

2.
Location of Files

For our own paper forms (Levels I and II) and indexes, we can physically arrange things nicely in simple numerical order. But with respect to the computer's own arrangement, that may involve a different story. Regardless of the word processing software that you elect to use, a directory or list of files can always be obtained during one of the early menu screens. Arranging that directory in accordance with your own choices or logic-based arrangements may not be quite so simple. Of course, it is not necessary if you use your Master Index Book.

If you can arrange the files in straight numerical order on your hard disk, then by all means do so. Of course, by arranging the files in numerical order, you will automatically be utilizing the arrangement called for by your Direct Reference Filing System.

Let us be clear about something at this point—It is not, however, critical that you *arrange* the form files in numerical order on your hard disk; your computer may have its own idea of how it will arrange disk text. Suffice it to say that they *will* be in order in your Master Form Book Index. For the time being, trust me when I say that your computer will have no problem whatsoever locating the file that is ''called,'' even though it may not be arranged in numerical order in its internal disk.

A good numerical arrangement of files on your directory will somewhat ease the eyestrain on the part of the user. However, as the numbers of files increase, so must the difficulty, regardless of how good that arrangement may be.

Of course there is a solution to this problem. As a matter of fact, your Master Form Book was designed specifically to allow you to locate file names quickly and easily, without having to scroll through several screens of your computer.

3.
Computer Slowdown

As the hard disk becomes full, the operations of the computer slow down. To lawyers, this is a ''too minor'' concern; for, we quite accurately assume that our computer has provided us with such incredible speed that a slight slowdown is not of major concern. But it should be.

When my secretary first complained, I did not pay attention to her, because I was quite pleased with the fact that the computer could, in terms of time saved, outperform the typewriter many times over. It was not until I *personally* sat down at the computer to prepare a file that I became aware of the differences in operating time for a full disk as opposed to a relatively empty one. As strange as it may sound, when you once get the taste of performing a function within two seconds, eight seconds seems like an awfully long time. The moral of this story is—The staff should always listen to secretarial complaints; the typist is there to produce a product as quickly and as efficiently as possible.

There are some methods by which speed can be increased; consider these few:

- *Enhancements and gadgets*—There are some extras that you can put on your computer to ''turbo charge'' it, in much the same fashion as a 16-year-old kid soups-up his automobile. Such gadgets exist and are being developed on a regular basis. You may wish to contact your hardware vendor for details.

- *Increased capacity*—The best way to provide increased capacity and speed is merely to upgrade your computer by adding an additional "Board." It is quite a simple matter to add additional capacity to the computers that are being sold today. The term "plug-in" is not a euphemism. The additional memory comes on convenient little modular boards that can be quickly and easily installed. They are not cheap; and before considering these "plug-ins," you should always compare the cost of purchasing a brand new computer that comes with the increased capacity, not to mention new technological enhancements that may accompany it.
- *Erase Unneeded Material*—The more text on your disk, the slower it will operate.

Floppy Disk Storage

Floppy disk storage is convenient, easy, and inexpensive. It is a simple method by which you can store great volumes of text into a relatively small amount of space, quickly and inexpensively. It has all but rendered microfilm storage obsolete. Personally, I like floppy disk storage because it is neat, convenient, and discrete. I can see, feel, touch, file, store, and physically label floppy disks.

Note that floppies should be thought of as *supplements,* not *substitutes* for hard disk storage. For, unlike hard disk storage, floppies do not permit immediate access to data. They must first be inserted, and booted, before data can be brought up. When a matter is stored on a hard disk, you can retrieve it by pushing a few mere buttons; no physical handling of materials is necessary. Everything can be accomplished at the keyboard. However, when using floppy disks, some physical operations are required. The user must first locate the disk, then copy the matter into the computer's memory, or onto its hard disk. The copied files become Working Files. The floppy disk must then be returned to its sleeve and placed into its proper position in the disk tray. This does not seem like a lot of work, and it is not. But it does take slightly longer due to the fact that more manual operations are involved.

There is another minor inconvenience with respect to updating and modifying. In particular, if a Master File is contained on hard disk, then modifying it should be a simple, one-step process. Of course, after the modification, it will be necessary to make the appropriate changes in your Master Form Book. However, if there are floppy disk backups, they will also have to be modified and updated. This can, however, normally be accomplished by simply copying the new updated files onto the old floppies.

With the foregoing in mind, consider the following recommendations:

1. Set aside ten *separate* floppy disks, one for each MAJOR CATEGORY (which includes a "0" Category for office forms); and
2. Label each floppy disk with a separate label:

	LITIGATION 1XX,XXX
Rev. 6/30/88	

Figure 4-4

3. The Master Files for each Category will be stored on the floppy disks. In addition, you should make one duplicate set of the disks to place somewhere for safekeeping. The months and years of effort that you will put into creating your polished Masters cannot be replaced.
4. Update your disks on a regular basis; this is quite simple and can be done quite quickly. As each Master File is updated or modified, you should, periodically, conform the other floppy disks. It is not necessary to update the floppies every single time that you make a change on one of the Masters contained on your hard disk. You might, however, get into the habit of updating or "conforming" them on a monthly or bi-monthly basis.

Added Digits and Extenders

Just because our decimal system uses a six-digit number, does not necessarily mean that you will be able to store up to 999,999 forms. Remember that several of the digits have specific meanings; the availability for use of the digits is therefore limited. The vast majority of firms, however, should be able to store all forms that will ever be needed, using six digits. If your firm cannot, remember that additional digits can be used, depending upon your software limitations. Most word processing programs permit up to eight alphanumeric characters.

The six-digit System should, as indicated, be quite adequate for most firms. Moreover, six characters would seem easy to remember and simple to repeat. But, some sub-groups that you might think up, may require more digits; if your software allows them, then, by all means, add the extra digits, *but be sure to add them at the end.*

The most fertile ground for expansion would involve Litigation files 189,000 through 189,999; recall that this particular set of forms would include Litigation matters in your state court of general jurisdiction, and would more specifically involve text citations of "Substantive Law" (see Figure 3-5 for your Litigation chart). This range would include created files that are not "swallowed up" by the remaining MAJOR CATEGORIES. Single citations or entire briefs involving various common law matters would be typical.

Even careful selectivity may not dispense with your need to store more than 999 files in that particular sub-group. Expansion of this system to seven digits will allow up to 9,999 files. But a word of caution—Do not expand the sub-group, "in this case—The Court System," unless you expand the entire Major Category, or else you will destroy the categorical arrangement of your file cabinet and computer storage system.

Moreover, it would not do any harm to expand the entire system to seven or even eight characters. You merely add "trailing zeros" to *all* of the forms or file names for the remainder of the System, even those that do not require the expanded numbers. It is noteworthy that a *seven*-digit form system would provide a nice distinguishing characteristic from your six-digit client file system.

Example 11

	6-Character System	*7-Character System*
Label	189,000	1,890,000
Comma Removed	189000	1890000
Alphanumeric	L89000	L890000

Figure 4-5

EXTENDERS are additions to existing file names. The ability to use extenders is carefully governed by the specifications of the software that you may be using. For example, your word processing software manual may contain a statement similar to this:

> For assigning names to your files, you may use up to eight alphanumeric characters. By using a decimal point, you can add an extender of three.

As we have suggested, the requirements for naming files will vary with your particular brand of word processing software. For the above "sample" software, consider the following examples:

Without extender	186345
With extender	186345.123

These extenders can come in quite handy, particularly if you wish to assign a separate file *name* to each individual *page* of your particular Master Form. The extenders allow you to increase your available number of file names. As a practical matter, they will permit you to have a quantity of names far beyond that which you will probably need. Of course, the use of the decimal point departs from our "pure integer" method. However, the use of the decimal digits will not, in any manner, interfere with your basic numbering structure. As indicated, the best way to use the digits would be to number each page of your masters.

A word of *caution* is necessary. Just because the word processing software permits you to use extenders, does not mean that it will allow you to use whatever characters or numbers you may choose. In some cases, the word processing software may require you to use a specific designation such as "doc" for all master files. Such a requirement would, of course, eliminate any benefits that you might otherwise realize from the use of extenders. Read your software manual carefully, and speak to your vendor about this *before* you purchase your word processing program.

5

Creating Your Forms and Masters

MAKING YOUR OWN MASTER FORM BOOK

There should be a *single* starting point for *all* of your office projects. And for your office, it is going to be a Master Form Book which will provide, or lead you to, your drafting forms, checklists, cross-references, court rules, masters, outlines, and every other conceivable drafting aid in your office. It is the ''one'' directory for every project or job that involves document production. And since that book is the focal point of your system, we will cover it first. Here is all that you need to create your own.

Required Materials:

- Labels
- Several Large Loose-leaf Three-Ring Binders
- Tabbed Dividers

With the few materials listed above, you are now going to create a reference that will cover all species of drafting implements. The book will cover your computer, your form file cabinet, and, it will even provide cross-references to closed client files that might be of help. Particularly, it will act as a guide to assist the following more specific functions:

- It will tell you what forms you have;
- It will tell you where they are;
- It will tell you what the forms look like (i.e., printed, photocopier-created, computer-stored, computer-created);
- It will provide hard copies of some forms;
- It will provide the Number of each form;
- It will provide the Identifier for each form;
- It will *even* provide information about forms that you do not yet have;
- It can, if you wish, be accompanied by as many alphabetical indexes as you care to create.

Setting up a loose-leaf book is not terribly complex; we all know how to pull the circular clips apart, insert pages, and close them. But there are some important, though simple, suggestions pertaining to the structure of your book that will save an appreciable amount of time during use. To present them, let's consider that structure, item by item.

Binders and Titles

I suggest that you *start* with a single book; i.e., loose-leaf binder. Admittedly, unless your firm is quite small, the forms will quickly outgrow that binder, requiring some added ones. For the time being, however, one book will best give you a handle on the overall scheme. Once that scheme or structure has been assembled, dividing the material into separate binders and making extra copies should be easy; we will cover the separation techniques shortly. Until the divisions occur, however, you can merely label the vinyl binder "Master Form Book."

Next, ten tabbed dividers will separate your book according to the nine Major Categories, in addition to a first tab allocated for generic office forms. The tabs will read:

Office XX,XXX	Tax 5XX,XXX
Litigation 1XX,XXX	Workers' Rights 6XX,XXX
Probate 2XX,XXX	Motor Vehicle 7XX,XXX
Corp. & Bus. 3XX,XXX	Administrative 8XX,XXX
Real Estate 4XX,XXX	Et. Al. 9XX,XXX

Figure 5-1

The numbers on the tabs, of course, represent the respective Major Categories. The Litigation tab, for example, suggests that each form falling within its scope will have a six digit number starting with a "1." For office forms, a "0" in the first position translates into a simple five-digit number.

An eleventh tab titled ALPH INDEX could be used for those of you who desire to create an alphabetical list of forms. Even if such an index is created, it should, nevertheless, be divided according to Major Category. This would provide separate alphabetical indexes for each Category. Creating one long list in pure alphabetical order is not practical. Personally, I believe that the time required to create and use any alphabetical index for your forms is marginally justified, at best.

If you elect to create a separate alphabetical index for each Category, the typing of them should be delayed until your Master Form Book has had a chance to "settle." After a substantial bank has been created, and some time has passed, you can create an index that may have some stability. Typing your index as you create your initial bank may later involve a substantial amount of retyping.

* * *

As I mentioned, after you get all of the components of your book assembled, you may realize that one binder will not suffice. In such a case, I recommend that you divide the books "by Category," to the extent possible. If, for example, your firm does litigation work only, you may find that you need two separate binders for Litigation alone. In such a case, your binders may be arranged and labeled like this:

Book 1 Office Forms (10,000 - 99,999)	*Book 2* Litigation (100,000-139,999)
Book 3 Litigation (140,000-199,999)	*Book 4* Remaining Categories (200,000-End)

Figure 5-2

There are no specific laws governing your expansion. Use and personal convenience are your only determinants. I like to keep things in *strict* numerical order; that is why I gave the relatively small Category 0 (Office Forms) its own book, instead of combining it with the other non-litigation Categories.

We are now going to consider the components of your book, individually.

Category Numbering Charts

Immediately following each tabbed divider should appear the numbering chart for the particular Category. The chart is the only component of your system that provides an overview of an entire area of law on a single page. It is your first reference tool for assigning numbers to masters and forms. So it makes sense that the chart should be the first page to hit your eyes upon turning the tabbed divider.

Your charts for all of the Major Categories are provided in Chapter 3. You may merely copy them if you wish.

The very first page of your Master Book will, therefore, contain a structural chart for your commonly used office forms. We have referred to this as Category Zero. It is a simple Category with nine Group Elements, four of which are reserved for your personal office structure (See Appendix A). You should keep copies of office forms in your book, as well as in your file cabinet.

Following this, you come to your first Major Category—Litigation. That Category, along with each of the remaining categories, will possess these items, in the order listed:

1. Tabbed Divider (Figure 5-1).
2. Category Numbering Chart (Chapter 3).
3. Index Pages (Appendix A).
4. Hard Copies of forms for Levels II, III, and IV (Level II is optional).

Index Pages

The index pages that appear first (after each chart) are the *most important* reference pages that you are going to create. They provide the most detailed information about your forms and form system. They will tell you what kind of forms you have, and which ones you do not have. They will tell you their type, physical structure, use, and location. These index pages will also provide an outline of the entire field of law represented by each Major Category.

You may create your own basic structure if you wish. However, the one that is provided for you (in Appendix A) has been very carefully designed and planned. Its purpose is to present a format that is easy on the eyes and yet packs the maximum amount of information on each single sheet of paper.

If you choose to stick with our suggested structure, you can get your book off to a fast start by using the index pages provided in Appendix A, just as they are. If you have a computer, you need only key them in, word for word. The decimal structure will permit you to easily add listings for any forms that do not appear.

Those without computers or word processors may wish to outline the index pages *before* typing them. You can use Appendix A as a starting point; then tailor the outline for your own office by merely adding and deleting items where appropriate. This should avoid excessive retyping at a later date.

Figure 5-3 provides a sample index page from Category 4 (Real Estate). Let's examine its structure carefully:

FEE SIMPLE ESTATES
(41X,XXX)

	411,XXX Options to Purchase		
411,010	Option Pur. Rep Buyer	II,III	Buyer's Favor
411,020	Option Pur. Rep Seller	II,III	Seller's Favor
	412,XXX Offers to Purchase		
412,000	Checklist	II	All offers
412,010	Offer Pur. C21	I,II	Century 21 Form
412,011	Offer Pur. LT	I,III	Lawyer's Title Form
412,012	Offer Pur. Form A	I	Longer Form
412,013	Offer Pur. Form B	I	Shorter Form
412,021	Offer Pur. Comm.	I	Commercial Property
	413,XXX Brokerage Forms		
413,000	All Listing Agreements	IV	Comprehensive
413,010	List. Agree. 2 Mo.	I	2-Month Listing
413,011	List. Agree. 3 Mo.	I	3-Month Listing
	414,XXX Disclosure Forms		
414,000	Disclosure Form		
	415,XXX Lending Institution Forms		
415,011	Loan App. Conv. BA	I	Conven. Loan B of A
415,012	Loan App. Conv. FF	I,II,III	First Federal
415,013	Loan App. Conv. FBB	I	First Benev. Bank
415,014	Loan App. Conv. BB	I	Bank B
415,021	Loan App. FHA. BA	I	FHA. Bank of America
415,022	Loan App. FHA. FF	I	First Federal
415,023	Loan App. FHA. FBB	0	First Benev. Bank
415,024	Loan App. FHA. BB	I	Bank B
415,031	Loan App. VA. BA	I	Veterans Admin. Loan
415,032	Loan App. VA. FF	I	First Federal
415,033	Loan App. VA. FBB	I	First Benev. Bank
415,034	Loan App. VA. BB	I	Bank B
415,101	TIL	0	Truth. Lend. Form
415,201	Escrow. Inst.	I	Escrow Instructions

Figure 5-3

Sample Index Page

Logic-Based Arrangement. The index for each Category is arranged strictly according to the numbering structure for that Category (per Chapter 3). In other words, the major groupings and sub-groupings within the Category appear in their logic-based order on the index pages. This means that the index is arranged according to your numbering charts. As previously indicated, a supplementary alphabetical index can be created at your option. Our sample index (Appendix A), however, is in *logical,* not alphabetical, order.

Once again, look at Figure 5-3; it represents the first page for the index of Category 4, Real Estate. (If you want to compare the page to its Category chart to get a broader picture, see Figure 3-16.) Notice the large heading at the top of the page that appears in block capitals—"FEE SIMPLE ESTATES." Observe the design of the number that appears immediately below it. In particular, the digits "41X,XXX" indicate that *every* number appearing underneath that major group element will start with the digits "41," to be followed by four additional digits. The "4," of course, represents the Category (Real Estate); it will not change. The "1" is the first element of the first major group. The Fee Simple Estate is, of course, the highest, and therefore, the "number-one" item in the real estate hierarchy (per chart in Figure 3-16).

I have selected "Options to Purchase" as the first forms for the Fee Simple Group. Look at the forms that appear immediately under the "Options to Purchase" heading (Figure 5-3); notice that the number "411,010" refers to those "options to purchase" to be used when your firm represents the buyer. Underneath that item is the same type of form; however, it would be used when the firm represents the seller. For that form, notice that a "2" appears as the fifth digit. For convenience, I let the "1" represent those forms that are to the buyer's favor, reserving the "2" for those that are to the seller's favor. *My* method is not that critical. If you find it easier to list the forms sequentially, then by all means do so (411,001 and 411,002, etc.). But by using the fifth digit, instead of the sixth, I kept the last (sixth) digit open, so that I could list up to nine different types of options for both sellers and buyers. Also, by keeping the last digit free (i.e., "0") where possible, it will be easier to insert new forms without having to renumber existing ones.

It is very important to *emphasize* that no great amount of thought should be given to the last three digits. They are there for *your* convenience. As long as the basic structure (i.e., the first two, preferably three, digits) is kept correct, you should have no trouble whatsoever finding any desired form.

With that in mind, look once again at the sample page (Figure 5-3). Toward the bottom appears the heading "414,XXX Disclosure Forms." Immediately below that and slightly to the left is the designation "414,000 Disclosure Form." You can think of this designation as a "placeholder," since it is obvious that there are no specific forms to fill that slot. To keep a "logical continuity" among the sub-headings, it may be desirable to periodically use these placeholders. In addition to providing continuity and at least one listing for each of the sub-headings, the placeholder avoids a "hole" in the form structure, which otherwise might leave the user to guess how it is filled. It also provides the index pages with a nice structure that is easy on the eyes.

Format of Page. Additions, deletions, and changes are going to occur periodically; the structure of your book must, therefore, be designed so that it can easily accommodate modification. Initially, these changes may be profuse. However, as your system becomes more complete and developed, it will not be necessary to change or alter pages quite so frequently. But in any event, it is important to utilize a structure that will keep your retyping of index pages to a minimum.

In case that it does not appear obvious from the sample page (Figure 5-3), the sub-headings are all self-contained by page. In other words, to the extent possible, if a given subgroup of forms occupies less than a full page, it should not be split up between two pages. If, for example, all of the Lending Institution forms would not have fit on the page represented by Figure 5-3, then that entire subgroup should have been started on a new page.

As a matter of practice, you may wish to *minimize* the amount of material that you put on *any* given index page. Remember that when the pencilled-in changes become numerous or messy, the entire index page should be retyped. And it is always easier to add things where there are greater numbers of pages, and fewer amounts of text per page.

Line Items. Notice from the sample page (Figure 5-3) that each form has one line consisting of four elements. These elements provide the most critical information about the form, at a glance. They are:

1. Form Number
2. Identifier
3. Level Indicator
4. Comments

- *FORM NUMBER*—First and foremost on each line is the form's identifying number. Such numbers determine the location of the form, and, of course, tell much about its content. Because all of the forms are arranged and listed in simple numerical order, it should never be difficult to determine just where a form is to be "plugged into the index," *after* its number has been assigned. Notice that a comma has been inserted (in standard fashion) after the third digit of each form number. This makes it much easier to read and verbalize. For some word processors, the computer file names *cannot* contain such a comma; for a ",'' is not alphanumeric. Nevertheless, just because you cannot use a comma on your computer screen, does not mean that it is against the law to keep your Master Index in nice readable form.
- *IDENTIFIER*—The next item of information is the Identifier, which serves a dual purpose. It provides a readable English description of the contents of the

form, and presents an abbreviation that can be typed on a label or hard copy. The rules for creating good identifiers were more specifically discussed in Chapter 3.

- *LEVEL INDICATOR*—As you may recall, there are five Levels of technology with respect to forms, prototypes, etc. The Level Indicator provides some very important information. It is presented as one of five *Roman* Numerals, to avoid confusion with the other numbers in your system.

  The *absence* of a Roman Numeral (or presence of a "O", zero) indicates that the form exists, but you *do not* have it. This should provide a signal to consider whether or not the missing form should be created, or otherwise procured. Theoretically, if you were to list *every form* that you may ever need (regardless of whether or not you now have it), you would never have to retype any index page. You would merely change each "O" to the appropriate Level Number for the forms that you obtain. Notice the "O" in the level column for Form 415,101 (Figure 5-3) indicating that a Truth in Lending Form exists but has not yet been obtained. You may wish to just leave the space blank, so that you will not have to erase the "O" when you finally do get the form.
  Notice that the Level Indicator gives your Master Index its unity and comprehensiveness. It brings together, in a single place, information about all of your forms, regardless of where or how they are stored, and even indicates those forms that you lack. We considered the levels in Chapter 1. Because of their importance to our discussion, I want to briefly review them:

  Level I—Printed forms, sample forms, and prototypes that are *obtained* by the firm and stored in file cabinet drawers.

  Level II—Copier-*created* forms, pull pages, and drafting sheets also stored in the file cabinet.

  Level III—Forms or text electronically, magnetically, or optically *stored* on a hard disk, laser disk, floppy disc, or in a dedicated word processor.

  Level IV—Computer-*generated* documents and forms.

  Level V—Documents *created* through Artificial Intelligence.

- *COMMENTS*—The last column can be used for special remarks or cross-references to client files, court rules, or even published cases. However, its primary purpose is to provide a definition for one or more of the identifier abbreviations that might not otherwise be obvious. For example, look at Figure 5-3, once again, and refer to item 412,010. It is obvious from the heading that appears immediately above it that the term "Offer Pur." refers to an Offer to Purchase. However, the designation "C21" may not be obvious. Therefore, the "Comments" column is used to point out that a "Century 21" form is being used. Should that same designation appear in a later form, close by, it will be obvious to the reader what the term C21 means, because it will have been previously defined. Therefore, for successive forms (underneath form

421,010), the space should be used to provide clarifications for any *other*, not previously ''defined'' portions of the identifier.

* * *

Let's consider a few specific examples of index listings for some common forms.

Example 1

412,000 Checklist II All offers

Without knowing what headings or titles precede this entry, it should be apparent that the form (or drafting tool) is, by its nature, generic; i.e., it will cover a variety of circumstances. As the Comments column suggests, it covers ''all offers'' to purchase (it is listed under the ''Offers to Purchase'' subheading; see Figure 5-3). The three zeros in the form number signal such a generic tool. Checklists in general will have this numeric property. As a rule, the ''more general'' the form, the greater the number of trailing zeros.

The ''II'' in the third column indicates that the checklist will be found in your file cabinet, at numerical position 412,000. Since the form is, by its nature, a condensed, comprehensive document, you may wish to keep a copy in your Master Book, regardless of whether or not you are computerized. The last, or ''Comments,'' column is designed to provide whatever additional information about the form that you may choose to include.

Example 2

413,000 All Listing Agree. IV Comprehensive

As with our prior example, the three trailing zeros on this form's number indicate its generic nature. Moreover, the ''IV'' in the Level column tells you that it is a comprehensive computer program that will be used to generate ''all listing agreements'' (see Chapter 9). The forms immediately listed underneath (see 413,010 and 413,011, Figure 5-3) are not necessarily obsolete, even though they are Level I forms. It may be desirable to keep these printed or ''official versions'' available in the file cabinet for reference, even though they can be computer-generated.

Example 3

415,023 Loan App.FHA.FBB O First Benev. Bank

In contrast to our prior generic examples, this is a very *specific* printed form. As the Identifier and Comments columns indicate, it is a Loan Application Form used by the First Benevelent Bank to process FHA loans.

The zero in the Level column indicates that your firm either chooses not to use the form or has yet to obtain it. In either event, the slot, though unused, *remains* to signal the user of the form's existence and place in the overall scheme of things.

Example 4

193,000 Discovery.Generally O See 183,XXX

Let's leave the Real Estate Category and consider an example from another realm. As the above form number indicates by its first digit ("1"), we are now squarely in the Litigation arena and in a Municipal Court (9).

As the Level Indicator suggests, the user chose to keep no discovery forms ("3") in the Municipal Group Slot. Instead, as the Comments column indicates, the reader is referred to the state court of general jurisdiction ("8"). The cross-reference suggests that the same forms are used for both the Municipal Court and the court of general jurisdiction. As we suggested earlier, the latter slot is used to store these overlapping items. The degree of overlap will, of course, vary from state to state.

The phrase "See 183,XXX" means that the user should examine, generally, *all forms* starting with numbers "183." The Comments column is also an excellent place to keep notes for short cross-references to court rules, citations, and client file numbers that may suggest where helpful case law can be found.

Example 5

244,001 Claims O Use 264,101 and 264,102

This form falls within the Mental Incompetent Group Element ("4") for Category 2 (Probate). As with our prior example, it contains cross-references. Note, however, that the cross-references are specific instead of general. That is because the claims forms:

264,101 Claim.Not. I Notice of Claim
264,102 Claim.Not.Hear I Not.Hearing—Claims

are used by this particular Probate Court for *all types* of *Estate Administration*, regardless of whether they involve minors (Group Element "3"), mental incompetents ("4"), physical incompetents ("5"), or *most commonly*, decedents ("6").

Alterations

The steps set forth below are designed to provide the most convenient and expedient methods for taking the basic framework provided, and tailoring it to your own specific day-to-day operations. The starting point for your System is Appendix A; it contains a full set of Index Pages designed to get your System started. As previously mentioned, to tailor these pages to suit your needs, you may want to make some deletions and additions. Afterwards, as you use your System on a regular basis, it will still undergo changes, but less frequently. Here are some suggestions.

1.
Deletions

As a rule, you should be slow to delete anything. Most of the forms in Appendix ''A'' have standard purposes, if not recognizable titles.

You might be surprised to learn how standardized forms have become throughout the country. The U.S. Constitution, Federal Statutes, and The Federal Rules of Civil Procedure have had a tremendous impact upon the names, titles, and basic forms used by the 50 states, even in non-federal matters. Many state court systems have adopted portions of the Federal Rules, word-for-word.

Litigation, the first Major Category, uses forms and names that are generally recognizable throughout the 50 states. Those names may vary somewhat, but their particular number and position in the overall structure should be fairly consistent. Therefore, it is far more probable, that if a given form in the Sample Index (Appendix A) has a name that you do not recognize, it should be *changed* and not deleted. Also, remember that just because a form is listed on the index does not necessarily mean that you must *currently* have it; nor does it mean that there will be any confusion between those forms that you have and those that you do not. Recall that the absence of a level number (or presence of a ''O'') should clearly distinguish those forms that you do *not* have.

For the other Categories, standardization may be even greater. Jets, telephone lines, and microwave dishes have increased commerce and homogeneity among the states. As a result, commercial and testamentary instruments are becoming more standardized as to *purpose,* despite the varying names and titles.

There is another good reason for being cautious about deletions. For, even though a given instrument may not be used in your particular state, you may nevertheless have occasion to come in contact with (or be required to handle) matters involving other states that may use such forms. Having the instrument listed on your index may give you some insight as to its use and function; at the very least, it will tell you how the instrument fits into the overall document structure and scheme.

Under no circumstances should you delete any major headings or subheadings merely because your firm does not practice in a particular area of law. Suffice it to say that there are very few, if any, areas of law that do not, at some time or another, overlap. You may never know when you will need to use those headings, at some time in the future, perhaps after your firm has expanded into new areas.

2.
Additions

The sample indexes provided for each of the Major Categories should deliver a good basic framework; we have covered hundreds of the most commonly used forms throughout the United States. To attempt to include every conceivable form would be impossible; their numbers are far too great. And even if we were to include all of the standardized forms, we could never hope to provide all of the personalized forms that you and your peers might decide to create.

With that in mind, we have presented some rather extensive indexes which are designed to accomplish two basic needs: (1) To include listings of some forms widely recognized throughout the United States, and (2) to provide enough of a framework to allow you to construct your own detailed scheme; that frame should guide decisions about where your additional entries are to be "plugged in."

Always refer to the chart *first,* when attempting to assign a number to a new form. Of course, once the number is properly assigned, it should be easy to put the form in its proper numerical position.

The Master Index can and should be used to assist the assignment of numbers. Hopefully, at least, one of the examples provided in Appendix A will get you "close." The sample forms that we provided in Chapter 3, with their "arrows" and number charts, can be particularly helpful, since they tend to provide a more dynamic picture of the numbering process.

3.
Changes

As previously indicated, forms and their titles are becoming somewhat standardized throughout the country. Even where federal law does not govern, it has an impact. The Federal Government does not, theoretically, have the right to dictate the manner in which clients structure their corporations or organize their employee benefit plans. It does, however, have the right to deny deductions and other tax breaks to those who do not comply with the "suggested" forms condoned and approved by the IRS. Therefore, whether we like it or not, when it comes to business in general, the Federal Government has created a rather uniform structure. And, as we all know, Federal laws change frequently, particularly those involving Federal Taxation. But just because the forms themselves may require revision, does *not* mean that the index entries must change. Your personal Federal tax return, for example, seems to change every year. But it has always been called "1040."

Where Congress has not created uniformity, various "uniform" statutes have. Perhaps the most notable is The Uniform Commercial Code. Individual states have the right to adopt the "U.C.C.," or portions of it, and virtually every state has. This means that many commercial and contractual provisions are standardized as a matter of law. As a result, many forms and their titles have become somewhat uniform throughout the states.

Despite the foregoing, there are still those areas left to state dominion and control. Likewise, there are forms whose names may vary from state to state. Whenever you recognize an incompatibility, by all means make the appropriate change. But, as previously discussed, be very cautious about making any deletions.

For example, in your state you may have a form called a "Petition for Probate of Will" (circa 241,001). For those who have died without wills, the pertinent form might be called a "Petition for Administration of Estate" (circa 241,002). A different state may use a single form for both types of proceedings, and call it a "Petition for Commencement of Proceedings" (circa 241,010). In Michigan, this last form did, in fact, replace the two prior petitions (and the Probate Court rules were amended accordingly). Where you encounter such a case, do not hesitate to change the form numbers.

Another example involves the very title of the courts and their respective forms. For example, the "Probate Court" of Ohio would exercise subject matter jurisdiction similar to the "Surrogates Court" of New York. So, if your firm happens to be in New York, then by all means change "Probate" to "Surrogate" wherever that Court title appears.

4.
Cross-Referencing

In some instances, you may wish to cross-reference matters instead of making deletions, additions, or changes. This cross-referencing tends to link up information that may vary from state to state.

As an example, let us refer, once again, to the Real Estate Category chart (Figure 3-16). The second element of the first major group is titled "Land Contracts." These devices permit buyers to purchase a "delayed fee interest." In other words, until the land contract is paid off, title is not transferred to the buyer. Therefore, in the hierarchy, we gave Land Contracts a second seat to Fee Simple Estates (which are created *immediately* when property is sold). Land contracts, however, are outlawed in states which require immediate conveyances or "nothing." If you were to travel to a state such as California and attempt to purchase property via a land contract, you would not be arrested;

however, your real estate broker might attempt to "fish" for the right term to permit you to accomplish your purpose legally. In the course of conversation, the term "trust deed" might arise (circa 418,310). Essentially, the trust deed creates a fee simple conveyance, with a mortgage interest back to the seller. So the "Trust Deed" may be the "closest thing" to a Land Contract. Both are designed for the seller's security. With that in mind, look at the notation that appears in the sample index (Appendix A), next to form 421,001.

Hard Copies

If you were to attempt to store all of your Printed Forms, Prototypes, and Masters in loose-leaf books, you might eventually need the Library of Congress to house them. And worse, copying every portion of the book for others may involve a full-time job. But relax; your Master Indexes make it unnecessary for you to overload your book. Some forms should be booked, to be sure; but many need not.

For each form that *is* to be placed in your book, we recommend that its identifier be placed in parentheses at the top of the page of the form (see Figure 5-4). The form's number should be placed on the lower right portion. This positioning will automatically provide a "page number" for the sheet. It would be a very good idea to number each separate page of a multiple page form. This could avoid confusion over misfiled or misplaced forms. It also facilitates page-flipping when trying to locate a particular page number.

In determining which forms to keep in your Master Book, it is important to first distinguish the index pages from the hard copies. The index pages will contain a listing of *every* form that you have in your entire office, regardless of species, location, or type. But that does not mean that you will want a hard copy of all of those forms in your book. The decisions in that regard should be determined by the *Level* of the form:

LEVEL I consists of printed fill-in forms, sample briefs, and other non-original matters taken from other sources. These items are normally clumsy and sometimes involve carbons, impression copies, or numerous pages. They do *not* go into your book. The information contained in your index pages should be adequate to steer the user quickly to the appropriate spot in the file cabinet where those forms are housed. Practically speaking, it makes no sense to keep copies of the potentially voluminous forms in your Book. Everyone should have easy access to them in centrally located cabinets.

LEVEL II forms, which are created by you and your photocopier, are generally meant to be kept in your file cabinet, so that multiple "ready-made" copies are available for immediate use. You will, however, want to keep a copy of some commonly used instruments in your Book. Much will depend upon whether or not you are computerized. If not, the absence of Level III forms will leave more room for Level II.

Your copier-created forms, pull pages, and drafting aids are a matter of choice. As a rule, it would be nice to have a complete set (with all relevant pull pages) of any form or instrument that is frequently used. However, if all such forms were placed in the book, it could become quite voluminous. I have a suggestion. For law firms with three or more drafters, where there is some degree of specialization, you might provide each with copies of *only* those categories that pertain to his or her specific area. Then, only one comprehensive (and centrally located) set of books would house everything.

LEVEL III forms are stored on your computer's disk. Hard copies of all Masters *must* be stored in your Book. As a matter of fact, an important purpose for the creation of the Book is to provide some permanent paper reference for those otherwise invisible magnetic impulses that only your computer can read.

For your computer-stored documents, you may be able to locate commonly used forms from memory by using the Direct Reference System (Chapter 3). In much the same fashion that you ''thumb through'' the file cabinet to locate a particular form, you *may* also ''glance through'' the form files on your computer's monitor. *However,* with respect to computer-stored information, most prefer to go *directly* to the particular file on the disk. This is because computer-stored information (unlike file drawer folders) does not permit easy scanning at a single glance. *The Master Index should, however, provide that glance,* even though it will not show the form itself.

With computer-stored forms, therefore, you have no choice. It is impossible to read coded electrons; so you should have a print-out (hard copy) of all forms that are stored on *both* your hard and floppy disks.

LEVEL IV does not consist of any forms or masters. Rather, it is comprised of ''computer programs'' commonly referred to as ''scripts'' or ''templates'' that are used for generating the final documents. If not unduly voluminous, a print-out of each program should be stored in its appropriate position. The programs should also be assigned form numbers. Chapter 9 provides more detail about this.

LEVEL V, Artificial Intelligence, is still a fuzzy concept. Technology is continuously moving beyond Level IV. This Ultimate Level assures that science will not leave your system behind. Like Level IV, Artificial Intelligence (however advanced) will always involve some type of program or set of algorithms. Hard copies of them should be stored in the Master Book.

FORM CREATION TECHNIQUES

It may be comforting to know that despite the several ''levels'' of form technology and an increasing variety in paper producing equipment, the basic

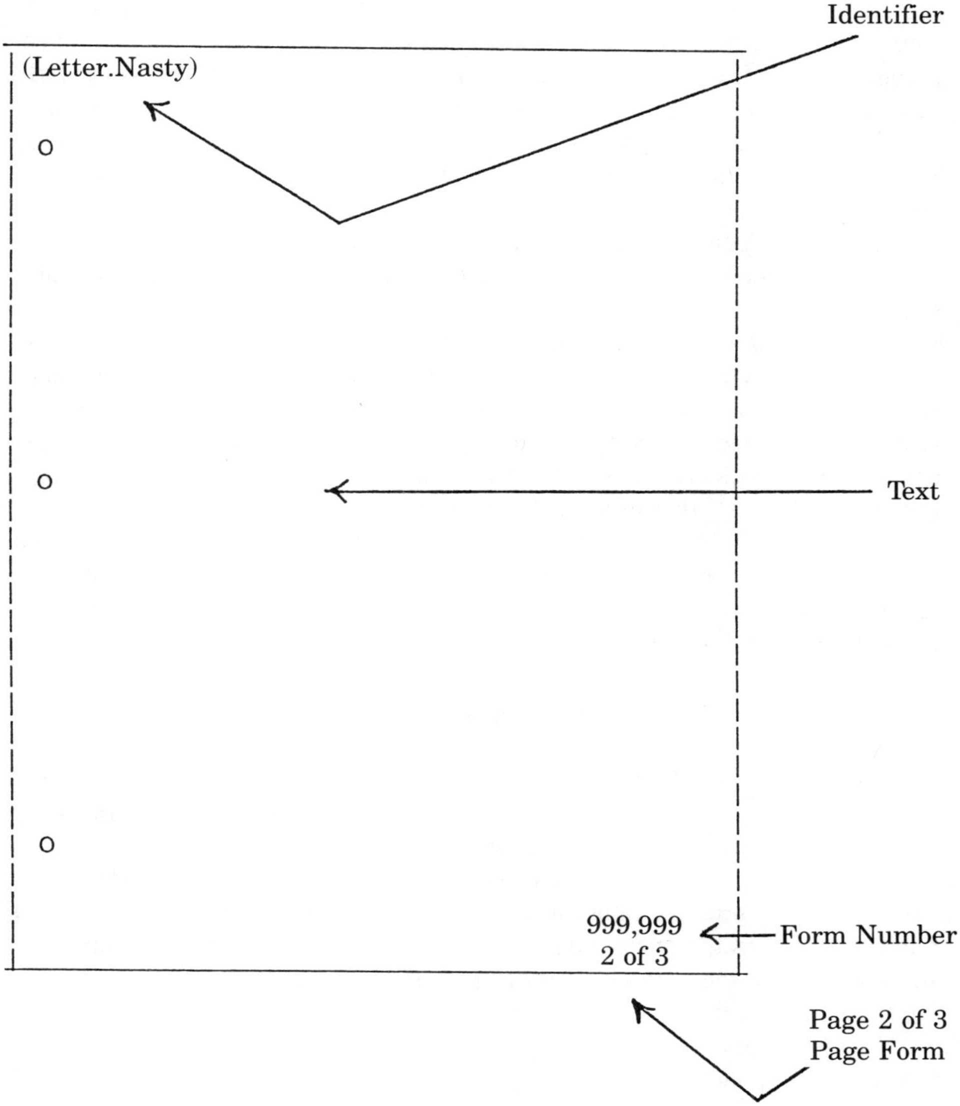

Figure 5-4

concepts pertaining to "page construction" remain relatively constant. So the discussions that follow should prove useful regardless of the present state of your office equipment.

Level I, of course, involves forms that are merely obtained from outside sources (see Chapter 3); they are created by others. So, our discussions of them pertain more to acquisition than creation. Levels IV and V (more particularly dealt with in Chapter 9) involve documents that are created by the computer. So, in this chapter, when we speak of ''creation techniques,'' we are primarily concerned with Levels II (photocopier creations) and III (forms created for computer storage).

Both Photocopiers and Computers can quickly reproduce boilerplate text. And although their capabilities are different, some important general principles pertain to both.

Some of the concepts concerning photocopier page constructions may seem archaic to those with computers. But the techniques are important, regardless of your office's level of technology. Just as airplane pilots make the best astronauts, those with a grasp of basic copier techniques will make the best creators of computerized forms. Moreover, the older technologies provide important ''basics'' that users of the newer machines too often overlook.

Throughout the latter portions of this chapter, the discussions and examples are tuned to specific areas of practice. Yet before diving into the specifics, there are some important matters that cut across categorical and technological lines of distinction. Let's consider them first.

How All Forms Are Constructed

Conceptually, it helps to think and plan in terms of *individual* pages. It doesn't always turn out that discrete points or provisions fit neatly into their own single pages, but that is the goal.

The computer's unique ability to move text about and balance it from page to page has obscured the importance of ''page structure.'' For those who must rely entirely upon the photocopier for the creation of forms, such concepts are still crucial. But they are also very important to those who are computerized. We will see why this is so as we proceed.

With the foregoing in mind, all forms consist of one or more of the following components:

1.
Base Page

Sometimes referred to as the ''solid page,'' this particular type of sheet does not change from instrument to instrument. In other words, the language remains constant, regardless of gender or plurality. It is the epitome of ''boilerplate'' text. A set of Corporate By-Laws is an example of a document consisting mostly of base pages. Lengthy trusts also frequently use language that can be placed on base pages (see also Figure 5-11). The base pages are the simplest and quickest items to deal with, and, of course, the least personalized. They require *no* added type, and, assuming that they were carefully constructed, no proofreading.

2. Pull Sheet

Sometimes referred to as a "choice page," or "pull page," this particular sheet can quickly be pulled from among folders and neatly inserted to create finished products. The concept suggests that there should be a variety of pages from which to choose, depending upon certain variables; these may include gender, plurality, corporate status, etc. They are simple to label, and easy to select (for an example, see Figure 5-10).

> *NOTE*—Recall that your Filing System allows you to number and name individual parts of forms. Base pages and Pull sheets are particularly convenient for this type of classification.

3. Fill-in Page

The fill-in page requires the addition of some typing, such as names, addresses, or other proper nouns. The first and last sheets of most instruments require this type of page. The fill-in pages are the most personalized, and are the fewest in number; yet they may consume more preparation time than all of the other pages combined (see Figure 5-9).

4. Typed Page

For some documents, there may be pages that contain so much personalized material that it may pay to type them from scratch. A cover sheet (which normally contains highly personalized data) provides an example of such a page.

5. Printed Page

There are those forms provided by courts and bureaucracies that call for lengthy, redundant information (Level I); in some instances, portions could be filled out, photocopied, and used for several different cases. This could save time and spare some monotony on the part of the typist, who would otherwise be required to read each one of the sometimes redundant, and often non-applicable, questions that appear on many bureaucratic forms. Computers can also be used, with some effort, to fill in these forms.

* * *

The Promissory Note provides a good example for illustrating some of the above concepts. Every such note must contain some method of identification for its maker(s). The ''maker'' is the person who signs the note and thereby promises to make the required payments. Let's examine four possible ways to refer to maker Willy Smith:

Reference A. Willy Smith (proper noun); this requires a typed or fill-in page.

Reference B. Him, he, or his (pronoun); this requires a pull sheet.

Reference C. The maker (regular noun); this may be used for a base page, if ''maker'' is to serve both singular and plural signers.

Reference D. The Undersigned (quasi-proper noun); this may always be used in a Base Page.

When you want to mention Willy by name (Reference A), typing will be required for *every* such use. Reference B should be *changed* for a feminine or neuter maker. The third term need never be changed for any *singular* maker; and if you accept that term as plural (where warranted), it need *never* be changed. The last term need *never* be changed, *regardless* of name, gender, or plurality. The word ''Undersigned'' is indeed a precious commodity for those desiring document production speed.

Dates are the ''second most troublesome'' concerns (second only to names). They are always present in any well-drafted note or writing. Here are some references to avoid having to type a date more than once:

a. The date first appearing on this contract;

b. The date of this document;

c. The date of execution (or some other well-defined event).

General Rules

With the preceding concepts in mind, here are some general, but nevertheless important, rules that pertain to all created forms:

I.
Think in Terms of Future Use

The whole purpose of taking the time to create a form is so that it may be used again, perhaps many times in the future, thereby saving time in preparation, research, typing, and proofreading. The form should be *broad* enough so that only minimal amounts of text need to be added as the form is used, and yet it must be *narrow* enough so that its use is totally applicable and tailored to the intended project. There is no such thing as a single form that will satisfy all of the day-to-day variables for a particular type of document.

II.
Look at What You Already Have

When you, or your peers, start to create masters, the process will be relatively new. But as time goes on, don't be surprised to find out that you may be creating new masters, when you should really be using your ''newly found text'' to update an existing Master File. This forgetfulness happens most often with respect to briefs and other pleadings.

As this rule suggests, your indexes must be kept up-to-date so that you will know what you have at all times. Your files will build up faster than you think.

III.
Eliminate Proper Names and Specific Facts

Client names and personal facts have no place in your forms or Masters. They belong in Working Files, not Master Files. Their presence in Master Files is dangerous and may lead to incredible embarrassment, and even malpractice. Blank spaces, asterisks, or other ''alert'' mechanisms should be used to indicate, on the forms, where things are to be added.

Violation of this rule will, sooner or later, lead to the careless use of a master containing the proper name of some client having no relation to the matter at hand. Particular attention should be given to ''factual arguments'' or other ''semi-personalized text'' contained in briefs, because they are more difficult to spot. This is due to the fact that personalized matter is often intertwined with the generic language contained in the forms.*

IV.
Use Paragraphs to Block and Structure Your Content

You might be surprised to learn how helpful the simple rules of grammar can be as you construct your forms. One such rule suggests that an individual paragraph (of any written composition) should express a single idea or point.

---

* For a light look at this very serious matter, see ''Microtransposedictus Gravis,'' Lipson, *Law Office Economics and Management,* Vol. XXVII, No. 3, Spring 1986, p. 302; ''A Reinfection of Microtransposedictus Gravis,'' *Legal Assistant Today,* Vol. 4, No. 4, March/April 1987, p. 28; ''Microtransposedictus Gravis,'' *The Docket,* Vol. 35, No. 4, January/February 1987, p. 11.

So too should the paragraphs of your forms express single thoughts or perform single functions. A single computer file (Level III) may provide several arguments to deliver a single message for use of briefs. Each argument, with its citations, should have its own paragraph.

Run-on paragraphs are difficult to read and, in general, signal poor draftsmanship. Individualized paragraphs, however, are simpler to digest, and lend themselves to *easy* deletion and manipulation. When in doubt, break the material up by creating a new paragraph; but remember that each paragraph should contain at least two sentences.

Thus, it is our suggestion that your paragraphs should form the individual building blocks to construct your forms. Readability, good appearance, and simplified drafting will all be served.

V.
Block Text by Page Where Possible

Any copier-created form (Level II) or master file (Level III) may, of course, contain several pages of text. Where possible, particular clauses or provisions would best occupy their *own* particular page or pages; this principle is crucial for Level II forms. But for Level III, which is less demanding (because the computer can assemble and move print easily from page to page), it nevertheless makes drafting that much more simple. A ''powers clause'' of a trust, for example, may run for several pages. It would be most convenient if the Bequest provisions were *not* mixed on any of the ''powers provision'' pages. Picking and selecting from among different powers provisions would be easier if they were not linked to extraneous provisions.

Where possible, paragraphs would best end on a page. Runover paragraphs are ''less easy'' to deal with when selecting text from your forms. I am not *just* speaking of widows (beginning lines of paragraphs that are ''stranded'' at the bottoms of pages), or orphans (ending lines of paragraphs at the tops of pages); but, where practical, all runover paragraphs should be avoided. When single pages of your Master Book are to be modified, you don't want to have to deal with other pages just because of runover text.

VI.
Segregate Variable or Fill-in Language from the Boilerplate Language

When creating masters or photocopies for future use, every effort should be directed toward *personalizing* the documents so that they do not appear to be standardized or ''formed.'' This is not a difficult task if a few simple steps are followed.

There should only be so much standardization by way of Base Pages and Pull Sheets. In addition, there must always be some fill-in information for names and addresses, at the very least. An important trick involves segregating the fill-in information from the Base Pages and Pull Sheets. This allows the number of Base Pages and Pull Sheets to be maximized. For, the greater the number of Base Pages and Pull Sheets, the fewer the number of sheets that must be typed on, arranged, and proofread. It is therefore much more economical to place as many fill-in items as you can on each fill-in page, rather than spreading them out among several pages. If constructed properly, the document will still maintain its personalized appearance.

Base pages, at least theoretically, should need no proofreading whatsoever; and Pull Sheets should need only a minimal amount of inspection to determine that the right sheet was used. Fill-in sheets, however, must be carefully proofed, since they contain customized and previously uninspected type.

> *CAUTION*—It only takes a single fill-in word to change a Base Page or Pull Sheet into a Fill-in Page. And it only takes a single personal pronoun to change a Base Page to a Pull Page.

Your biggest problem, while implementing the preceding rules, will involve provisions and text portions that do not conveniently fill a page and then end abruptly. Language that might otherwise be perfect for use as a Base Page, for example, may be a few lines too short or too long. For computerized storage (Level III), no one really cares about the length of text on the individual pages of the Master Book. But when the actual output corresponds to the pages of the Master, assembly is easier; this is particularly true where page number limitations are involved.

To solve the problem, we must start with the proposition that you should *never* cut needed text just to make a page "come out even," *nor* should you add text that might change or confuse the intended meanings; but, practically speaking, there is room for a small amount of leeway where very small amounts are to be added or subtracted. Consider some possible solutions:

- When the text is only two or three lines short of a page, an extra blank line might be added to the top to give the page balance.
- Where the text is only a few words too long, careful proofreading may indicate that a small cut might improve the language.
- Text can always be added to "fill out" pages, but only in very small doses.
- It is quite natural for pages to end "in the middle" if a new title or subheading is going to follow.

The above "page balancing" suggestions should not, under any circumstances, be permitted to interfere with or compromise good draftsmanship. But where the opportunity presents itself, they may lead to more complete pages.

VII.
Use Pronouns Freely for Pull Pages but Avoid Generic Terms

The classic pronouns ''he,'' ''she,'' ''it,'' and their various forms should be used in order to maximize the total number of Pull Sheets. However, proper names should also be sprinkled freely throughout the fill-in pages; this will keep the document personalized.

There has been a temptation, however, by some draftpersons to carry the process one step further by using generic language. For example, we have all seen form wills that seemed unconcerned about the fact that females actually exist; such a will, though it is executed by the female, nevertheless contains the possessive pronoun ''his'' when referring to the testator throughout the entire will. There would then appear at the end of the document a clause similar to this:

> Words used in the singular, neuter, or masculine are to be construed in the plural, masculine, or feminine where applicable.

Like the generic products in the supermarket, using this language to justify generic pronouns looks cheap, and it makes the document appear to be cheap. There is no need for this. It cannot be that much more expensive to create a set of alternate ''pull sheets'' for female clients. Quality should be improved, not degraded through automation. The indiscriminate use of the generic pronouns provide what is, perhaps, the best example of a *misuse* of automation techniques.

VIII.
Increase Your Bank

Without a doubt, the single greatest restraint and impediment to building a massive, thorough form bank has been the lack of a retrieval system to cope with the volume. The more forms that were created, the more difficult it was to find any one. Alphabetical systems *never* coped with the subtle variations among similarly named forms. I believe that this factor alone has accounted for the failure of firms to increase their form banks dramatically. The value of the time lost by the lack of a single form will far exceed the extra pennies occasioned by an over-supply.

The Direct Reference System (Chapter 3) was designed to remove the impediment. With the system, you should be able to store your forms and reusable text, regardless of number, and retrieve them instantly. So, if in doubt about whether or not to create a form for any given project, *do* it.

IX. *Create "Packages" Where Applicable*

A ''Package'' might be thought of as a complete set of documents for a particular job, together with all ancillary letters, affidavits, etc. The package is, in essence, a master that consists of all these writings.

Where the ratio of base pages to non-base pages is high, there is a greater likelihood that it would ''pay'' to incorporate the project into a single master form or ''package.'' For, the master is really nothing more than pre-fabricated text that has already been created; therefore, the expense of changing this ''already existing'' language into a master should be minimal. As a corollary, where the ratio of pull pages is high, it may pay to create alternative packages.

Specific Rules

Each of our Major Categories has its own particular quirks with respect to document classification, storage, and use. But, when it comes to drafting techniques and structures, we can quite accurately lump our discussions into four basic types.

First are the writings known as *pleadings*. These may appear to be within the exclusive domain of Category 1 (Litigation), but they are also extensively employed by Category 6 (Labor), and used sporadically by firms that specialize in practice before one or more Administrative Agencies (Category 8). Pleadings are, in essence, governed by very specific rules, and sometimes even page number limitations. They are used whenever a court or other tribunal is involved.

Second are the writings that we refer to broadly as *documents*. They concentrate heavily in Categories 2 (where estate planning is involved) and 3 (Corporate and Business), and have occasion to show up in the other categories. Everything from wills, trusts, and corporate merger agreements, to simple promissory notes might fall within this second type.

Third and last are the *riders* or attachments that are appended to those Level I forms that we do not have the authority to replace altogether. Categories 4 (Real Estate), 5 (Tax), 7 (Motor Vehicle), and 8 (Administrative Agency) make heavy use of such additions.

There is a ''fourth type'' that deals more with internal firm affairs than client products. Before tackling the Major Categories, we are going to consider these special ''Housekeeping'' papers thoroughly; they are very important. Sometimes called ''Category O,'' I refer to them merely as General Office Forms.

OFFICE FORMS

The first papers that you confront as you open your form file drawers, will be your General Office Forms. These sheets deserve their favored position; for they will be pulled, used, referred to, and replaced more often than any other papers in your office. They comprise the epitome of Level II (copier-created forms) and should be kept in the form drawer in heavy supply.

As we use the term, "office forms" refers to those handy questionnaires, medical authorizations, retainer agreements, status sheets, incorporation checklists, and papers that simplify repeated procedures. An ample supply and variety of these forms is indispensable to the efficient operation of any law firm. With respect to quantity and availability, they are either *immediately available* or they are *worthless*.

The forms are normally tailored to the specific needs of the given office and serve some very important, though often overlooked, functions. Consider these goals:

Characteristics of Office Forms

1.
They Should Provide a Checklist

The presentation of the "checklist" is perhaps one of the most important functions inherent in any "housekeeping" form. It is nearly impossible to remember all of the detailed information necessary to consider with respect to any given case. And more often than not, it is incredibly easy to get side-tracked and forget completely the basic information that is needed.

Young lawyers, for *example,* seem to have an incredible propensity for writing down the most esoteric thoughts and impressions while interviewing clients. This is well and good; however, it is too often the case that complete names, addresses, or telephone numbers of the client are completely omitted, along with other critical information necessary to perform *any* required service.

So in summary, a well-devised form should provide an automatic checklist of prompts to assure that the critical information will not be forgotten. It is this most important information that is often the most monotonous, and least exciting; this means that it is often the most overlooked.

2.
They Should Provide Speed
with Respect to
Obtaining and Recording Information

It is far faster and simpler to check boxes, fill in blanks, and strike portions of text than it is to write things out in longhand. The better the construction techniques that you employ, the faster the information can be obtained and recorded. Some of those techniques are more thoroughly discussed hereunder.

3.
They Should Provide Immediate Availability

Assuming that the forms are kept in proper supply and in accordance with the document location principles set forth in Chapter 3, the user should have a means of immediate access to information that is needed quickly and consistently. If information is to be transcribed, or retainer agreements (or medical authorizations) are to be executed, the time savings can be somewhat dramatic; for, most of the forms and agreements can be filled in by hand, signed, dated, and completely executed at once. Time will be saved by *not* having to dictate, type, proofread, and retype the document.

4.
They Should Provide an Important Communication Device

If constructed properly, office forms are neat and clean in appearance. Such sheets can be more easily read and processed by other members of the firm.

Information obtained from structured forms can be interpreted far more accurately and rapidly than handwritten or oral instructions. It is far easier and much less time-consuming, for example, to train a typist (or other member of the office staff) about "what to do if a check-mark appears in box A." This type of instruction is far more precise and discrete than typical written or oral commands.

Dictated memos also provide excellent communication devices; however, the created forms that we are discussing have *several distinct advantages,* the most important of which include a *structured* format, *predictable* data, and a *defined* place where the information can be located.

Memos are particularly useful when dictated "to a client file," to set forth and explain some of those more esoteric aspects of the client's case. However, with respect to "basic information," the prepared office form is a far superior device.

5.
They Should Provide Managerial Control

A surprisingly small number of well-drafted and efficiently stored office forms can provide you with an immediate clear view of how a given case, or group of cases, or even the operation of the entire office, is running. The status sheet, for example, is a very important document which should contain all basic information concerning any client matter. It should be carefully devised and constructed.

* * *

No two law offices are alike; each should have its own set of forms designed to suit its own particular needs and clientele. But by the same token, other law firms that specialize in your category or categories will utilize similar skills and require similar data. So some consideration should be given to the forms that you have already developed and tested. They should provide your starting point.

The suggestions and rules that follow can be used to help you create new office forms or update your old ones. We present them in their chronological order of construction.

Construction of Office Forms

First
Create a List of Basic Forms

Regardless of your firm's size, specialty, or makeup, there is some basic information that will always be required. Consider some necessary forms:

- Status sheet
- Billing or time sheet
- Hourly retainer agreement
- Retainer Agreements
- Medical authorizations
- Checklists and questionnaires for specific types of cases (i.e., personal injury litigation questionnaire)
- Trial preparation sheets

Second
Give Thought to New Forms

The office forms set forth in the preceding checklist are by no means exhaustive. As a matter of fact, whenever you find yourself requesting repeated information from a client, regardless of the nature of that information, or whenever you find yourself writing the same information repeatedly, you should always consider creating a form or checklist.

Third
Think the Form Through and Then Sketch It Out

Give some thought to the form before sketching an outline; however, do not spend too much time on it, for, no matter how much forethought you might devote to a given form, until it is actually tested, it will *never* be complete. It seems that no matter how many times you might revise a form, and think that it is complete and perfect, additional items will show up during actual use. Therefore, do the best you can, but then go to the next step.

Fourth
Make the Form as Comprehensive and as Multi-Functional as Possible

Try to get a large quantity of information on a single sheet of paper, and, *if possible,* avoid using multiple sheets. This literally means that as much information as possible should be crammed onto the single page; however, in no event, should less-than-adequate room be provided for fill-in information. That is perhaps one of the most aggravating attributes of most forms.

A single sheet should serve as many related functions as possible. A time or billing sheet, for example, should contain all related information pertaining to hours billed; but it should also include information that might be helpful to the users and recipients.

Items to be recorded simultaneously should appear on the same form. Billable Hours and Advanced Costs, for example, go hand in hand. They are recorded together, and therefore should be record*able* together. Also, since billing sheet users always refer to their calendars, it might help to copy a mini-calendar on the sheet itself. Figure 5-5 provides a sample Billing Sheet for a small firm.

Fifth
Polish, Arrange, and Adjust

For the reasons set forth above, it is necessary to test the form, revise it, and then test it again before starting mass production. This multiple revision process will also enable you to "polish the form" by condensing, adding, deleting, and arranging material.

It is much easier to polish and adjust the print on the form after seeing a rough print out of it. Only then can you see how the words and blanks appear on the page.

Some techniques are quite simple and somewhat self-evident. For example, blank spaces for dates require very little space; for names and addresses, ample space should be provided.

Where there are a limited number of possible choices for a given item of information, the "check box" method should be used. With respect to taking down the information and communicating it, the box method is by far the best. For situations where there are only two choices, the "strike through" method is the best. (For example—Client [does] [does not] have liability insurance.)

19___

MONTH

____

ATTORNEY

____

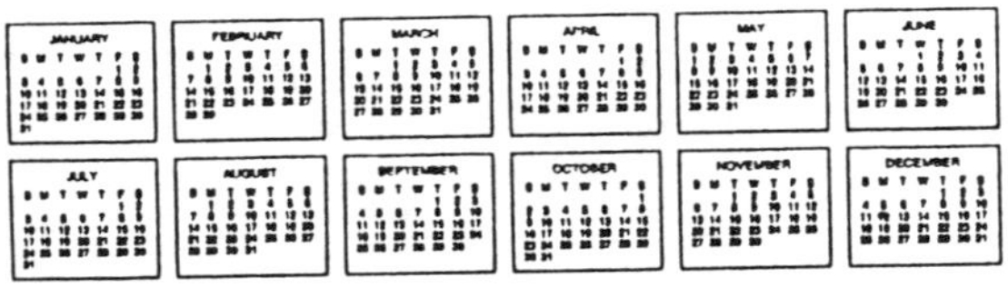

DATE	CLIENT-FILE NO.	WORK PERFORMED	TIME	COSTS

CHECK IF POSTED ___ PAGE __ OF __

Figure 5-5

Sixth
Mass-Produce

Running out of the form is foolish and timewasting. At its most extreme level, it may mean that you have used the last copy and can no longer perpetuate it.

Most office forms rarely change. So our rule of ''oversupply'' (General Rule VIII), should apply that much more vigorously.

PLEADINGS

Litigation is an intellectual, oral, and above all—a *paper* war; pleadings must be ready immediately. For, as with any war, speed is critical. You may be called upon to provide a brief right in the middle of a trial, with less than 12 hours' notice.

Quantity translates into speed. The greater the number of forms in your bank, the greater the chance that those numbers will include the form that you need.

Level I

Before discussing our more creative Levels (II and above), a brief word should be said about Level I forms, since they are quite common in the Litigation arena. You should always have a *thorough bank* of pre-printed forms and pleadings (i.e., subpoenas, praecipes, summonses, etc.), particularly those that are supplied by the courts. And with respect to accumulation, it would be a good idea to ''get them all at once.'' The best use of your time suggests that whenever you are next in a given court, obtain several bunches or pads of all forms that the court provides, particularly those which are free or come at minimal cost.

The next best source would be the form stores (often office supply stores), and services that pre-print commonly used forms in accordance with applicable local court rules. Of course, these sources should be tapped only after ''free'' sources are exhausted. There are some forms that you may wish to obtain and photocopy, such as Summonses and other commonly printed forms that do not use multi-part carbons or impression copies.

Level II

CAUTION! The techniques that we will next discuss, provide some examples wherein photocopiers may provide documents more rapidly than computers. Under no circumstances does this mean that the copier should be thought of as a substitute for a computer. The photocopier can be used as a powerful supplement, but generally there is *no substitute* for a computer.

The computer is a miracle device when it comes to most document-preparation tasks. However, for stable, repeatedly used forms, you can often pull the pages from a file cabinet drawer faster than you can retrieve them from your computer's data base. And thus, with a little bit of planning and preparation, the photocopier can provide a very powerful substitute for straight typing. This is because many of the pleadings that we use in a given case are no different than those that we have submitted, and re-submitted, on numerous prior occasions. The copier is not a substitute for the computer, but it can still be expanded beyond conventional use. Moreover, even with a computer, there are some pleadings that are constant enough to keep in the file cabinet instead of on disk.

With the preceding in mind, I want to consider for a moment the all-important *Interrogatory* as an example. When properly used, this can be one of the most important litigation tools available. It is more than just a discovery device; notwithstanding its technical limitations, The Interrogatory can be used for determining facts and obtaining admissions from the opposition. In any event, it is an important tool, and one that will provide an excellent example, since it is one of those pleadings that should be ''ready to go'' as soon as litigation gets under way.

Quite simply, interrogatories consist of a ''usual'' face sheet, some introductory language, and a series of numbered questions. Here are some techniques to facilitate the drafting process; these methods apply to other pleadings, as well as interrogatories:

1. *Multifacing*

In addition to the heading and the names of the parties, the first few pages contain some rather standard introductory language indicating the name of the person or party to whom the interrogatories are directed, a time limit for submitting answers (as determined by the applicable court rules), and some of the usual cautionary threats as to what will happen if the questions are not properly answered and submitted. In particular, the language does not change very much from case to case.

It makes little sense to retype the same language every time that you send out a set of interrogatories. Therefore, it is a simple matter of tailoring, constructing, and preparing a single set of face sheets to be used for all situations within a given court. There is a problem however; in particular, the required pronouns in the face sheet will depend upon whether or not the interrogatories are being submitted to a plaintiff or a defendant. They may also depend upon whether or not the interrogatories are being submitted *by* a plaintiff, defendant, or multiple parties. Our problem is slightly reduced, however, because good practice requires that we *not* submit any given set of interrogatories to more than one person; separate sets should go to each person or entity.

Instead of leaving blank spaces on the form, or using a "transvestite" definitions page to indicate that males may be females, and vice versa, I recommend the preparation of alternate pages that avoid such pronouns altogether. In other words, one face sheet might contain the language: "The Plaintiff is required to answer each of the questions under oath, within the time permitted by law"; however, an alternative page would use the word "Defendant" in place of "Plaintiff."

This may seem, at first glance, to involve some unnecessary work with respect to preparation. But in truth, consider how easy it would be to prepare these sheets all at once. Moreover, contrast that preparation time with the amount of time required to go back and re-draft the language, or even retype it, every single time that you want to submit a set of interrogatories in the future. I think you will find that the ability to have these pages on a "ready to go" basis will, in the long run, save a great deal of time. Computerized or not, these pages could then be pulled faster than they can be lazer-printed.

You should not be unduly concerned about having places to store these alternative sheets. If you will, notice that the Discovery Division of the Litigation Category has its own numbers for face sheets (see Figure 3-3). For example, all of your face sheets will bear the form number structure (for federal court) 133,2XX. This "leaves room" for 99 different combinations, far more than you will ever need. You might consider a topical breakdown for the face sheets, in any manner you choose; here is one suggestion:

1. Submission to defendant, by singular plaintiff.
2. Submission to defendant, by plural plaintiffs.
3. Submission to plaintiff, by singular defendant.
4. Submission to plaintiff, by plural defendants.

An interrogatory face sheet, for example, directed to a defendant by a singular plaintiff would bear form number 133,211. Likewise, face sheets to be used by plural plaintiffs would bear number 133,121, etc. For want of a better term, I refer to this "multiplication" of a single form as "multifacing." The purpose behind it, in summary, is to have the forms there and ready for use, *immediately*.

2.
Pull Page Techniques

It seems that every good set of interrogatories is composed of three types of questions. First, there are those that are asked *all the time*. Exemplifying this group are questions directed toward the identity of the person submitting answers, the identity of witnesses, and, perhaps, past criminal records. Depending upon the court and your particular state, the same questions come up repeatedly, as well they should; for, certain information should *always* be requested, regardless of the type of litigation involved. Think of these questions as forming your base pages.

Second, are those questions that seem to come in "blocks," depending upon the type of litigation involved. For example, if your firm is defending a personal injury case of any kind, be it assault, battery, or automobile negligence, you will submit questions to the plaintiff pertaining to physical injuries. But, in addition, you will *automatically* want to submit questions pertaining to medical reports, lost wages, and interim earnings. For such questions, you should form a group or "set" of pull pages, all directed toward an "injured plaintiff." You will find that Discovery Division Number Four (see Chapter 3) should accommodate several different sets. In particular, for a state court, the number structure 183,4XX should accommodate up to a 99 sets.

You could keep several of these copied sets in a single folder. Each page of each set would, of course, be unnumbered until use. The preparer could insert the pages at will. It may also pay to keep the interrogatories unnumbered, unless you structure them with a number-letter combination, in which case, you could number the individual questions. But even that is not necessary. You could quickly insert the pages in the typewriter, and number the questions consecutively, after you have assembled your completed set. Each group of questions pertaining to a particular topic could be placed in a separate folder. Or, each entire set could be placed in its own folder; such a form might contain the following label:

Interrog.Injury.Plain.	183,411

Figure 5-6

The third type of question that should accompany any well-drafted set of interrogatories will involve some personalization. There should always be some questions directed toward the specific allegations contained in the Complaint, or other principle pleading filed on behalf of the interrogated party. These questions could be placed toward the end, or after the introductory base questions, as you may see fit. They comprise your fill-in or typed pages.

Both your base pages and pull sheets should be constructed in such a way that pages are neatly filled. This should not be too difficult to accomplish. In any event, the material to be added should be minimal, depending upon your ability to make thorough use of base pages and pull sheets.

3. *Packaging*

This concept implies that there are certain types of pleadings that are mailed out in sets. For example, your Motion to Compel Answers to Interrogatories will *always* be accompanied by an (a) Affidavit, (b) Notice of Hearing, (c) Proof of Mailing or Service, and a (d) Brief. (The Federal Rules of Civil Procedure and the rules of most state courts require briefs.) In addition, your motion should contain certain allegations common to all such motions, such as: the date the interrogatories were submitted, the fact that they haven't been answered, and perhaps a few niceties about the opposition.

There is no doubt that all of the above pleadings should be contained in *one file* or "package," so that all of the required documents can "go out" together, automatically, without requiring you to guess about enclosures, or causing you to waste time preparing those seldom-changing items.

Employment of this technique should save time, and a lot of it. Forms can be grouped together as "packages" and given a single form number. The concept is a valuable one, *with* or without the computer. With one, of course, the form preparation and modification processes can be completed that much more quickly. This brings us to our next level.

Level III

Small or large portions of text, that are computerized, can be rearranged, changed, moved, deleted, and added to, in much the same fashion as copier-created text. But the computer can move at far greater speed. And it is this speed that gives the computer its incredible power with respect to the rapid preparation of pleadings and documents.

Moreover, remember that the same form construction principles and numbering scheme may be applied to the text stored in both your computer and file cabinet. This is important; for you may wish to keep certain interrogatory sets in both places.

For those with computers, the last technique discussed (packaging) should always be considered as a strong option. The storage capabilities of the computer are far greater than those of your file cabinet. Therefore, instead of keeping a separate file, for questions pertaining to lost wages (for example), you may wish to create entire sets of personal injury interrogatories that include *all* of the relevant questions. A simple copy function (available on most word processors) enables you to take a large block of text and insert it into another document. Therefore, by using the copy function for material that you previously put on base pages and pull pages, that material could easily and quickly (in a matter of seconds) be copied over into different sets of interrogatories. You could put together such entire packages and have them "ready to go" for any situation that may arise.

Specific questions, the kind that must be hand-typed, can very easily be added to your existing data, regardless of whether or not it is a part of any package. If, however, the "package concept" is involved, the fill-in or typed questions should be kept together.

* * *

I now want to move our discussions from "Interrogatories" to "Briefs." Unlike interrogatories (whose basic elements remain fixed), briefs contain citations and arguments, both of which are ever-changing. Using copier (Level II) techniques, such as those discussed, will work for firms who use similar arguments repeatedly; but, when it comes to citations of law, Level III will always be superior. Computers simply handle changes, insertions, and deletions with greater speed.

Detailed Example of a Brief

It is now time to present a very detailed Example that will encompass and explain many of the principles considered thus far. Bearing in mind that a Master File may vary in length from a single sentence to several hundred pages, we are going to keep our example very short. Of course, the same principles and steps that we are about to outline should apply to any file regardless of size. So as you analyze our relatively short example, try to envision lengthier versions; only then can you gain full appreciation of the amount of time to be saved. With that in mind, consider the Example.

> *FACTS:* Refusals to comply with discovery requests (i.e., Interrogatories, Document Requests, Depositions, etc.) during the course of civil litigation result in the courts' most common motion. As a matter of fact, the number of motions to compel discovery outnumber all other motions combined. So, if your firm is involved in litigation, you can expect to file motions compelling discovery on a regular basis. As a matter of fact, your master form file should contain several form motions and briefs ready for immediate use.
>
> Our particular problem is this—Assume that you are involved in litigation representing a plaintiff who has, on numerous occasions, sought discovery against a reluctant defendant. As a matter of fact, the defendant has failed to show up for depositions and also failed to produce required documents.

You must now prepare a motion for a default judgment due to the defendant's failure to comply with discovery. To keep our text limited, we are going to assume that your brief must be limited to two pages in length. Also, *remember* that we are now dealing with the creation stage; in particular, you do not have an *existing* master to accomplish what you need.

With the foregoing in mind, let us now consider our procedure, step-by-step:

Someone will proceed to dictate the motion, accompanying brief, supporting affidavit, notice of hearing, proof of service, and enclosures. Anyone can prepare these documents, but an attorney must review and sign them. At some point in time, you may wish to make a single master out of the entire package. However, for purpose of our example, we are going to assume that your master will deal only with the accompanying brief. So let us backtrack for a moment by assuming that you have completed your motion and are now preparing to dictate your supporting brief.

Step 1

Prepare the preliminary portions of your brief, and the factual allegations, together with some arguments about the willful misconduct on the part of the defendant's attorney and his client for failure to properly respond to your discovery request (See ''FACTS'' portion of Figure 5-7).

You will have already opened a working file and assigned an appropriate number; say:

L87201MD (The client file number is 187,201)

In accordance with our discussions set forth in Chapter 4, notice the first digit was changed from a ''1'' to an ''L.'' This operation should become almost instinctive; recall that is to ensure that the number will not take on the name of an existing Master. In order to further insure that the working file won't be confused with some master, two additional characters have been added to the file. The letters ''MD'' are your way of remembering that this involves a Motion for Default. After naming your working file, you will then proceed to type the preliminary portion of your brief.

Step 2

Assume now that you have just finished a paragraph, and decided that it is time to insert an argument, statement, or citation that you may wish to use again for a different case (or for this case) at some time in the future. You must now assign a number and identifier based on the content of your insertion.

Look at the boldfaced portion of Figure 5-7; that is, the portion of text that you are now preparing to formate. Refer either to your Master Form Book or your Litigation Chart; both should be kept closely at hand.

You will already know that the first digit, which, of course, represents the Litigation Major Category, should be a (1). You will also know, without even looking at the chart, that you are dealing with a Federal District Court, and, therefore, your second digit will consist of a (3). From your chart, you will see that discovery is the third stage of your litigation proceeding and, therefore, your third digit will have a (3). For a determination of your next digit, you may look to the optional subdivision set forth in Figure 3-3. You will see that item "8" consists of "recent decisions." With this in mind, you may come up with the following number:

133,801

The number alone says that you have chosen—The first file (01), dealing with recent decisions (8) pertaining to discovery (3) in Federal District Court (3). If, however, you are in a hurry, and do not have time to check your Master Form Book, you may assign the inferior digits (4th, 5th, and 6th) quickly and randomly; the number can then be adjusted after you have finished your pleading and mailed it. But *never* put it off beyond that time. And *never* assign a file name that has already been used; *this may cause erasure of a pre-existing file*.

After becoming familiar with the system and your book, assigning digits will become easy. So do not be troubled by your initial confusion and lack of speed.

In addition to assigning a file number, you should always provide an identifier to be used for your hard copy (Figure 5-8) and the appropriate index page of the Master Form Book. It is not necessary to identify the items represented by the first three digits. Their mere positions on the index sheet and the headings that precede them will have already provided that information. Therefore, consider this identifier:

Mot.Default.willful

Step 3

Now that you have provided a file name and identifier, prepare your Master. At this point, it is best that you polish the master and put it in the Master Book, but only if you have taken the time to give it a *proper* number. If not, then resume with Step 4, and perform those duties after your pleadings have been finished.

Step 4

After creating the master, you will *immediately* make a hard copy of it, punch three holes in that hard copy, and thereafter place it in its appropriate place in the Master Form Book. You will then immediately change the appropriate sheet of the Master Index to indicate the addition.

Following the above procedures, you then proceed to perform a "copy over." (The exact name of the function may vary depending upon your brand of software.) Specifically, you will merely copy the Master *into* the Working File so that the material becomes part of it. You then resume your normal operations and proceed to complete the pleading for filing. The master (Figure 5-8) will remain intact; the working file will now include the material from the Master File (per Figure 5-7).

* * *

When the foregoing procedures have been completed, you will have two separate items. First, you will have the complete set of the pleadings that you just prepared, ready to be filed and served upon the enemy attorney. Second, you will have a master that you can use for subsequent purposes. The working file will eventually be erased (per Chapter 4). However, the master file will be saved permanently.

UNITED STATES DISTRICT COURT
FOR THE EASTERN DISTRICT OF MICHIGAN

JOHN SMITH,

Plaintiff,

v. Civil Action No. 372807

DAN DILATORY,
Defendant.
____________________/

BRIEF IN SUPPORT OF MOTION TO DISMISS ACTION FOR FAILURE TO PERMIT DISCOVERY

Plaintiff, by and through his attorneys Coleman, Lipson, and Bradford, Professional Corporation, hereby submits the following brief in support of the attached motion:

FACTS:

The Defendant, Dan Dilatory has repeatedly refused to show up for his depositions. More particularly, in accordance with the affidavit attached to

Figure 5-7

the motion, Defendant failed to show up on June 15, 19xx for a properly noticed deposition, and again failed to appear for a deposition on October 20, 19xx. He again failed to appear for his rescheduled deposition on August 15, 19yy.

The Defendant has not provided any adequate excuses whatsoever, stating only that one of his many pets coincidentally happened to die on each of the preceding dates. The most recent date according to the Defendant (by way of correspondence through his attorney) involved the death of a pet goldfish.

In addition to the preceding problems, the defendant has also failed to produce any of the documents requested repeatedly, pursuant to Rule 34 of the Federal Rules.

Under the circumstances, we believe that sanctions should be imposed upon the Defendant. In this case, a default judgment is warranted.

APPLICABLE LAW

It is clear, that where refusals to comply with discovery requests are repeated and willful, the court should impose sanctions. In this regard, Rule 37 (d) of the Federal Rules of Civil Procedure states as follows:

> If a party or an officer or managing agent of a party willfully fails to appear before the officer who is to take his deposition, after being served with a proper notice, or fails to serve answers to interrogatories submitted under Rule 33, after proper service of such interrogatories, the court on motion and notice may strike out all or any part of any pleading of that party, or dismiss the action or proceedings or any part thereof or enter a judgment by <u>default against that party</u> (emphasis supplied).

It has been specifically held that, where a defendant has acted willfully, sanctions would be justified. In one particular decision, a defendant failed to appear at his deposition on numerous occasions. Moreover, it was determined that the defendant's behavior did not result from an inability to comply with the numerous notices of deposition that were properly filed and served. In that case, the court not only issued a default judgment against the defendant, but also assessed fees and costs. *Shawmut Boston International Banking Corp. v. DuquePena*, 767 F.2d 1504 (11 Circuit, Fla., 19xx).

As in the Shawmut case, our particular Defendant acted willfully and failed to show for depositions on repeated occasions, without an adequate excuse. Therefore, a default judgment should be entered against the Defendant.

Respectfully submitted,

COLEMAN, LIPSON, and BRADFORD

Figure 5-7 (Cont'd.)

Professional Corporation

Ashley S. Lipson

DATED:

Figure 5-7 (Cont'd.)

USING THE MASTER IN THE FUTURE

Do not be misled by my rather picky description of the Master creation process. The great deal of detail was for the purpose of simplifying a process that might be totally strange to you. But under no circumstances should you get the impression that the preceding steps and operations were unnecessarily time-consuming; they were not. And after the procedures have been used for a period of time, they will become second nature. Moreover, in truth, the actual additional time required to execute the steps is *very minimal*.

Regardless of how you view the previous procedures, *using* the masters is much simpler than creating them. And the timesaving benefits could be astronomical. Let us now use our prior example and assume that, sometime later, you wanted to reuse the Master that you just created. Consider these steps.

Step 1

Proceed to prepare your motion and supporting documents in the same manner as before. Stop when you come to a point where you want to use the material from the Master that you previously created. If there are any doubts about whether or not you have the Master available, you should always refer to your Master Form Book Index. Also, your Master Form Book should contain a hard copy of each Master File (See Figure 5-8).

Step 2

Having come to the point where you want to use the Master File, perform a simple ''copy function'' to get a copy of the master placed into your working file. When through, resume work on the working file.

* * *

Following is a hard copy of the Master (Figure 5-8). Notice the identifier in the upper left portion; it is parenthesized, so as to separate it from the remainder of the text. The file name (or number) is placed on the lower right portion of *each* page. (In this example, there is only one page.)

The body contains only that portion of the prior brief (Figure 5-7) that is to be reused for future briefs. The language was constructed with this "generic" use in mind.

(Mot.Default.Willful)

It is clear that where refusals to comply with discovery requests are repeated and willful, the court should impose sanctions. In this regard, Rule 37 (d) of the Federal Rules of Civil Procedure states as follows:

> If a party or an officer or managing agent of a party willfully fails to appear before the officer who is to take his deposition, after being served with a proper notice, or fails to serve answers to interrogatories submitted under Rule 33, after proper service of such interrogatories, the court on motion and notice may strike out all or any part of any pleading of that party, or dismiss the action or proceedings or any part thereof or enter a judgment by default against that party (emphasis supplied).

It has been specifically held that where a defendant has acted willfully, sanctions would be justified. In one particular decision, a defendant failed to appear at his deposition on numerous occasions. Moreover, it was determined that the defendant's behavior did not result from an inability to comply with the numerous notices of deposition that were properly filed and served. In that case, the court not only issued a default judgment against the defendant, but also assessed fees and costs. *Shawmut Boston International Banking Corp. v. DuquePena*, 767 F.2d 1504 (11 Circuit, Fla., 1985).

133,801
Page 1 of 1

Figure 5-8

Notice in Figure 5-8 that the *underlining* for part of Federal Rule 37(d) has been omitted. If, however, you examine Figure 5-7, you will notice the very same quotation has the words "default against that party" underlined. By keeping the Master without underlineations, you can underline (for emphasis) whatever portion of the rule that applies, *after* the language has been placed in the working file. If, for example, you represented the Defendant and filed a Motion *against* the Plaintiff, you might wish to underline the "dismissal" provisions instead of those pertaining to "default." Using this method, the same text can be used for both situations.

DOCUMENTS

Only the Monks worshipped duplication and repetition. The rest of us, it seems, tolerate it. But there has been some progress, even in the legal profession. Several hundred years ago when a barrister first instructed his secretary to prepare Smith's will by using Jones' as a model, that lawyer launched a major attack upon the profession's most time-consuming fault—duplication of effort; perhaps it only took a single moment of genius for him to deduce that a deceased "Jones" was not a whole lot different from a deceased "Smith." But this use of the "form" has since become the predicate for almost every major drafting tool. More important, it has also served as a "thought-saving" device. When put to its best purposes, the user can put everything that he or she has into a polished, complete instrument, designed to serve as a model for repeated use.

Lengthy documents and instruments normally encompass a lot of planning, thinking, and polishing. They are often the end product of generations of legal wisdom, often obtained through trial and error. The Categories: Two (Probate —particularly with respect to estate planning), Three (Corporate and Business), and Four (Real Estate) are among the heaviest contributors of lengthy documents.

The range of items encompassed by our reference to "Documents" is endless, and might technically include every writing on the planet that is not a printed form, pleading, or rider. For our purposes, however, we are concerned primarily with those lengthy writings that your firm might be required to produce on a regular basis; short writings and letters need no special attention. The principles considered thus far should suffice. So we are therefore interested in things such as: lengthy contracts, estate plans, pension plans, etc.

The Joint Trust, an increasingly popular estate planning device, provides an excellent example of a typical "document." As we shall soon see, it contains all of the page structures that we previously analyzed. There are those paragraphs requiring extensive added type, those requiring minimal additions, and straight boilerplate language requiring nothing. Here are some examples of the drafting tools for each.

Figure 5-9 presents that portion of the trust containing the greatest amount of fill-in material. As previously discussed, as much "fill-in material" as possible should be "bunched" into as few pages as possible:

JOINT LIVING TRUST AGREEMENT

THIS AGREEMENT, made this _______ day of __________, 19___, by and between ____

____

Figure 5-9

and ____,
of ________________, Michigan (hereinafter referred to as the "Settlors," and sometimes as the "Settlor"), and______________________________
and____
of ____________________________________, Michigan (hereinafter referred to as the "Trustees," and sometimes as the "Trustee").

WHEREAS, the Settlors have certain property interests that they desire to place in trust for the purposes hereinafter mentioned; and

WHEREAS, the Trustees are willing to accept such trust.

NOW, THEREFORE, the parties agree as follows:

ARTICLE I

BENEFICIARIES

The Settlors are the primary beneficiaries during their respective lifetimes. The Settlors are husband and wife, and all references in this Trust Agreement to the Settlors, or the surviving Settlor are to them, or the survivor of them. The Settlors have ________________________ (child) (children), ____,
born ____,
and ____,
born ____,
and ____,
born ________________.

Figure 5-9 (Cont'd.)

Figure 5-10 presents one of several possible alternatives, depending upon desired distribution ages:

1. *Income and Principal.* Until such time as there is no living child of the Settlors under the age of twenty-three (23) years, the Trustee is granted discretion to distribute all or any part of the net income not used to maintain a residence, together with all or any part of the principal of the Children's Trust, equally or unequally, among the Settlors' children and Descendants as the Trustee may deem necessary for their health, support, maintenance, and education. Any undistributed net income shall be accumulated and added annually to the principal of the Trust. The Trustee shall consider all receipts and other resources which the Trustee knows are available to each beneficiary for those specific purposes and shall consider the standard of living to which each beneficiary is accustomed. The Trustee is granted discretion to expend such part or all of the income and principal of the Children's Trust as to afford any of the beneficiaries an opportunity to obtain a college or university education, or graduate studies, or both, or any course of higher learning commensurate with the ability and inclination of each such

Figure 5-10

beneficiary to apply himself both diligently and seriously to such purpose. No later adjustment shall be made to compensate for unequal distributions made among beneficiaries pursuant to this subsection 1. It is the Settlors' primary concern to provide for the health, support, maintenance, and education of the Settlor's children and descendants who are under the age of twenty-three (23) years rather than the preservation of principal for distribution upon termination of the Trust.

Figure 5-10 (Cont'd.)

Figure 5-11 provides an excellent example of boilerplate language that will never vary from document to document, regardless of gender or plurality. The term ''Trustee'' is a generic proper noun that ignores gender and plurality:

Section 6.2 Exoneration of Trustee

No person who deals with the Trustee shall be bound to see to the application of any asset delivered to the Trustee, or to inquire into the authority for, or propriety of, any action taken or not taken by the Trustee. The Trustee shall not be liable for acts or omissions in administering a trust, except for that Trustee's own actual fraud, gross negligence, or willful misconduct. No trustee shall be responsible for any act or omission of any other Trustee. If the Trustee becomes liable as Trustee to any other person who is not a beneficiary, in connection with matters not within the Trustee's control and not due to the Trustee's actual fraud, gross negligence, or willful misconduct, the Trustee shall be entitled to indemnity out of the trust assets. No successor Trustee or additional Trustee shall incur any liability as a result of qualifying as a Trustee before receiving an account of the previous administration of a trust.

Figure 5-11

The rules of construction pertaining to our sample joint trust might very well apply to any lengthy document. So let's examine our three selected pages very carefully.

Figure 5-9 is the first page of the trust; as a fill-in page it is heavily personalized, and well it should be. For, it is the first page that the client will see; and it may be one of the very few pages that he or she will take the trouble to read. We can thus conclude that the first pages should be heavily personalized, and therefore be fill-in pages.

As a corollary, the last page or pages should also consist of typed or fill-in material. They will contain the necessary names, dates, and signatures.

Any pages involving added material must always receive special attention, particularly with respect to proofreading. So, as our general construction rules indicated, where possible, fill-in material should be bunched together so as to minimize the number of such fill-in pages. Ideally, the document would have two fill-in pages, one at the beginning, and the other at the end; the rest would consist of pull pages (Figure 5-10) and base pages (Figure 5-11). Fill-in material that is buried in the middle of lengthy documents should be avoided if practical.

Pull pages are of rare concern to those who are computerized. For, it is common knowledge that every word processor has the ability to move text about, from page to page, without any regard as to whether it is boilerplate or not. It freely mixes the two without "thinking." Computer users do not share the same *critical* concern for such mixtures as those who rely solely upon the photocopier for document construction.

Notwithstanding the computer's ability to arrange your pages, there are some very definite advantages to be derived from maintaining some separation of pages by content. *First,* it will be easier to select individual boilerplate pages where portions or parts of forms are needed. While drafting, or giving drafting instructions, you can refer easily to those specific pages of a master that you wish to use, and those that you want to omit. It is clumsy and time-consuming to have to use or refer to parts of pages.

Second, there will be less chance for some incredibly embarrassing mixtures of boilerplate language with proper names that bare no relation whatsoever to your working file. Where base pages and pull sheets are kept separate from fill-in pages, these mixtures should not occur. Also, boilerplate language is not as carefully read as fill-in pages *must* be; boilerplate tends to put readers to sleep.

Third, good forms must be modified and updated periodically. Often, the need arises to modify only portions of documents. Even if the revisions cover several pages, the outdated material is always easier to zero in on when the pages are classified according to type (i.e., base, pull, or fill-in sheet).

Fourth, your Master Book will contain forms that are arranged and numbered by page (see Figure 5-4). This reason alone is sufficient to warrant "content consciousness," as you construct your large documents.

RIDERS

Technically, a "Rider" is an attachment or addition to a printed form. I like to think of the finished document as a marriage between Level I and a created form (from Level II or III).

The printed form often contains very fine print that has "been around for awhile," and is therefore "trusted" by the signing parties. Of course, it never seems to leave enough space for fill-in material or special provisions that the parties may desire to add.

At your choosing, if your office is not computerized, the hybridization between Levels I and III could, of course, come together in the form of Level II. In particular, you may wish to store your form leases or construction contracts together with pull pages for your addendums. But do not be confused, copies of printed forms remain in Level I. Anything that *you* create with your photocopier becomes Level II. The distinctions are not important, except for purposes of our discussions; for, Levels I and II always go in file cabinet folders, in any event.

If your firm is heavily engaged in performing work for clients who deal with commercial or real estate transactions, you may wish to keep a solid bank of form options, offers, and leases. Even though such "stored text" might be more efficiently handled on a computer, there is nevertheless room for increasing efficiency by using pull pages for addendums. A good rider should *always* identify:

a. The date of the attached (printed form) instrument;

b. The date of execution of the Rider itself;

c. The parties to the attached instrument.

d. The signatures of the Parties to the Rider; and

e. The title of the attached instrument, if any.

Because real estate makes heavy use of the "Rider," an excellent opportunity exists for stocking different riders, containing a wide variety of provisions. Here is one sample:

RIDER TO LAND CONTRACT, DATED ________________________.
BETWEEN ____________________________________, AS SELLER,
AND ____________________________________, AS PURCHASER.

In the event any inconsistency between this Rider and the Land Contract form to which it is attached shall occur, the provisions of this Rider shall govern and control.

Substantial Principal Payment at
Expiration of Land Contract

It is hereby acknowledged by the parties hereto that the monthly installments are insufficient to pay this Land Contract in full during the term hereof and that a substantial principal payment will be due at the expiration of the term hereof.

Late Payment Charge

Purchaser will pay to the Seller a "late payment charge" of_______ (_____) Dollars for any installment of principal and interest when paid more than fifteen (15) days after the due date thereof.

____
Purchaser

____
Seller

DATE:

Figure 5-12

6

Choosing and Using Equipment

Because of its data-intensive nature and logic-based structure, the law firm is in the best position to profit from the "miracle machines" that have been flowing onto the market in recent years. By all indications, the stream of new equipment is going to continue. Nevertheless, lawyers are slow, and reluctant, to capitalize. We are simply too impatient, busy, and unwilling to "shop" and compare among an infinity of features and models of microprocessing hardware.

You are the people that we lawyers depend upon, when sophisticated equipment is to be purchased. As a primary user, the skilled secretary can fully appreciate the technical features to which most lawyers are oblivious. Paralegals are expected to have familiarity with the technical aspects of document production, which, of course, is "equipment dependent." And administrators are in a key position to determine and dictate hardware purchases. Though lawyers are the actual purchasers, studies have shown that they want to be the *least* involved. Lawyers would prefer to deal with legalese rather than computerese.

This chapter is designed to provide information that will help you determine the best use for your firm's current equipment, and its future purchases. It is not geared to any particular makes or models. So the suggestions and principles should not become obsolete, or "dated." Rather, the discussions should provide a general framework, along with some specific tips.

A focus upon specific brands would not be practical. Their numbers exceed anything that we have ever encountered for any prior product or industry. And new advances occur daily. No single entity, not even Consumer Reports, could hope to be familiar with the 3,000 plus brands of computers, along with the hundreds of thousands of items of software, not to mention all of the peripherals that are constantly being developed. However, as a programmer, and one who has been involved with several systems, I can come pretty close to the mark with respect to your needs by providing some information about features and vendors in general. Monthly magazines are the best providers of up-to-date information about specific brands.

You may or may not be pleased to know that when it comes to asking equipment vendors simple questions, I am as fed up as you are by the overly technical jargon that is supposed to serve as an answer. As one who has examined equipment and programmed and studied computers, I can truly sympathize with those of you who are more concerned about producing paper than fiddling with buttons. So I am going to try my best to keep the discussions simple and precise.

THE TYPEWRITER

Those of you who are more traditional in your approach to law office equipment may take heart in knowing that although computer systems may come and go, the typewriter will always remain. It is still the basic and most indispensable tool of the law office. No other instrument has ever been nearly as effective when it comes to striking a single character onto a specific point on a piece of paper.

Your Present Use

Under no circumstances should you plan to dispose of your typewriter merely because you are in the process of purchasing a computer-printer combination. For as long as there are multi-part forms, fill-in-the-blank documents, deeds, applications, and an endless unpredictable variety of items requiring ''quick type,'' the typewriter will always be necessary.

The Decision to Upgrade

Like every other machine the microchip has invaded the typewriter, causing it to exhibit some very beneficial, computer-like capabilities. In many respects, the modern typewriter is like a mini-word processor. It is not a substitute for a good computer, but it can be an excellent supplement.

Many typewriters have features that closely resemble those of the computer. With the following characteristics, your typewriter could provide an emergency backup, if the computer goes down or is in use:

- Several kilobytes of memory, so that small amounts of text can be stored for repeated use;
- A small window to view text before it is transferred to paper;
- A spellchecker that comes with a stored dictionary;
- An auto-correcting device, that permits the erasure of an entire line;
- Automatic centering;
- Right margin justification with automatic text wrap-around.

RULE-OF-THUMB—For any *new* equipment, particularly a new typewriter involving new characteristics, test it.

We could discuss some of the newer typewriters at length. But technologically, this piece of machinery has already received adequate space.

THE PHOTOCOPIER

When it comes to inexpensive paper production and duplication, nothing can match the combined flexibility, quality, and speed of the modern photocopier. For the majority of available copiers that produce original-like copies, the machine is far more than a mere duplicating device. If employed to its best use, this equipment can be used to create, produce, and modify any manner of document.

Photocopiers provide rapid, consistent output, which translates into readily available supplies and varieties of needed forms. In the last chapter we analyzed the output; now let's look at the equipment.

Developing a Large Bank

Through the methods discussed in the preceding chapter, your photocopier should be used to develop a large, substantial bank of those forms and documents least likely to change. If you have a computer, so much the better—you have a tool that can rapidly perform revisions and modifications. Without the computer, the copier is your *principal* automation device. So, in either event, a close examination is warranted.

The Decision to Purchase or Upgrade

Because of continuously advancing technology (similar to that of the microprocessor), photocopiers have been getting better and cheaper, faster. There is no reason to believe that this trend will end soon. Because of this, the market for used photocopiers is such that it may very well pay for you to keep your old one as a backup, after purchasing a new model.

To determine the number of photocopiers that would best serve your office, measure the distances from the typists' desks to the nearest available copiers. Make your measurements with this in mind—The need to make photocopies is the number-one distraction when it comes to pulling a typist away from the desk, frequently, and for long *periods* of time.

Prices, brands, sizes, and capabilities will vary significantly. Since the machine is one that generally requires continuous maintenance, it is *critical* to pick a copier that is manufactured and serviced by a large, reputable company. For, if the corporation that manufactures and maintains the machine goes out of business, so does your copier.

It is noteworthy that while "interviewing copiers," most vendors are very eager to provide a sample machine for use and testing. By all means take advantage of this. There is no better testing than testing "in the field." Also, you may be provided with an opportunity to perform some heavy duplicating jobs at the vendor's expense, as you legitimately give the machine its acid test.

With the foregoing in mind, we have provided a check-list of the most important items in their order of importance. Price will, of course, vary with respect to the features presented. But the following checklist should provide your basic factors. Following the list, each of the items will be discussed more thoroughly:

1. Reproduction quality
2. Reproduction time
3. Maintenance structure
4. Maintenance contract
5. Choices of paper size
6. Feeder capabilities
7. Two-sided copy function
8. Sorting and collating functions
9. Reduction/enlargement capabilities
10. Color capabilities
11. Crispness
12. Edge eraser
13. Digital control and image manipulation
14. Price per copy

In conjunction with the preceding checklist, here is the more detailed information to consider with respect to each item.

1.
Reproduction Quality

As opposed to the very small "personal copiers," you will, no doubt, want something that has the speed and capacity of what is sometimes referred to as a "favored office copier" or a "high volume" copier. These are buzz words for the "typical office copier." Most, if not all, office copiers will provide very high quality output. The copy is often indistinguishable from the original; and this makes it difficult to compare output quality among different copiers. But there is a trick for figuring out which copier delivers the best reproduction.

The method is really simple. Take a document, preferably one of the testing patterns used by the vendor, and make a copy of it on the machine to be tested. Then take that copy and make a copy of it. Then make a copy of that copy, followed by a copy of *that* copy. Continue on down through as many generations of reproduced copies as it takes before the image begins to disintegrate. The greater the number, the better the machine. All copiers should be able to go down at least five to seven generations without *any* noticeable disintegration.

There is also a simple rule-of-thumb to guide you—If you go with one of the major brands, you can be pretty well assured that the quality of the copier will be acceptable. When interviewing the best known brands, you should be most concerned about prices and maintenance fees; someone has to pay for all of the promotional and advertising expenses.

2.
Reproduction Time

With respect to the time that it takes for the copier to produce each individual page, there are *two* factors to consider. That is because, for multiple copies, it takes longer to produce the first copy than it does to make any subsequent multiple copy.

The response times will, of course, vary with respect to the size and quality of the copier (which will, in turn, be directly related to the cost of the machine). Of the two factors, for the lawyer, the multiple copy response time is most important. But the ''first copy'' time should *always* be questioned and tested. A copier that produces split-second multiples may be worthless if it ''takes forever'' to get the first copy.

At the lower end of the copier spectrum, the inexpensive personal machines can be expected to take from three to six seconds to produce a single copy. For the average law firm, this response time would be far too slow, even for a backup copier. At the other end of the spectrum are the high volume machines which can be expected to produce copies in less than one second. Some will reproduce at speeds of up to 100 copies per minute.

Before thinking that these slight differences in time are insignificant, be sure to test a given machine carefully. Particular attention and weight should be given to the opinions of the user secretaries.

3.
Maintenance Structure

Look for modular or cartridge construction. That type of machine facilitates the rapid replacement of bad parts, and correction of malfunctions. As you probably know, today it is easier, and cheaper, to replace things than it is to repair them.

4.
Maintenance Contract

Substantial attention should be directed to maintenance contracts. Things with moving parts will always break down; and, like cars, copiers will always have lots of moving parts. It is a good bet that your copiers will need maintenance and repair more frequently than any other item in the document production chain.

Beware of contracts that are not fixed as to amount. In order to sell the machine, the vendor may provide you with a "low-ball" figure for the first year, which may translate into a substantial increase later. Such further increases should be defined, listed, or otherwise "capped." And, above all, the service contract should provide for annual sums that are not dependent upon the prior years' history and frequency of service.

Deadlines, such as 24 hours, should be specified as maximum delay times for the repairman to show up. For problems that cannot be corrected quickly, an adequate spare or "loaner" should be provided.

5.
Choices of Paper Size

Today, photocopiers can be expected to reproduce copies up to 11″ x 17″. All copiers are expected to provide an alternative of 8½″ x 11″ paper and 8½″ x 13″ paper. Occasionally, there may be a requirement for 8½″ x 14″ paper. Partially due to the extraordinary influence of the computer, courts throughout the United States are gradually *requiring* 8½″ x 11″ paper for all pleadings.

6.
Feeder Capabilities

Feeders are substantial time-saving devices. Papers need only be placed in a feeder tray, and, with the push of a button, the user is free to leave and perform other duties. For any firm that produces briefs, trusts, or other lengthy documents, the automatic feeder is indispensable.

There are distinctions among feeders. There is the Semi-Automatic Feeder, which requires someone to hand-feed the copies into the machine. Then there is the Automatic Feeder which allows papers to be stacked up in a tray, to be *automatically* fed into the machine. In addition, there are those Automatic Feeders which will recirculate pages automatically for two-sided copies.

Feeders should *always* be tested carefully; their very nature suggests that they are prone to continuous problems and foul-ups. For, it is not easy, even in this day and age, for a machine to single out extremely thin items such as pieces of paper, and feed them through a system repeatedly. Therefore, particular attention should be paid to the manner and frequency of feeder breakdowns.

Some feeders are sensitive to paper that is not "perfectly" static-free, or "perfectly" flat, so when testing a feeder, use as many different types of paper as are available.

7.
Two-Sided Copy Function

The ability to make two-sided copies can be somewhat valuable to reduce the size of files. It can also save paper where the photocopier is used for lengthy research projects which involve duplicating several pages of text.

The ability to make two-sided copies is not, however, crucial. It is more of a luxury item than a necessity. Always keep in mind how difficult it is to flip through pages of a client's file and attempt to read two-sided documents.

8.
Sorting and Collating Functions

Separating, inspecting, and arranging multiple copies can consume a lot of time. A copier that will sort numerous copies can be of great value, particularly where multiple copies of large instruments are involved.

With an automatic sorter, the user can place the work on a tray, push the ''sort'' option, select the desired number of copies, depress ''start,'' and walk away. So, needless to say, this feature saves time.

9.
Reduction/Expansion Capabilities

It is to be noted that when creating forms, masters, or documents, whenever type size is reduced, the result is a very fine, professional, and almost ''print-like'' appearance. Also, the ability to put large amounts of text on a single page by way of reduction could be very important and valuable, particularly when creating office forms.

Expansion functions can provide valuable tools for creating demonstrative blowups or exhibits for use during trial. They can also come in handy for research projects involving cases or head notes with small print.

10.
Color Capabilities

The ability to produce documents in color has never been a major consideration of the legal profession. As a matter of fact, the first document ever produced contained pretty much the same black-white character combinations as the documents being produced today. But with respect to the future, who knows? Perhaps the day may come when you can start making pretty documents. Nor should you rule out color as a potential enhancement for brochures and newsletters.

11.
Crispness

It is disconcerting to watch the quality of your copies slowly fade as the toner runs low. You never really know when it is optimal to switch cartridges or toner. For want of a better adjective, a ''crisp'' copier will provide nice, dark output up until the toner runs out; this is preferable.

12.
Edge Eraser

The ability to erase or eliminate those shadowy edges around partial pages can be quite valuable. Where parts of documents are ''assembled'' on the copier, a neater and cleaner result can be obtained.

13.
Digital Manipulation of Image

This ''final straw'' involves the ability of the photocopier to digitally store information, and then rearrange it in the form of altered output using microprocessor techniques. In other words, after a document is placed on the photocopier plate, its image is reduced to numerical representations and then stored in a microprocessor; thereafter, the user can enhance, change, and rearrange the resulting output just as if it were a hard copy of some computer file.

This has a not-so-obvious disadvantage to it. While the feature may be an incredible device for document preparation and perfection, it also presents a very serious evidentiary problem. This machine represents the first copier of its kind that is specifically designed to reproduce an image that is *not* a ''true copy.'' This is significant; for the concept of the ''true'' or ''accurate'' reproduction was something that courts had been accepting for years. Now this may change.

The presence of a microchip may also signal the presence of sensors that automatically adjust exposures, and paper sizes. In any event, this feature has ushered in the start of a merger between the copier and the computer. The day will come when the former will cease to exist as a separate tool.

14.
Price per Copy

This ''last but not least'' factor can be very complicated. It will, of course, depend somewhat upon the selection of the preceding enhancements. Computing it accurately can be futile. But some information can be obtained from the vendor.

* * *

In the last analysis, the major brands should be interviewed, tested, and considered. Remember that the duplicating machine is one of the most important items of equipment in your office. It should be chosen carefully.

THE DICTAPHONE

The dictaphone is still an extremely ubiquitous item of equipment. It is not the most efficient; but it is nevertheless very necessary. There are some other very important media for getting thoughts from the brain onto paper. As might be expected, the computer is playing an ever-increasing role in this particular function. And it is doing so from several different angles.

With the computer, we have the ability to pull pieces of text as we would a puzzle, placing them into a given order and letting the machine do the rest. Therefore, the need for actual verbal dictation is reduced. The dictating machine is, therefore, not the device of the future. It wastes incredible amounts of time, requiring one individual to spend time talking and another an equal or greater amount of time listening. In addition, such matters must always be proofread carefully, which often results in retyping, which, in turn, results in a redraft and then more proofreading.

Nevertheless, for whatever use the dictation equipment will serve, it will always be around for giving instructions to computers, if not people. At the very least, the equipment will be needed for dictation which directs the text manipulations for your office computer.

Using the Best Communication Techniques

The ability to *properly* communicate with the typist is paramount. Documents, or parts thereof, should be quickly identifiable with single, unambiguous language or numeric code. Here are some elementary tips for the paralegal that the typist will truly appreciate:

- Dictate paragraph starts, and punctuation where possible.
- Spell difficult words, particularly if they are right in front of you. It is foolish to require the typist to look up a word when you are staring at it.
- Identify master files by *both* their numbers and their identifiers. Be very specific when describing placement (for example—"Insert the file after the first paragraph, following the word 'country.' ")
- Where separate tapes are used, the very first words on the tape should identify its sequence number and its side (for example—"This is tape two, side one," etc.).
- Frequently, play back portions that you have dictated to make sure that the voice is clear and understandable. When the typist wants to "get something out," it is extremely aggravating to be held up by a single, unintelligible word.
- When finished be sure to tell the typist to ignore everything else on the remainder of the tape, so that he or she does not have to waste time listening ahead.

Handling of Material and Data

The physical handling of data, before it emerges in the form of a written document, can be quite a sensitive matter. For, it is at this stage that data is most flimsy and capable of being lost, and never again found. There is a simple, and yet very important, procedure that we follow in our office. That is this—

> *RULE-OF-THUMB—Before* erasing anything, always make sure that you are left with two separate physical embodiments of the document *after* erasure.

This is an important rule since it is a most horrifying experience to lose several hours of original dictation or work. Therefore, as you are dictating onto the tape or dictaphone, save your notes. When you are through, you will at least have rough notes plus the tape. This is important since notes can get lost, and tapes can very easily be erased accidentally. At this point, your document is still in two forms, one of which will serve as a backup.

After the document has been typed and copies made, then, and only then, should the tape be erased. At the very worst, if your file burns, a copy of the document will be on file with the court or in the possession of the client.

This rule-of-thumb is extremely important with respect to computer storage. For there may be a temptation to key a document into the computer, and then erase the tapes before a print-out or "hard copy" is obtained. Although disk crashes are becoming rarer as technology improves, they nevertheless occur. And you may lose massive amounts of data, should your disk foul up. Therefore, there are several safety measures that can be taken to provide a backup, such as saving an extra copy of the material on a floppy disk. This will provide two sources, one floppy and one hard disk file. The point is this—Do not erase the tapes until you get a hard copy from your computer; that is the safest way to proceed.

THE COMPUTER

The Direct Reference Form Filing System (Chapter 3) was invented before the micro-invasion of the legal profession began. At the time of its development, it was the only pure, logic-based system of its kind. To my knowledge it still is. The benefits were not dependent upon the computer, even though its decimal structure caused it to mesh perfectly with computer technology, like two tangent gears. The ultimate wedding between system and computer can produce a remarkable magnification of the already time-saving capabilities of the non-computer version of the Direct Reference Filing System.

The nice thing about the filing methods is that you need not have a computer in place in your office to construct the system. Whenever the computer does arrive, the system will automatically welcome it. So you need not disrupt your present office system for a second. Nothing has to be *re*arranged or *re*numbered. This means that you can take a giant, cost-efficient step (you can't get anymore cost-efficient than "free") toward automating your office before you even decide which computer system to buy.

As we shall see throughout this chapter, the advantages and costs of today's microprocessors are such that *no* office should be without one. The word processing capabilities alone make it somewhat unreasonable to delay purchasing a computer any longer.

The Decision to Buy

For those of you who do not yet have a computer, we can start out with a non-technical, indisputable piece of advice:

BUY ONE!

Because of the relative price and the incredible capabilities of today's microprocessors (particularly with respect to the legal profession), there is simply no debate. Once you use one, as the cliché goes, you will wonder how you lived without it.

Perhaps the benefits of the computer can be emphasized by providing a rather extreme example—For those of you who are not computerized, consider giving up all of your machinery, typewriter included, so that all legal documents would be drafted by hand, page-by-page, without carbon paper to handle duplication. In effect, to go from the computer back to the typewriter would be nothing less than the equivalent of going from the typewriter back to hand-drafted documents. Perhaps this will give you some idea of just how incredibly efficient and productive the modern computer can be.

Admittedly, computer shopping can be perplexing. Most of the confusion, particularly with respect to the legal profession, has resulted from a delayed entry into the market by computer vendors. Superimpose upon that problem at least 3,000 different brands of computers, with as many languages. But now things are becoming standardized, *very* standardized. With respect to the hows, whys, and details of purchasing, we are going to provide some helpful tips that are both simple and condensed.

I do not intend to engage in a lot of philosophical conversation about the technical specifications of the various choices that you have; quite frankly I do not feel that you are interested in digital circuits or electronic impulses. I also feel, contrary to many other authors, that your decision-making process is minimal at best. In other words there are some "things that you need," and I am going to tell you quite simply what they are. With that in mind, let's consider the basics.

Whom Do I Contact?

There are two basic attitudes that must be examined before you contact anyone. As might be expected, the answers to the remaining questions will depend heavily upon which choice suits your firm's philosophy:

Choice 1: Contact the largest and most reputable vendors and buy *only* from among the *very largest* brand names (those manufacturers that have not yet filed for Chapter 11 Bankruptcy). This means that the product will cost *more*, but, there will be less aggravation, lost time, and problems.

The premium price that you will pay for your product entitles you to a bit of extra security with respect to backup assistance and maintenance. It also provides a sympathetic "shop" to take your problems to, and people familiar with your situation in the event that you need to have your equipment altered or upgraded.

Choice 2: Sometimes referred to as the "Grey Market," it provides alternative equipment that is compatible, and sometimes nearly identical, to the machinery provided by the brand names; often the only difference is that of price. These off-brand computers cost substantially less.

To find the Grey Market, you need only look in any popular computer magazine or journal; they are readily available at your local book store. Beware that this alternative is strictly for those who wish to operate on a do-it-yourself basis. It is recommended for those of you who are computer buffs or have access to someone who is quite familiar with computer equipment.

When you deal in the Grey Market, you do so at your own risk. Unlike the situation involving a local vendor who can provide service contracts and warranties, there is a bit more uncertainty in dealing with products through the mail. But nevertheless, some such companies offer valid warranties. And, believe it or not, some of those companies may even be around long enough to honor them.

Author's Choice: Grey Market, Black Market, or White Market, it makes no difference to me; the Comprehensive Computer Document System (Chapter 4) is compatible with every make of computer in existence. There are simply no incompatible microprocessors. However, with respect to the better investment, unless you have a great deal of time to spend, and waste, I would suggest the first alternative. If not the first alternative, then I would recommend a well-known, competitive brand of computer that is compatible with the top-name models. Under no circumstances will you want to get a strange, "off-brand" that is non-compatible.

The idea of compatibility with the major brands is extremely important for one simple reason—All of the software vendors, and those who sell peripherals, do so for the major brands. Therefore, the major computer brands will be able to run a greater variety of programs, and utilize a much greater variety of peripherals, than will the incompatible off-brands. With respect to the Grey Market, it is simply a matter of being absolutely certain that the off-brands are totally compatible with the major brands.

What Are the Key Aspects of "Compatibility"?

Choosing a particular format for your computer is not quite as easy as picking out a video cassette recorder. Many of you may remember shopping for a VCR as your last bout with two inconsistent formats (Beta and VHS). Those seeking to buy a computer will face similar, but more complex, decisions.

As with the purchase of my first VCR, I delayed buying a computer until it appeared that some victor would emerge in the war of the competing formats. When it became apparent that the VHS format was going to beat Beta, I purchased a VHS even though the popular journals indicated that the Beta was mechanically superior. In the microprocessor arena, there were (and still are) many competing systems. But, when it appeared that IBM and its "MS-DOS" format was going to become prevalent in the office setting, I committed the resources of our office to the IBM-PC XT.

The format that I chose remains exceptionally popular and should be found in thousands of law offices for years to come. Nevertheless, IBM has come out with newer systems that are *not* compatible with MS-DOS. Will one of these become the system of the future? Maybe; maybe not.

Those who remember IBM's small personal computer will understand that this giant of computer manufacturers is just as capable of producing a dud as any other innovator. So, from this we may conclude that it is not enough to pick the right company. You must also pick the right format or model.

Checklist: As much as the manufacturers may desire standardization, keeping the products compatible is not easy. This is partially due to the fact that microprocessors keep getting better and faster; it is not possible to keep the later generation machines compatible with the former. With that in mind, here are the key components to consider when testing for compatibility:

- Operating System
- Floppy Drive Size
- Keyboard Configuration

The operating system is the structure or built-in program that controls all of the other programs that you are going to run on your machine. Think of it as the connector between your hardware and software. It isn't quite "hardware'' because it is an actual program, with algorithms and logic-based instructions. On the other hand, it isn't quite like ''software,'' because you can't conveniently select, discard, change, or create it at your choosing. Rather it is a go-between.

MS-DOS is currently IBM's most popular operating system; it is in wide use in law offices in all states. OS/2 is a newer IBM offering which may or may not take hold. As for the future, I am rooting for the UNIX operating system because it was designed for use on a variety of different computers.

For the micro, there are two standard types of floppy disk. Most of us are familiar with the flexible 5¼ inch, thin floppy disk. A newer 3½-inch disk is a smaller but thicker item, commonly referred to as a ''micro-floppy.'' Its popularity is increasing while that of the standard floppy is decreasing; this is due to the micro's ability to store almost twice as much data, with less chance for damage or crash. The two formats are incompatible, but material can be transferred, as long as you have at least one of each type of drive.

Several years ago, IBM won acclaim for its keyboard's design. Since then, it has became quite standard; and you may find similar configurations for computers that are otherwise totally incompatible. In addition to the 26 letters, 10 decimal digits, and standard typewriter characters, for any keyboard that you are considering, expect to find:

At least 10 function keys

A ''Return'' or ''Enter'' key

Shift, Control, and Alternate keys

4 cursor movement (arrow keys) directives

An ''Insert'' and ''Delete'' key

What is Partial Compatibility?

If you purchase an IBM PC from a reputable dealer, and that machine contains an IBM logo, you may truthfully state that your equipment is ''100% IBM compatible.'' If not, you have something less. This does not mean that all IBM clones are less than adequate matches; indeed, there are some pretty good ones that sell for quite a bit less than those displaying the IBM trademark. And for the most part, the more popular brands of software should have no problem running. But some programs may run slowly or with glitches; and one never knows what type of bugs may pop up on machines that were not specifically tested by IBM software developers. Also it is difficult to predict how more sophisticated future software will run.

> *CAUTION!* When it comes to the intentional misuse of terminology, hardware vendors are worse than used car salesmen. I have heard vendors emphatically state ''This machine (referring to some clone)

is exactly the same as an IBM, except for the label.'' Be distrustful of such statements, even if you trust your vendor; they are often false.

As opposed to clones which often claim to be 100% compatible, there are those computers that advertise and claim to be ''partially compatible'' with other machines. This can be a plus where one major brand which, in addition to being able to run ''its own'' software, can run programs designed for another major brand.

It is is worth noting that there are programs specifically designed to allow a computer to run software that would otherwise be considered totally imcompatible with its particular operating system. These ''emulators,'' as they are called, are relatively inexpensive, and will normally list (on their packages) several major brands of software that will run. For our purposes, it is worth noting that major products involving word processing and data base management are normally included.

If I Want to Get My Feet Wet Gradually, but Want the Ability to Expand Later, What Minimum Requirements Should I Demand Now?

Today's computers are tailor-made for addition, enlargement, enhancement, and expansion, particularly the major brands. Terms such as ''modular construction'' and plug-in ''boards'' suggest ease and flexibility when it comes to adding enhancements. However, with respect to the basics that you should demand for any computer, here is a small, but nevertheless basic and critical, checklist. With respect to these items, *do not* shop price:

- At least a 20-megabyte hard disk.
- At least 512K of RAM (Random Access Memory); 640K is becoming a standard minimum.
- At least one floppy disk drive.
- Ports for a printer and a mouse.

For those of you who do not understand completely, or even minimally, the significance of the above terms, do not worry. It is not important that you understand them; it is only important that you see to it that your vendor supplies them.

For those of you who are interested in the above terms, we can provide a brief summary. The first two refer to the capacity or ''horse power'' of the computer. These are minimal requirements in today's market; the storage is needed to enable your machine to handle the software that you will need with an appropriate amount of speed.

The third item, the floppy disk drive, enables you to store a limitless amount of text on small floppy disks. These floppy disks, unlike the hard disks, can be removed from the computer and stored in bins. With respect to the last item on the list, you will need a ''port'' (plug-in) for a printer, (which you will certainly want) and a port for a ''mouse.'' Your peculiar need for this item (see Chapter 9) involves some state-of-the art software that you may, or may not, be interested in at this juncture. The point is that you *may*, some time in the future, want such capabilities. So even though you may not wish to purchase a mouse at this point, you may certainly want the capability.

What About Word Processing Machines?

Today, we call them ''Dedicated Word Processor,'' meaning that the machines are dedicated exclusively to word processing functions. However, unless they are capable of utilizing the continuing technological and developmental improvements of the software industry in general, it might be best to think of them as being dedicated to obsolescence.

Personally, I don't like a microprocessor which is limited to a single function. Although it claims to be entirely ''dedicated'' to producing text, I question the dedicated processor's ability to utilize the new, and rather remarkable, software packages and word processing utilities presently available for ''normal computers.'' The ''Dedicated Word Processor'' is, by definition, limited.

The non-microprocessor word processor is all but obsolete. Regardless of whether it is an old, mag-card machine (short for ''magnetic card system) or a less-antiquated system which employs magnetic tape, such word processors are nevertheless obsolete. Their capabilities and document manipulation potentials are dwarfed by the current microcomputer. And for reasons that we will consider shortly, even modern dedicated micro-word processors are limited, by comparison.

How Should I Deal with the Vendors?

Contrary to popular belief, vendors from the largest companies will ''wheel and deal'' to a limited extent. Like automobile salespeople, they have their margins of profit and will do their best to maximize it. Do not be afraid to negotiate, particularly when you are buying several items of merchandise, such as word processing programs or printers. In such cases, you should be sure to ask the vendor for some kind of reduced rate. The vendor will no doubt be aware of the impact of the Grey Market; he will know that you will always be able to get the equipment cheaper through the mail.

The following list has a dual purpose; it can be used to negotiate or determine what services are available from your vendor. It can also be used as a checklist for comparing vendors. With that in mind, consider the elements:

- Is there a trained, educated employee who will be servicing your account after the sale?
- What warranties and guarantees are provided?
- Is there any on-site or classroom training provided? At what cost?
- Does your particular vendor have any expertise with respect to legal software?
- How long has the company been in business? Is it part of a large national chain?
- What peripherals are kept in stock? Is there a large store in which adequate supplies are kept on hand?
- Are there trained technicians capable of repairing the equipment quickly?
- Is there a toll-free hotline that is not constantly busy?

When you purchase your computer, you are certainly going to want other items to connect (interface) to it. The computer alone is worth nothing. You will *automatically* need a monitor (picture screen), a printer, and a modem if you intend to use a legal database. You will certainly also want a word processing program. And most important of all, you will want someone who will be able to connect all of these things together in a completed chain; this can be tricky and time-consuming.

IMPORTANT! When you negotiate with your vendor, *make certain* that he agrees to come out to your office and set everything up. And what is even more critical is that you insist upon seeing a single sentence printed on a single sheet of paper. This will mean that everything is working. Under no circumstances should you agree to any other arrangement.

I have heard countless incidences where the vendor would set everything up and something would not match, or an additional part, link, or cable would be needed. Moreover, some technical expertise will be required to see to it that your word processing program is properly implanted on your hard disk, and that the printer is "set to handle" that program.

There are dozens of tiny little adjustments that need to be made. There is no point in discussing each of these items with the vendor; he will certainly have you at a disadvantage. He will know what has to be done; you will not. Buying a computer *is not* similar to buying a new automobile. It will not start running as soon as you turn the key. But there is a simple solution—Reach an agreement whereby the vendor agrees to install the system and guarantee that it will print a single, simple sentence using your word processing program. Once this agreement is struck, problems with interfacing, serial ports, parallel ports, and any other number of concerns will become *his* problems and not *yours*.

Should I Get a Service Contract?

There was a time when computers, particularly those containing hard disks, were heavy, bulky, fragile items. Extraordinarily expensive "on-site" service contracts were quite common and necessary. Today, it may not hurt to have a service contract; however, if you have a second or a backup computer, most service contracts would *not* be cost effective.

The primary "gamble" with respect to the service contract involves the risk that more money will be paid out in repairs than in service contract payments. As previously stated, there was a time when this was a pretty good gamble. Today, however, repairs are relatively inexpensive. But more important, computers are breaking down less frequently. As the technology advances, the improvements continue, and the cost of repairs has been coming down. Therefore, if you can afford the gamble, you should not get a service contract. Statistically, if something does *not* go wrong within the warranty period, there is a good chance that it never will (during the useful life of the equipment).

What Can I Expect in the Way of Help?

If you purchase an item via the Grey Market, or by mail, expect very little help. In most cases, the vendors will not even promise to provide assistance.

If you purchase from a local vendor, you will be promised a variety of things, such as "backup," "help," "support," etc. And you can expect to receive some help; however, remember that most errors are not the fault of the computer. Therefore, your local vendor may inform you of a policy involving "idiot charges." These involve situations where *you* may be convinced that a failure of the system to operate is the fault of the computer hardware; however, in truth this is rarely ever the case, and it is becoming even more rare as time goes on. As most all plane crashes are attributable to "pilot error," not equipment, most computer crashes are attributable to "operator error," and not the hardware.

Where Can I Learn More About Hardware?

Books, magazines, and seminars are good "stock" places to pick up information of any sort. I also recommend talking to vendors; they will have the latest information on new systems.

> *CAUTION!* Vendors are the best source of immediate product information. But they will always slant their recommendations in favor of their in-stock items. Always talk to several *competing* dealers before buying.

For continuous and reliable information concerning hardware (and software) that pertains to The Legal Profession, I strongly recommend subscribing to the literature published by The Section of Economics of The American Bar Association and its Computer Division. There is no better source of timely information for the profession, regardless of specialization.

Integrating Your Computer and Document System

As indicated in Chapter 4, setting up your computer document system involves little more than a movement of forms from your form file drawer to your computer. But, it is important to note that this transition can be accomplished gradually, as gradually as you may wish. As a matter of fact, any given form, other than the ones that must remain in the drawer, can be subject to the "concurrent jurisdiction" of both the form drawer and the computer.

The Decision to Upgrade

As previously indicated, today, computers are built for easy expansion and additions of peripherals. However, perhaps your biggest decision may involve the implementation of a "local area network," sometimes referred to as a LAN, or the installation of multi-user terminals.

When the firm purchases its first computer, only one or two people may have occasion to use it. But later, several different people may desire immediate access via their own terminals. Networking involves separate computers (not just "dummy terminals") that are linked or interconnected so that the users can share information.

In addition to sharing data, computers can also be arranged to allow a use of some of the peripherals that we will shortly discuss. But more is involved for satisfying the complex hardware and software requirements necessary to establish a true network.

Networking can be a complicated affair. I single it out for preliminary consideration because it is *not* one of those enhancements that you can easily implement *after* you have a system in place. On the contrary, if networking or multi-user terminals are anticipated, such matters should be discussed with your vendor at the time that you initially purchase or upgrade your present system.

The term "multi-user" refers to the use of "dummy terminals" (keyboards) that permit people from different stations to share other items of hardware. Several people might thus be provided with access to printers, hard disks, etc.

Your Peripherals and Add-Ons

The enhancements offered by today's computers extend far beyond mere word processing abilities and capabilities. They have the ability to perform some rather incredible functions. The following is considered as a checklist of the peripherals that are available.

1. *Printer*

Of all peripherals, the printer is certainly your most important add-on; it is destined to become the busiest piece of equipment in your office. When it breaks down, your office breaks down. As strange as it may seem, the computer/printer combination is so fast and efficient that your office staff will be quickly spoiled. And even though your old, reliable typewriter remains willing and able, nevertheless, if the computer or printer stops, a feeling of total helplessness will engulf your office and your paper production capabilities. So efficient are today's printers, that once you have a good one, you will wonder how you ever lived without it.

To give you some bearing with respect to laser printer technology, there are helium-neon lasers capable of producing more than 20,000 lines per minute. You probably don't need that kind of speed. But it is something to think about as you listen to your strike-printer produce a once-thought-of rapid tune.

Due to the position of current technology and the rapidly declining prices, it is foolish to buy anything other than the best for your particular office. Let me be more specific—essentially, there are three types of printers out on the market: (1) Dot Matrix, (2) Daisy Wheel, and (3) Laser. The Dot Matrix is the cheapest, and below the quality required for your office. The Daisy Wheel is the most ubiquitous printer; however, due to the incredible capabilities and the declining prices of the Laser printers, the Daisy is rapidly being replaced as the leader.

After owning, using, and studying the various types of printers, I *strongly* recommend that you consider the purchase of a Laser printer. They are by far the best printers on the market, and with respect to price, there is no comparison; some Laser printers are now under $2,000. In general, they cost more than Dot Matrix printers; however, they are cheaper in the long run. If you currently employ a Laser printer in your office, there is no need to tell you of its benefits. If you do not have one, consider these characteristics:

- They are *faster* than anything that you have previously encountered; they look like, and sound like, a small photocopier; they pump out pages of print just about as fast;
- They are as quiet, or quieter, than a photocopier;
- They have very few moving parts, meaning that in the long run, maintenance costs should be lower than those of your mechanical printers;
- They are very high quality; most come with multiple fonts and other features, some of which allow very high-quality Desktop Publishing (with newspaper-like graphics and fonts).

Unlike any strike printers, there are no ribbons to fool around with or replace; nor are there any problems with respect to messy toners, such as those encountered when dealing with photocopiers. The laser printer has a type of modular and cartridge construction. So when a current printer cartridge wears out, it is merely replaced. These cartridges last far longer than printer or typewriter ribbons.

When dealing with vendors and interviewing machines, you should pay particular attention to the font manipulation capabilities and graphics capabilities. The items on the above list will become apparent, and easy to view by mere demonstration. You will notice immediately how quickly, quietly, and easily the laser printer will produce documents. In much the same fashion as a photocopier, however, expect the first page printed to be delayed, perhaps for several seconds. Following this initial delay, the copies that follow should come almost immediately, in much the same fashion as your photocopier.

The ability to provide graphics may not be very important to you. Such capabilities will depend not only upon the type of printer that you buy, but also upon your software and hardware. Most firms do not seem to care a great deal about graphics capabilities.

Font, however, is another matter. The ability to switch font effortlessly, or in the middle of a document, is something that I consider quite valuable. It seems that there is nothing quite so professional looking or pleasing to the eye as footnotes or headings or titles, that are different from the font of the main body. Such switches not only look professional, but also enhance readability. Fonts may be built-in, insertable via cartridges, or available within software.

As discussed previously, if such capabilities are being purchased, you should insist upon seeing them, in print, before the vendor receives your check and exits your office. Perhaps even more so than the other peripherals, the printer's capabilities should be quick and easy to demonstrate.

When "shopping price" for laser printers, be sure to inquire about "cost per page." The print cartridges are the principal expense items. A more expensive machine may result in a substantial savings in the long run.

2.
Modem

The modem is your device for communicating with the outside world. It brings to your desk, the law libraries of the country and some important user-group databases. It also provides an immediate shopping list of values and services, right at your fingertips (See Chapter 8).

Quite simply, the modem connects your computer to your telephone lines, which are in turn connected to other computers and databases throughout the United States. This permits you to research very large legal databases, without ever leaving your office.

Once a clumsy device that you physically placed your telephone upon, the modem now is placed "invisibly" inside the computer. A designated telephone line will be used as you download data into your computer ("downloading" is nothing more than retrieving data from an outside source bank).

3.
Optical Scanner

The optical scanner is a truly remarkable device that permits the computer to photographically read a page of text (and graphics) and feed it directly into the computer's central processing unit. The significance of this device is substantial; for the first time print from a page may be entered by a means other than a secretary's fingertips.

As the device is perfected, information will be transmittable from documents, cases, or virtually any source (including pictorial information) to the computer immediately. This means that once the data is entered into the computer, it may be adjusted, changed, or manipulated at will, before it is output in the form of a printed page.

Think of the possibilities, particularly with respect to lengthy citations or paragraphs from contracts. Instead of hand-typing the information, line by line, you can do it mechanically, all at once. This will greatly facilitate the creation, and especially the revision, process for any lengthy writing. For virtually any situation involving the transmission of lengthy text into your own data manipulation process, the optical scanner can save an incredible amount of time and effort.

As with the laser printer, this "miracle machine" now has a relatively small price tag on it. Once very expensive, clumsy, and inaccurate, current optical scanners may now be purchased for as low as under $1,000, and today's models are less error-prone.

Most of the technological problems were resolved not by major changes in the hardware, but rather by advances in computer software. In any event, the optical scanner is something that you should look into if you are in the habit of retyping from text instead of a dictating machine.

There is only one way to interview optical scanners; test them by repeated use. Under *no* circumstances should you limit your experiment to text produced by your own printer. This serves no purpose whatsoever, since the last thing that you would want to scan would be material that you already have in your computer's databank. Instead, consider this brief checklist:

- Casebook text (large print)
- Casebook text (small print)
- Pleadings prepared by other offices

- Textbook
- Handprinted notes
- Handwritten notes
- Graphics
- Photographs

The above list covers a fairly broad spectrum, and you should not expect a $1,500 optical scanner to be able to accurately reproduce each of the above items. As a matter of fact, the scanner's ability to even consider the last three items will be dependent upon hardware and software limitations. For the items higher up on the list, you can draw your own conclusions. If the scanner cannot, with a fairly high degree of accuracy, reproduce text from a case book, then that scanner may very well be of limited value to you.

When testing the scanner, do not be too tolerant of errors. During your initial encounter with the machine, you may be extremely impressed to see a page quickly reproduced that has only three or four errors on it. However, it may take more time to locate and correct errors than it would to retype entire pages. In such a case, the scanner is obviously not cost effective. However, as previously indicated, the technology is now at the point where you should give serious consideration to the device. It is safe to say that your need for an optical scanner will be directly proportional to the amount of text that you copy from outside sources.

When interviewing scanners, here is a brief checklist of things to watch for:

- How many errors per page, on the average?
- Is it compatible with your word processing software?
- Paper handling capabilities (will it handle single sheets and bound material)?
- Will the paper feeder permit the ''stacking'' of multiple sheets, or does it require a ''one-at-a-time'' feeding? And if stacking is permitted, how many pages will fit in the feeder tray?
- How many pages scanned per minute?
- Will it handle proportional typefaces?
- How does it handle ''halftones'' and text with weak resolution?

For those of you who are involved in lengthy litigation or lawsuits involving mass documents, an optical scanner may very well be a ''must.'' And even for those who do not handle such cases, mild litigation may, in and of itself, warrant the purchase.

If you handle litigation, you have probably had occasion to prepare a pleading known as ''Answers to Interrogatories.'' It is often one of the most painful and time-consuming items on your agenda since it involves communication from your client. Most Federal District Courts, and many State Courts, now require you to repeat each question that your enemy has provided, before each answer. This, of course, involves straight retyping. If the information was first fed into the scanner, then you would only be required to type the answers after the questions; much duplication of effort would be avoided. But consider a situation where your scanner could translate handwritten notes; in such a case, you could have your client prepare handwritten answers, and then do nothing more than cut and paste them below the typewritten questions from the enemy attorney.

For other specialties, the scanner can be of equal value. For Estate Planners, you could build up a massive computer form bank, almost instantly. Merely obtain copies of your favorite trust and will instruments. Label them in accordance with your form numbering system (Chapter 3), scan them, feed them into your computer, and you are ready to go. Also, imagine the amount of time that can be saved with respect to revisions of lengthy boilerplate language for employee benefit plans.

For law firms in general, a scanner can mean getting rid of the old "once indispensable" fax machine. By installing a simple "fax board" in the computer, the scanner can be used to transmit and receive the usual photocopies of documents; but it will also provide the power to digitize and store images on the computer's disk. This is something that a fax machine cannot do.

4. *Mouse*

As a replacement for the boredom of typing and using keys as input, the mouse provides a quick selection device by which information and choices may be fed into the computer with the simple movement of a wrist and a single finger. It is not necessary to actually lift one's fingers or hands off of the mechanical surface.

At this point in time, you may very well consider the mouse to be a luxury. However, with the computer industry, luxuries have a habit of rapidly spoiling their users and becoming indispensable necessities.

Much of the modern software that is being developed today is tailor-made for mouse operation. For this reason alone, the peripheral should be considered. It is very inexpensive, to be sure.

To gain some idea of how the mouse works, examine Figure 6-1. Notice that the computer screen is displaying three possible alternatives for the user to select. The pointer (dark arrow) is positioned at Choice 1, causing that position to be boxed (or highlighted). If Choice 1 were desired, the user would punch the button on the mouse (lower left corner), to notify the computer of that selection.

If, however, Choice 3 were desired, the user would move the mouse along the path of the dotted arrow (below); the pointer on the screen would follow suit. The Choice 3 portion would then become highlighted. The user would then punch the button, causing the computer to select that item. Sound difficult? It isn't; the hand-finger movements take a second or two, at most.

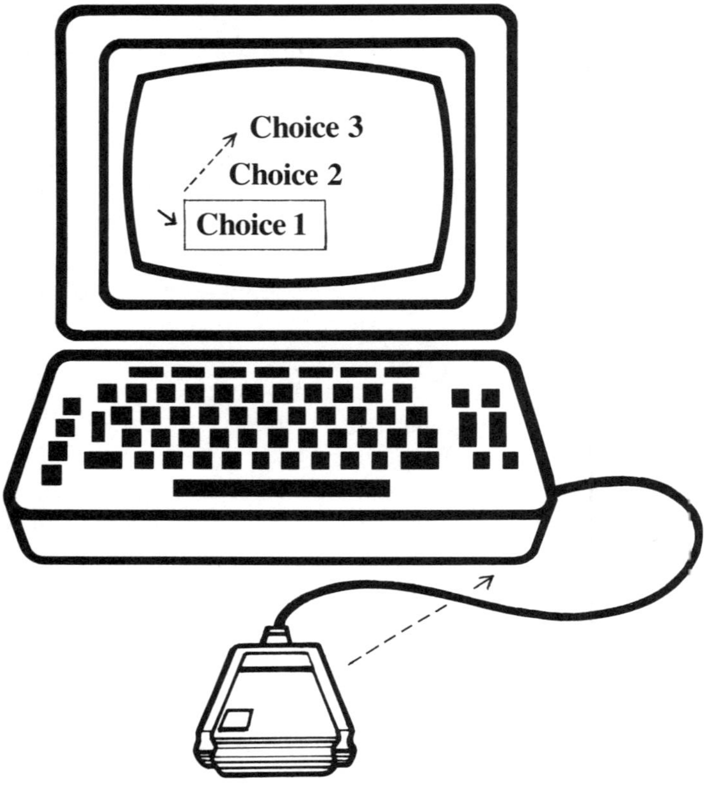

Figure 6-1

In Chapter 9, we are going to consider an important item of software for the legal profession (Document Modeler Language). The use of the program can be greatly enhanced through the use of a mouse for input procedures.

5.
Acoustical Input Device

This is, no doubt, the input device of the future. Still in its experimental stages, this particular item of machinery is the final step for getting information from the human mind directly into the computer. It also seems to be a device that is intent upon putting many secretaries out of business. The item, in effect, permits voice to be translated directly into print.

When interviewing voice-to-computer input devices, the key characteristic will involve the machine's ability to distinguish the various patterns of human speech. At some point, the machine, or its software, will be required to separate, for example, drafting instructions from actual text. It will have to know when to capitalize words, and how to spell them. These latter capabilities are no real challenges for today's software. If you have a spell-checker, you are already aware of the fact that the machines can probably spell better than you could ever hope to. However, the ability to distinguish between the other characteristics will still be very important. Homonyms will certainly present a very definite challenge; these are words that sound alike, but have different meanings (i.e., bear, bare, etc.). It is assumed that the software will eventually have the ability to analyze the word's position and use in the sentence, and determine the proper spelling. Consider this acid test when interviewing one of these machines:

> Is it right, Mr. Wright, that your employer refuses to bear in mind the bare essentials with respect to providing shelter from the bears during the camp-out?

The acoustical input device is an item which, for the next several years, will undergo substantial changes and improvements. Those of you who are curious about artificial intelligence may be interested in knowing that this device is only one step away from creating robots that will follow human commands. In essence, that is precisely what the printer does when it follows your voice instructions.

7

Choosing Your Software and "Paper" Ware

Software is a generic term commonly used to refer to a never-ending variety of purchasable computer programs. These are the programs that make the computer perform its limitless functions and tricks. For those with computers, this chapter is your legal-software primer. Those without should consider it as an argument for purchasing hardware that can open the door to features that we are going to consider. Computer non-users may also be interested in our discussions pertaining to manual systems and devices. They are, however, intended to *supplement* the automated aspects of your office and should not be construed as reasons for failing to computerize.

You might think of software as the "records" that your phonograph (hardware) plays. But the analogy ends there. For, phonograph records do not interact with one another; nor do they interact with the user or change their contents to suit that user. But software does all of these strange things.

There is software to serve every conceivable need and desire. Did you know that there are programs that work within word processors which do nothing but verify the structure (not the content) of your citations? In addition, there are dozens of other types of single function software that will continue to pop up in journals, bookstores, and computermarts. However, we are going to focus on the "major" items that are of greatest concern to you and your profession.

It is important to recognize the benefits that can be derived from the miraculous software that is available; but you should not let these products blind you to the fact that in certain instances, simple, intelligently designed manual systems (which I refer to simply as "paper-ware") may suffice. More often than not, an efficient firm will have a mixture of well-selected software and paper-ware. This, then, brings us to the first topic.

YOUR CURRENT MANUAL SYSTEMS

Before rushing to introduce any complex systems or software into your office, keep this in mind—speed, accuracy, and, above all, simplicity form the greatest triumvirate of efficiency for your office. When repetition or volume becomes great enough to outweigh the benefits of manual simplicity, computer software should enter the picture; for, the word "computer" does not translate to "free ride." Some input of work is always required; human hands are needed to key in, manipulate, and retrieve data.

We are going to treat software as an additional tool to consider—nothing more, nothing less. For some law offices, a singular item of software may, by itself, justify the purchase of an entire computer system just to run it. But your firm does not need every program and gimmick available. Some firms may be better off *without* certain relatively inexpensive programs, even though that firm may already possess the requisite hardware. Much will depend upon the particular layout of your office.

To assist your decision-making process, detailed information about software can be obtained from vendors, magazines, and computer stores. Legal software is continuously advertised in the various bar journals and legal publications. In response to a simple letter, software sellers will be pleased to bombard you with brochures, tutorials, booklets, demonstration disks, and other specific data. Therefore, we are going to concentrate on information intended to give you an *overall* picture of the software scene, along with some basic tips.

The differing types of software should fall into one of three pigeonholes: (1) You should buy it, regardless of the size of your firm; (2) an intelligent purchase depends upon your firm's size, structure, specialty, and its volume of business; and (3) you shouldn't buy it.

You will be way ahead of most if you can just identify which of the three slots your firm falls into for any given product. The following sections should provide some help.

WORD PROCESSING

The word processor is mightier than the pen. Like the typewriter, the pen is clumsy and unforgiving; both record thoughts character by character, word by word. And once those words are written, they are cumbersome to change.

The computer-word processor can record those same thoughts, but by pages instead of characters. Its features help perform routine functions quickly and effortlessly, and with as little duplication of effort as possible. If you do not have a computer to run such a program, then you should buy one. Because this software fits squarely into the first pigeonhole, *no* office should be without one.

For the legal profession, word processors are truly revolutionizing the manner in which lawyers, paralegals, and secretaries are producing documents. Initially, the greatest impact was upon the secretary; however, the powerful and fast text manipulation features have had a corresponding impact upon everyone else's ability to construct documents accurately and rapidly.

Your Dictionary Checklist

The following dictionary is designed to accomplish two things simultaneously. First, it should provide you with a working knowledge of some of the basic terms pertaining to word processing software. Second, it will present a checklist of items and functions that you might expect from your potential purchase. Consider any listed feature accompanied by a "(+)" as absolutely mandatory. For more detailed information, always consult the manual for your particular model and brand of software; or better yet, make the vendor explain the listed features:

- *ASCII*—American National Standard Code for Information Interchange, it is a standard by which binary numbers (capable of being understood by the computer) are internationally assigned to represent letters and other characters. It forms the character base for most operating systems and word processing utilities. It includes all 26 letters of the alphabet (upper and lower cases), the ten numerical integers, a blank space, and some of the most common symbols (.,$, =, +, -, etc.).
- *AUTOSAVE* (+)—An important feature that causes text to be saved automatically when the lights go out. Without this device, a power failure may cause you to lose all of the work that has been keyed in but not yet saved to disc. The feature will guarantee that in the event of a power failure, no more than a single page will ever be lost. A good Autosaver should cause your work to be saved to disc automatically upon exiting the "create" or "edit" modes.
- *BLOCK MOVE* (+)—A function which involves the simple, but important ability to "pluck out" a chunk of text, and move it to another part of the document.
- *COPY FUNCTION*—Allows you to copy a block of text into another document, or another portion of the same document, without erasing the original block.
- *CUTTING AND PASTING*—A process which refers to the general ability to move blocks of text from one part of the document to another. To accomplish this, you should not be required to pre-define spacings. In other words, you should be able to pick out entire paragraphs, and squeeze them in between two adjacent sentences if you so choose. The program should automatically "make room" for the new text in its new spot, while "closing up the hole" caused by its departure from the old space.
- *DELETE* (+)—This term is somewhat self-evident; it is a good test of speed for the word processor. You should be able to delete large amounts of text very fast. You should not have to move the cursor, letter by letter, or word by word, in order to accomplish a deletion. But a word of caution is warranted—As the speed and ease of deletion increases, so must the care and attention of the operator.
- *DOCUMENT ASSEMBLY*—A term which generically refers to special features which allow you to use your macros to "automatically assemble" documents from boilerplate language contained in different files or masters. In a "strictly" word processing environment, the feature will provide a very minor form of the more potent tools discussed in Chapter 9.
- *FONT*—Pertains to the size and style of print that appears on the paper. An important feature is the ability to change fonts in midstream. Documents can look quite professional and attractive when multi-fonts are utilized. This feature will, of course, be dependent, not only upon your software, but also upon the capabilities of your printer.

- *FOOTNOTE SPACER*—A feature which arranges pages containing footnotes; i.e., pages are automatically ended at an appropriate spot so as to allow enough room for footnotes at the bottom.
- *GLOBAL SEARCH AND REPLACE* (+)—A function which permits you to direct the computer to automatically change a word, term, or character string everywhere that it appears in the document, "all at once," without physically tracking down each individual string. For example, if you wanted to change "Plaintiff" to "Defendant" everywhere in the document, you should *not* have to read through the text to find each "Plaintiff." One set of keystrokes should do the job.
  BE CAREFUL—this is one of those "think before you punch" features. For example, assume that you told the computer to change "Plaintiff" to "Plaintiffs" because you wanted to pluralize the term throughout the document. In essence you might tell the computer to add an "s" to each character string—"Plaintiff." You might be surprised, however, to find some resulting words that look like this:

  Plaintiffss
  Plaintiffs's
  Plaintiffss'

  Remember, in the word processing setting, the computer does not "look to see" if an "s" is *already* there. It blindly obeys the command. *NOTE*: The addition of a blank space at the end of the search term ("Plaintiff") would solve this *particular* problem; careful thought may, however, be required to anticipate and solve others.
- *HEADERS AND FOOTERS* (+)—Pertain to page numbers and whatever additional text you may require at the beginning or end of each page. Every processor should be able to number pages consecutively *without* any numerous keystrokes. Respectable software will also enable you to define start and stop numbers, in case you do not want to begin numbering with page "1," or, correspondingly, if you do not want to number the pages all the way to the end.
- *INSERTION* (+)—The ability to "plug" blocks of text into the middle of paragraphs or sentences. Some programs will allow you to move the cursor to the point of insertion, so that as you type, you can watch the words to the right being "pushed over" to make room for the inserted text. Other programs will "blank out" everything after the insertion point when the "insert" button is pushed; hitting the key a second time will cause the disappeared material to reappear at its proper point (immediately after the inserted text).
- *JUSTIFICATION* (+)—Refers to the ability to "line up" the right-hand margin by causing variable spacing between the words on each line. The result is a "printed page" look for your documents.
- *MACRO-COMMANDS*—In addition to storing boilerplate text, a macro captures and saves repetitive keystroke commands for future use. This feature can

be particularly helpful for avoiding the repetitious busywork involved in setting up formats, spacers, footers, etc.

- *MERGE* (+)—A capability which allows you to take data from two files, and blend them into a single document. The feature can be particularly valuable where documents are repeatedly sent to the same addresses over a period of time. Litigation correspondence and pleadings provide excellent examples.
- *SEARCH AND REPLACE*—See Global Search and Replace.
- *SPELL-CHECKER*—A built-in dictionary that signals the user as to any spellings that do not appear in it. A good program will allow you to add words, such as proper nouns or legal jargon. And an even better word processor will contain a dictionary with legal terms.
- *SORT COMMANDS*—Valuable tools for arranging lists in numerical or alphabetical order.
- *TEXT CONFORMITY*—A measure of the degree to which the text on the screen matches the text that ends up on the printed page; the greater the degree of text conformity, the easier it is for the typist to read. See WYSIWYG.
- *WINDOW*—Allows you to look at two or more pages of text on the screen at the same time.
- *WORDWRAP*—See Wraparound.
- *WRAPAROUND* (+)—A common feature which permits the word processor to automatically balance words on lines so that no single word will be split between two lines.
- *WYSIWYG* (Pronounced ''wiswig'')—An acronym for ''what you see (on the monitor) is what you get (on paper).'' It refers to the software's ability to make the screen look like your actual printed page.

The foregoing terms are among the most standardized; however, the list was not quite as easy to assemble as you might expect. Each word processing vendor seems to take delight in creating its own special terminology. So, if you find any terms in your prospective word processing package that are remotely similar, they may define one of the functions just described.

* * *

When shopping for a software package, factors such as compatibility, support, quality, and future updates require that you purchase a major brand. For a quick rule-of-thumb as to which word processing programs are ''major brands,'' you need only count the number of books at your local bookstore that are devoted to the program. It might help to glance through some of those books before you select your software.

Compatibility Considerations

You should have no trouble whatsoever finding a major brand of word processor that conforms to your computer document system (Chapter 4). But just in case, here are two simple requirements:

- You should be permitted to assign a file name of up to at least eight alphanumeric characters.
- There should not be any strange features that name your files for you.

Before leaving this subject I want to mention WordPerfect (TM), particularly versions 5.0 et seq. Normally, I avoid mentioning brand names, because of the ever-changing market. But in addition to having *all* of the features contained in our Dictionary Checklist, WordPerfect claims to be the long-awaited software designed with the legal profession in mind. There is reason to believe the claim. In addition to the inclusion of a 50,000-word legal/medical spell-checker dictionary, the software places great emphasis upon macros and boilerplate movement. This focus seems to mesh well with your new systems' emphasis upon text manipulation and arrangement.

BILLING, PAYING, AND ACCOUNTING

Countless programs are available to perform every manner of accounting operation and function. However, this is not the time to shop price. Primary considerations should center upon your firm's particular needs. So your accountant should be the first person that you consult. The firm's bookkeeper comes next. With that in mind, the information that follows is designed to familiarize you with types of products that are available, and to keep them in proper perspective as your staff makes its decision.

Keeping Billing Simple

Those of you who are administrators know that to get associates to keep good time records on a regular basis is like pulling teeth. Studies have shown that as a rule, a very high percentage of attorneys fail to properly bill for all of the time that they put into a given matter. And those that postpone or delay marking their time sheets (so that they can later estimate their billable hours) always end up on the losing side of the guessing game. Therefore, it is critical that whatever billing system is employed, it must be uncomplicated, easy to operate, and immediately accessible to the user.

I have seen systems that required as much recordkeeping as actual attorney work. Some had stickers, multiple postings, and other strange varieties of time-wasting, paper-generating exercises. The best systems, however, are the simplest, requiring the least amount of work, and generating the least amount of paper.

Look at the simple, yet comprehensive billing sheet (Figure 5-5) that was constructed as a sample office form for Chapter 5. It is concise, simple to read, and easily "keyed" if your office is computerized. Nothing could be quicker, except perhaps direct coding for those offices with a computer terminal on every desk. But even without a computer, good "paper-ware systems" can work efficiently.

Notice that the sheet (Figure 5-5) provides space for the attorney to fill in four pieces of information with respect to any legal service performed; the "COSTS" column can be billed or charged simultaneously. There is, therefore, no separate sheet for cost accounting.

Incentives for procrastination should be avoided at all costs. The calendar at the top of the sheet provides a quick reference in case the attorney cannot remember the present date, or the date that some prior services were performed.

Experience has shown that each person tends to use his or her own acronyms and abbreviations for work performed. Computerization, of course, will require standardization if symbols or short abbreviations are to be effective. And if they are employed, those symbols should be listed on the billing sheet for quick viewing by the user.

Posting time *from* the sheet is a simple matter. At the end of each month, or biweekly period, as the case may be, someone could pick up the sheet from each attorney and post the information *directly* from the time sheets to a ledger or computer.

Notice, therefore, that the entire system could operate with very few pieces of paper—a billing sheet for each attorney, and a statement for each client. There are no stick labels, carbon copies, or multiple sheets to be placed into booklets or processed. I doubt that there is a simpler system.

In the event that a separate ledger is required for cost accounting, the bookkeeper can simply extract whatever information is needed from the "COSTS" column. That particular column can be used for all billable costs such as parking fees, telephone charges, and copier costs. The simplicity of the system should not, in any shape or form, interfere with any accounting system that you or your firm's accountant may decide to utilize.

Billing Software

The billing package is one of the most common items of software available for use by the legal profession; there are many from which to choose.

Perhaps the following guidelines could be of assistance, while shopping. Ask the vendor whether or not the software:

- Provides a simple, easy-to-use, and understandable menu. (Ask to see it.)
- Permits entry of data with few key strokes, and, of course, with less required time than it would take to perform the task manually.
- Allows a billing for each transaction (or work item) in chronological order of transaction, with "billed time" and "costs advanced" automatically separated on the statement.
- Allows you to show detailed written descriptions of services rendered. (An advanced system should provide the option of itemizing charges or delivering a statement with no detail whatsoever.)
- Provides options for billing on demand or by cycle, at your choosing.
- Produces bills which reflect client advances (retainer balances) and credits.
- Allows different cases or matters for a single client to be put on the same bill.
- Provides for linkage between accounts receivable records and a general ledger so that totals flow automatically into the desired entry positions.
- Provides for the generation of a variety of sorts and reports by client, billing period, etc.

Pegboard Payables Systems

I am a very strong proponent of pegboard check systems. With all of the office methods that multiply work or duplicate effort, there are few systems, indeed, that move in the opposite direction by combining multiple functions into singular tasks. Pegboards provide an ideal example of this latter type of efficiency device.

As each check is written out, the date, payee, and amount are automatically transferred to the underlying ledger sheet. This results from the carbon strip placed on the reverse side of each check. It means that the information will appear both on the check and on the ledger sheet, even though it was written only *once*. The procedure makes most recording errors a thing of the past.

Most pegboard system checks are designed so that they can be placed in a window envelope, with the addresses appearing in their proper positions. This can be particularly helpful for developing a simple accounts payable system. So, by writing a check, one would automatically have made a journal entry and addressed an envelope; think of this as killing *three* birds with the same stone.

Spreadsheets

There are, perhaps, as many different accounting systems as there are law firms and accountants. Each seems to have its own quirks and special characteristics. The specifics of financial structuring are matters that should always involve some consultation with the firm's accountant.

As a general rule, you should favor software that is specifically designed for the legal profession. You will be able to find a copious supply of advertisements in many of your firm's bar journals and legal publications. However, if you don't have time to shop or experiment, you might try an extremely popular item of software known as Lotus 1-2-3 (TM); it's simple, proven, inexpensive, well-established, and no bookstore lacks its subject matter. Think of it as a starter program that will provide familiarity with spreadsheets, in general. It also contains a utility that lets you construct your own databases.

CONTROLLING AND DOCKETING YOUR DATES

Most of you already know how critical it is to maintain a proper system for keeping track of dates. For most firms, it is a life-death function. The legal environment consists of trials, hearings, meetings, conferences, mediations, and due dates for documents. When dates are missed, the punishment is unlike that imposed upon the members of any other profession; you pay, and pay dearly. Clients can suffer defaults, sanctions, and costs.

Perhaps more than any other industry, professional liability insurance carriers are becoming increasingly aware of the importance to be placed upon a good docket and calendar system. Malpractice cases and rates are on the rise, and the insurers are well aware of the fact that the greatest percentage of problems is caused by missed dates. Indeed, there was a time when the *only* basis for liability imposed upon a lawyer involved a missed Statute of Limitations. Currently, the missed appointment, trial, or deadline, still constitutes an overwhelming cause for professional liability. This is the reason why your firm's malpractice insurance carrier sends detailed questions concerning your calendar and docketing systems.

The bottom line is this—There is no reason for *not* keeping a simple, precise, and accurate calendar system. It should be maintained and watched by virtually everyone in the office, and the procedures pertaining to it should be obeyed religiously. And, if your firm specializes in litigation, the amount of caution should be doubled.

Calendar Basics

Before you get whisked away into the realm of electronic ticklers and computerized docket control, consider this—The more movements required to perform a single function, the more complex that function becomes; and correspondingly, the greater the chance of foul-up. When it comes to calendar and docket control, you should be far more concerned about accuracy than speed.

So before you even remotely consider instituting some complex paper-tickler system, or other structure, consider the basic techniques set forth in the following list:

A. *Dates received by mail*

1. A designated secretary (or clerk) opens mail (Everyone else keeps "hands off");
2. Secretary segregates office and junk mail from client file correspondence;
3. Secretary automatically pulls client file for each item of correspondence pertaining to it;
4. Secretary examines mail to determine whether or not there are any dates or scheduling orders, and if so, makes the appropriate entry both on the responsible attorney's calendar and on a large office calendar centrally posted in the secretarial area;
5. File will be placed upon attorney's desk with information, thereby informing him or her of the date;
6. Secretary will remind attorney at least two days prior to hearing.

B. *Dates received by telephone*

1. Whoever receives call will see to it that date is posted on both responsible attorney's calendar and office calendar;
2. Secretary will remind attorney at least two days prior to hearing.

Paper Products and Ticklers

As a rule-of-thumb, you should be very cautious about any *new* system that purports to regulate the manner in which the firm's associates are going to keep track of important dates. In my lifetime, I have seen some pretty bad systems. I once worked in an office that had a tickler system that generated more paper than a Wall Street tickertape parade. The system was resented and not followed.

If used properly, ticklers, tabs, dividers, and pads often provide some effective, inexpensive methods for organizing and controlling office operations and procedures. Neatness, organization, and predictability are crucial accompaniments. If they can be enhanced by relatively inexpensive paper products, they should be considered. But you should always question *any* system that generates more work or paper than is absolutely necessary.

If your firm is small, a simple calendar system should serve as a reminder, a date-setter, and a tickler. Such a system should provide a central calendar (normally kept in a common secretarial area), along with separate calendars for each associate. The system should work well, depending upon how busy your firm is. Of course, if you are too busy to use a simple calendar system, you may need software to complicate your life.

If you have happened upon or created a decent manual system, *make certain* that everyone in the office is aware of the manner in which it is to function. The docketing chain is only as strong as its weakest supporter.

Docket Software

Computer programs are available to perform some rather remarkable feats with respect to calendar control. But before you get overly intrigued or hypnotized with the features that we are about to discuss, be sure to ask this question—*Can I perform the operations just as accurately and easily by hand*? If so, then you should question the purchase of any calendar docketing software. The size of your firm will be relevant, though not determinative.

Above all, remember that unlike simple manual systems, using software requires accuracy in reporting dates to the computer operator (or keying them in yourself), seeing to it that the proper reports are generated at the proper time, and seeing to it that the proper associate obtains the reports when they should be obtained. Does all this sound self-defeating? Well, it may be for some firms.

For firms that can maintain simple, accurate, and efficient offices, the involvement of all these additional functions may do nothing more than create potentials for foul-up. And remember, a bad system is like a bad tire; it is worth *less* than nothing to you. Nevertheless, if your firm is a large one, or if the docketing problems are getting out of hand, then software may provide the solution. With that in mind, consider these features.

1.
Input—Output

The calendar software forms a database of sorts; more particularly, information is input, and substantially the same information is output, but in different forms and arrangements. The input is a simple matter; someone must physically key in the dates, times, and other relevant information pertaining to the calendared events.

The input function may be centralized (i.e., from one terminal), or it may be "decentralized" (i.e., available from different terminals). In any event, there must be some coordination among all of the input mechanisms to insure that the responsibilities for obtaining, transmitting, and inputting the information are clear.

With respect to *output*, there are two essential possibilities; they are: (1) the screen or monitor, and (2) paper printouts or reports. In either event, if information is not readily available, the system will be worse than worthless.

2.
Forms of Reports

Essentially, docket control software is measured by its ability to generate a variety of different reports. You should be able to obtain, for example, a report of all cases, for all attorneys with respect to a defined *period.* In addition, the program should be able to generate specific reports:

a. by Date (i.e., all matters for a given date);
b. by Attorney (i.e., all matters for a given attorney, for some defined period);
c. by Subject Matter (i.e., all personal injury briefs that are due for a given period);
d. by Case Name (i.e., all matters scheduled for a given case);
e. by Activity (i.e., all types of a certain activity, such as depositions);
f. by Location (i.e., all matters scheduled for a given court or even a given conference room).

There was a time when, in the litigation arena, the court dates were provided piecemeal, one at a time. Today, however, courts are becoming infatuated with "scheduling orders" that provide all future dates for a given case, including discovery cutoffs, pre-trial conference appointments, and mediation schedules. Because of this, reports can provide better pictures, further into the future.

3.
Default Entries

Don't be misled by the heading; it does not pertain to situations where someone has been defaulted for failure to appear. Rather, it refers to defaults with respect to information that was not otherwise provided to the computer.

For example, assume that a given hearing date has been set in a given case. But the person who entered the information did not input the location. The program may (based on prior information), nevertheless, provide the judge, room number, and court location. It would do so "by default," based upon previously entered data.

I am extremely suspicious of this "beneficial" feature of calendar software. It could be dangerous and counterproductive. For it should not be the business of the computer to guess as to location (or any other factor). If anyone is to make the assumption, let it be the someone with information; and if an assumption is not adequate, someone should check further for the information. Far too often, hearing rooms, judges, and even buildings will change during the course of litigation. It is far less dangerous to *omit* such information than it is to provide *wrong* information, or information "by default." If something is missing, we have a tendency to find it; if something is written, we tend to accept it as correct. So if the software has such a default feature, it should also have a method for "turning it off," permanently.

4.
Codes and Safeguards

Think of how awful it would be if a firm clown, or worse yet, an inventive enemy attorney, were to obtain access to your docketing system. Chaos could result. Therefore, as with any data that is critical to the operation of your firm, there must be an access code or some other type of *security* to assure that the calendar is not tampered with or improperly used.

In addition to intentional mischief, a far greater threat involves accidental erasures. This is not a simple matter; for, as you know, dates, times, and places change and are erased on a continuous basis. If your firm has ever handled arbitrations or litigation matters on a regular basis, you know that dates and times shift repeatedly and constantly. Therefore, it is necessary to erase *some* data; however, an erasure of the wrong data could result in serious problems. While it is not possible to avoid improper erasure, the software should be operable with a minimal encouragement of human error.

5.
Scheduling Auxiliary Services

As you schedule important dates or events, there is a tendency to overlook those individuals who may not play a central role in the given activity. They are, nevertheless, extremely important people, who often include witnesses, notaries, court reporters, videotape cameramen, hotel reservationists, etc. Often, with one of these people missing, the central event may, indeed, be in jeopardy.

Imagine trying to hold a will ceremony in the evening without the requisite number of witnesses, or conducting a deposition without a court reporter. Because each of many adjournments could involve a barrage of adjustments and telephone calls (where these ancillary people may be omitted), the computer may, if used properly, far outshine the human hand, by providing prompts and reminders.

6.
Boolean Search Capabilities

In addition to sorting capabilities and report generation, there should be features permitting basic Boolean searches (see Chapter 8). The Boolean search capabilities should insure that you would be able to find any "character string," regardless of whether or not it fell within any of the generic report categories that the software may offer. For example, if you wanted a printout of all matters scheduled for the "Holiday Inn," you should be able to plug that string variable (i.e., "Holiday Inn") into your search tool and generate your own listing, even though the software may *lack* a specific "location" report generator.

7.
Changes and Foul-Ups

After the subject event has occurred, it is quite possible that something else might need to be scheduled as a result. This is normally the case with respect to adjournments, continuances, and even cancellations. Therefore, there should be some method by which the computer prompts the individual to report back to it as to what transpired on the date of the said event, so that matters can be rescheduled if necessary.

8.
Instructions as to Procedures

Instructions, guidelines, and procedures must be ultra-clear. If there is *any* ambiguity, there will certainly be error, and, if there is error, the entire purpose of the system will be defeated. Therefore, notwithstanding all of the capabilities set forth above, the methods for entering and retrieving data at a very basic level must be *extra* simple and understandable by everyone involved in the docketing process.

9.
Demonstration Program

A clear and concise demonstration program should accompany each item of calendar software. It is *not* a tool to be learned through trial and error.

CONFLICTS OF INTEREST

It is not a good idea for two members of the same law firm to represent opposing parties in any matter; excepting unusual circumstances, the Canons of Ethics prohibit such conduct. But often, the existence of a conflict of interest is not obvious or self-evident. The larger the law firm, the greater the problems. These problems, which involve an overview of the firm's clientele, normally fall upon the administrator's shoulders.

Conflicts of interest may be quite subtle or hidden. One member of a large law firm may, for example, start suit against a former client (or partner of that client), who was represented by a former member of the law firm, without ever being aware of these prior relationships. Often conflicts are quite innocently established, but nonetheless improper.

How do you protect against conflicts of interest? First, you need a list of people and companies (perhaps even related entities) that the firm has represented, or currently represents. Second, you will want to apply an ethical standard; according to the Canons, you will want to avoid *even* the appearance of impropriety. So if there is a *chance* of a conflict or a possibility that the client's interests might be compromised, serious consideration should be given to refusing representation.

It is questionable whether or not software has an advantage over a simple, but often sizable paper list of clients; essentially, that is all that "conflicts checking" consists of—a list. As the firm grows, so does the complexity of its client relationships. The value of computerized conflict checks increases, along with the complexity. So we should put this type of software in our second pigeonhole (i.e., whether or not you need it, depends upon your firm's structure and size).

Here are some factors that may aid your selection process. In particular, you might ask your prospective vendor if the program:

- Allows a variety of search methods, including Boolean, phonetic, and proximity searches;
- Allows access to other firm databases, particularly those containing names of former clients;
- Identifies name changes;
- Allows editing;
- Allows a variety of sorts and resulting reports;
- Identifies the type of case or matter involved in prior representations, the business of the client, other lawyers involved, and other pertinent information;
- Prohibits opening new files without running a conflicts check; and
- Provides simple screen information in addition to written reports.

DESKTOP PUBLISHING

Did you ever wonder how many typesetters it took to arrange the words on your daily newspaper, so that they fit neatly into columns and around all of the photos and charts? I don't claim to have the answer, but today these people are being replaced with relatively inexpensive software.

You can assemble text in columns, similar in appearance to a newspaper. Graphics, headlines, and multi-font type are all at your fingertips for newsletters, firm resumes, and brochures. Desktop publishing also provides a simple, effective way to perform inexpensive marketing by using in-house resources.

LITIGATION CONTROL

Sometimes referred to as ''Litigation Support,'' other times ''Litigation Management,'' the software is primarily concerned with managing, sorting, listing, indexing, and controlling voluminous amounts of documentary evidence. There are four basic types of text storage systems.

Full Text

Often called ''The Entire Text Method,'' or ''Free Text Method,'' this system requires that the subject documents be keyed into the system, in their entirety. This can be quite expensive, depending upon the size of the project. With Boolean search techniques (See Chapter 8), it does, however, permit the rapid location of documents or character strings, once the tedious entry process has been completed.

Abstract

There are several different abstracting methods that are used to avoid the storage of ''full text.'' The most common include the use of summaries, codes, and text-selection methods to abbreviate and represent the entire documents. The last method would utilize methods similar to a full text system.

Index

Indexing characteristics are, in reality, present in all software systems that relate to litigation management or control. Codes, symbols, and abbreviations are used to represent lengthy writings. These reduction methods enable the computer to rapidly provide lists and reports designed to identify the location and content of the more lengthy documents.

Integrated

As the name implies, an integrated system will employ a combination of the preceding three methods. As might be expected, it allows the maximum flexibility.

As you may have correctly gathered from the preceding discussions, there is no ''free ride'' with respect to work. Evidentiary documents must always be analyzed and carefully considered, regardless of whether or not a computerized system is used.

Selection of the proper software package can only occur after careful study of the particular litigation setting. If in doubt, integrated systems should provide flexibility. This is important, since the course of a lawsuit is often difficult to predict. Issues, parties, and strategies may change frequently.

8

Databases

There is no need to feel intimidated or confused by talk of "Databases" or "Data Files." A database is nothing more than a *place* where you put, store, and periodically retrieve data. Your form filing system (Chapters 3 and 4) is essentially a private database. As a matter of fact, your form file drawer could likewise be considered as a database of sorts; however, today, use of the term generally denotes computer storage.

You could refer to the hard disk (or floppy) that contains text for each of your Nine Categories, as one, or nine separate, databases. There are no size or space limitations with respect to the term; a database could, theoretically, comprise several sentences or it could consist of the entire text of millions of cases (similar to those of some major law book publishers soon to be discussed). The form files (masters) that you created to be stored in your database, can each be thought of as one of several data files.

Your use of databases is not, however, limited to those of your own creation. With your computer, a simple modem (Chapter 6), and a telephone, you may reach out across the world and tap into hundreds of databases within seconds. Now the law libraries of the world and the cases contained in them can be placed at your fingertips at a relatively small cost.

Do not think that your access need be limited to the legal databases. On the contrary, there are medical databases, stock market reports, encyclopedias, and an ever increasing variety of ''on line'' information that may prove valuable to your firm. In addition to the commercial databases, there are private user groups, or ''clubs,'' that maintain their own databases for use by members who pay an annual membership fee. In essence, the database should be thought of as nothing more complex than an electronic library that can be constructed by anyone, using relatively inexpensive computer equipment.

THE COMMERCIAL LEGAL DATABASES

If you wanted to create your own commercially saleable database, it would not be difficult. First, take some text or information that is of value to someone and store it on your hard disk; then connect your firm's computer to the telephone system by using a modem. Next, shield or limit access to the data by creating some appropriate code words (referred to as an ''access code''). And finally, offer to sell to anyone, a right of access to your database, for a charge that is based upon each customer's connect time, or the quantity of data retrieved. Essentially, this is all that you should need to create your own commercial database; of course, your customers must have access to a computer and a modem of their own in order to ''talk to,'' and retrieve information from, your database. Such were the steps followed by those who created the first databases for use by the legal profession.

As time goes on, information is being pumped into the legal databases at a rapidly increasing rate. Also, retrieval methods are becoming faster and cheaper, allowing you to obtain information on a daily basis much faster than you could receive advance sheets by mail. The time is fast approaching when the need to maintain large, bulky, and expensive law libraries will become a thing of the past.

The Big Four

The hats of the legal profession should go off to the pioneers of the legal databases (Lexis, Phinet, Veralex, Westlaw); for they are revolutionizing the manner in which we obtain our most critical and vital information—Case Law. The time will come, and relatively soon, when most of the research conducted by the legal profession will be done via computer. The computerized bases may not yet be perfect, and we may not yet be entirely in tune with their retrieval methods, but things are improving continuously. Consider a brief checklist of some important advantages over traditional book research:

- The information is at your fingertips, without leaving your office, often without even leaving your desk.
- You have access to massive libraries that even the largest law firms could not hope to maintain.
- Your information will be more current than any library because that information comes directly from the publisher at the speed of electricity, not U.S. Mail.
- Your firm can save money by maintaining less of a law library and, of course, less in the way of yearly update fees.
- Your research time should be shorter than it would be if you used traditional research methods.
- Your research will be far more accurate and thorough, since computers can conduct searches of millions of pages in seconds.
- Printouts can be obtained immediately without quarters and photocopiers.

On a very large scale, many law book publishers have taken steps to see to it that each of the above advantages are increasing in terms of speed, efficiency, and reliability. As time goes on, the services should improve; and yet, due to competition, costs should come down.

Special benefits are to be derived by the *non*-megafirm; for, now the smaller firms can have access to the same libraries as do the giant firms. The electronic database is just one more example of an electronic equalizer, designed to give the small firm the same power as the big ones.

There is some important insight to be gained from examining the four pioneers of the field. There are differences; and those differences highlight some of the key considerations with respect to the selection of a database. So, let's consider them, in alphabetical order.

1. *Lexis**

While it may or may not be the *best* database, Lexis is certainly the *largest*, boasting over 3 million cases and other documents. It was first introduced for use by the legal profession in 1973; that entitles it to be labeled as a pioneer in the field of legal databases.

---

* Lexis is a trade name of Mead Data Central.

In addition to the complete texts of all federal statutes, codes, and regulations, the database contains the published Supreme Court Reports of all of the states of the United States, together with the published appellate reports of most. In addition to federal decisions, it provides rulings by the Federal Trade Commission, the Securities and Exchange Commission, and Congressional Reports. It is also keyed into the American Law Reports (ALR) series. In the foreign sphere, Lexis provides statutes and laws of the United Kingdom and France. Lexis also includes both the reported and unreported cases of the European Court of Justice.

The database maintains special libraries pertaining to Tax Law, Securities, Energy, Labor, Bankruptcy, Trade Regulations, International Trade, Admiralty, Communications, Patents, Copyrights, and Trademarks. It claims to publish the full text of more than 800,000 U.S. patents.

In addition to the foregoing, Lexis claims that its database contains more than 8,000,000 full text articles from over 125 magazines, newspapers, newsletters, and wire services. It also provides a variety of financial and related reference material. Such information is being added every day, and so, the items that we have listed should be considered only as examples; they by no means exhaust the information contained in this enormous database.

Cases can be shepardized and updated by using Lexis. Lexis claims to add some of its new cases within 48 hours of decision.

Notwithstanding its size and the fact that it publishes a very wide variety of decisions from various courts throughout the United States, Lexis is, nevertheless, at a disadvantage of sorts, when compared to Westlaw; the reason for this is that Westlaw, unlike Lexis, has access to the National Reporter System (which is published by West Publishing Company). In the minds of some, however, Lexis would have an edge when it comes to sheer size and quantity, and greater ease with respect to query searches.

2.
*Phinet**

Tax firms will want to consider this rather specialized database as an extremely powerful resource. It is limited to tax matters, to be sure; however, pursuant to a cross-user arrangement, subscribers to Phinet can obtain access to the powerful Westlaw database.

When compared to Lexis, Phinet must be considered a relative newcomer to the computer database scene. However, it proudly points to its link to Prentice Hall, and the Simon and Schuster Professional Information Services Group for its parentage; these entities have combined credentials, including more than 70 years of experience and over 80 looseleaf services and related

* Phinet is a trade name of Prentice Hall Information Network.

periodicals in the fields of Taxation, Business and Management, Labor, Personnel, and Estate and Financial Planning. This would certainly seem to give it some type of head start.

Some of the special features of Phinet include its special reduced rates for customers who already subscribe to Prentice Hall's Federal Estate and Gift Tax, and Federal Income Tax Services. The database also provides a method whereby once a search is conducted, the results lead the user directly to the appropriate page of the looseleaf services; this method can cut use time and printing costs.

Phinet claims to have some of the best developed, and "easiest to use" special command functions for searching and obtaining information. This is an important factor, particularly since time is normally the key factor in determining the cost of any given research project.

3.
*Veralex**

Veralex claims to have the full text of all of the federal, state, and administrative cases found in Lexis; this would, of course, include the U.S. Supreme Court Reporter, the Court of Appeals Reports, and cases from the Federal District Courts. The Veralex Base also includes reports from all 50 states and the District of Columbia. Like Lexis, Veralex includes the full text database of the ALR (American Law Reports).

Veralex further claims to have an edge with respect to the manner in which it prices its time. It charges a small amount for each case examined, along with a reduced rate based upon the total number of minutes of "connect time." You may wish to compare this combination to the straight-connect-time method of billing that most of the other databases utilize.

Veralex next claims, as do the others, to have its own special tools for obtaining cases quickly and easily. As with most of the other databases, these devices are, however, undergoing change and improvement.

4.
*Westlaw**

One might consider Westlaw as the heavyweight of the legal databases. In addition to a very large variety of separate services and information bases, Westlaw has access to the powerful National Reporter System, together with the United States Code, the U.S. Supreme Court Opinions, U.S. Court of Appeals Opinions, U.S. District Court Opinions, the Code of Federal

* Veralex is a trade name of Veracorp, which is a wholly owned subsidiary of the Lawyer's Cooperative Publishing Company.

* Westlaw is a trade name of West Publishing Company.

Regulations, and the Federal Register. As with the other databases, Westlaw allows you to shephardize and update; this can be accomplished by a few simple keystrokes.

With its key numbering system, the books published by West Publishing Company were tailor-made and structured for the age of the micro-computer. Like your computerized document system (discussed in Chapter 4), it was created and designed with a numerical-logical base, thereby causing it to mesh with the methods and structures of the microprocessor. The West Systems, and those presented in this book, are not, however, the same.

West, being the publisher of law books that it is, carefully edits its material. There is a trade-off, however. When compared to Lexis, the searches are more time-consuming and cumbersome.

How to Work Them

There are as many different types of research gimmicks and aids as there are sets of law books. All are designed to help you zero in on a specific topic of law, or even a single case. Most of the methods are good; however, others do nothing but create headaches, aggravation, and barriers.

The gimmicks are designed to get you to a specific set of cases, provided that you already have some specific information, such as a case name, or citation. Those of you who are shy about engaging in full-blown query searches (which we are going to discuss momentarily) may be pleased to know that most of the time, you will be provided with a case name or cite. So you may wish to zero-in on the simple special features of your database.

Without a case name or citation, it may be necessary to conduct a full-text search of the entire database for a phrase (character string) that will be shared *only* by those cases that you desire. Predicated upon simple Boolean logic, in terms of power, the potential capabilities for this type of research *dwarf* all other research methods and tools combined. To get some idea of how the system works, consider this example:

> Assume that you want to find reported case law pertaining to flammable undergarments or pajamas and you do *not* have access to a database. You could use any one of a number of publishing tools. The West ''key word'' index may or may not be of help. Perhaps the digests may be of help, or you may wish to consult a secondary source that specializes in tort law and start the research there. In any event, as simple as the project sounds, it will, of course, take some time, and you may have to use an outside library.
>
> Having found only a few cases involving products liability, you want to be ''sure'' about your research. So you go back and check *all* of

> the millions of cases throughout the 50 states and locate *every one* where the term ''flammable underwear'' or ''flammable garments'' appears. How do you do that? You might flip through every single page of every single reported case in the entire National Reporter System. You may wish to look at every single paragraph—because you want to know every single case that *even uses* the term ''flammable pajamas'' or ''flammable undergarments.''
>
> Estimate, if you will, how long such a search would take. Years, decades, or a lifetime?

The simple fact of the matter is that with a computer and access to the appropriate legal database, you could conduct the same detailed search of an entire database within a matter of seconds. And, it would be far more accurate and complete than a search conducted by any human being, even if allowed decades of time. In effect, the computer will search through every single case contained in its bank, page by page, word by word, and even character by character.

In summary, the actual capabilities of the computer with respect to conducting legal research are staggering. Indeed, even that literature which brags most about the capabilities of the databases must be considered modest.

The real trick then is to be able to select the appropriate words and phrases in such a manner as to zero in on desired text or cases. With this skill, and *nothing else*, there is no need for indexes, cross-references, or digests.

PRINCIPLES OF DATABASE (BOOLEAN) LOGIC

Recall that a database consists of stored text, nothing more, nothing less. Westlaw's database, for example, consists in part, of the National Reporter System; so all of the cases stored in that system are part of the Westlaw database. This means that the body of each case, the opinion portion, the titles, as well as the dates and footnotes, are all part and parcel of the text. For a full-text search the computer does not distinguish between the heading, the names of the parties, the name of the judge, or the citations. Everything stored with respect to the given case will be considered by the computer as nothing more than strings of characters (i.e., text).

Let us start with a simple example and illustrate some basic points:

EXAMPLE:

> Consider a relatively simple research project involving injuries sustained as the result of an automobile's exploding gas tank. Such an

incident occurred on more than many occasions when Ford Pinto automobiles were rear-ended.

Sample Search I—The Disjunctive:

FORD PINTO

Under principles of normal Boolean logic, the above example would be considered as one *character string* consisting of ten characters. The blank space is considered to be a character just as any other letter, number, or symbol on your computer's ''typewriter keys.'' *However*, the commercial databases have their own special treatments with respect to the manner in which character strings are handled. This is done for convenience and speed. Westlaw, for example, would treat the above example as two separate character strings, the first consisting of four characters and the second consisting of five characters. The blank space (in Westlaw) represents the *disjunctive connector* ''OR.'' This means that a Westlaw query search will yield *all cases* in the databank that contain the word ''Ford,'' and, in addition thereto, it will return all cases that contain the term ''Pinto.'' Notice, therefore, that the disjunctive will always *expand* the number of cases to be returned.

With respect to the above example, you should expect your computer screen to tell you that a very large number of cases satisfies your request. Included, for example, would be all cases containing the word ''Ford,'' regardless of whether or not Ford was involved in the litigation. Also, it would return the number of all of the cases using the word ''Pinto,'' regardless of whether the Ford Pinto was involved. As a matter of fact, you might receive cases involving a dispute over horses. The above boxed phrase could have been written in ''normal'' disjunctive form:

FORD OR PINTO

and it would yield the same results.

Sample Search II—The Conjunctive:

FORD AND PINTO

The above example will yield *only* those cases that contain *both* the term ''Ford'' and ''Pinto,'' anywhere in the given case. Unless *both* words are present, the computer will ''pass the case by.'' Notice that the *conjunctive connector* ''and'' will cause a reduction with respect to the number of results. In other words, it will limit or ''narrow the search.''

Sample Search III—Combination:

GAS OR EXPLOSION AND PINTO AND FORD

In normal Boolean logic, the conjunctive (and) takes priority over the disjunctive (or). This means that you may not get the result that you might otherwise expect. As a matter of fact, parentheses should be used to insure that you would get your intended result.

Examine Sample Search III. If we were to use parentheses, the Search Command for:

Gas or (Explosion and Pinto and Ford)

Is *not* the same as:

Gas or Explosion and (Pinto and Ford)

In the first first example (supra), *all cases* containing the word "Gas" will be returned. But in the second example, the search will not return a case with "Gas" *unless* both "Pinto" *and* "Ford" *also* appear somewhere in the case. The position of the parentheses is therefore quite important.

Westlaw Format

The search symbols and methods used by Westlaw have become quite common with respect to legal databases. Here are the rules:

1. A blank space is used for the disjunctive (or).
2. An ampersand (&) is used for the conjunctive (and).
3. "/s" denotes a conjunctive, where both elements fall within the same sentence, but they need not be in any order.

EXAMPLE:

Ford /s Pinto

Would yield every case where the two words appeared together in any single sentence. So the query:

Pinto /s Ford

Would yield the same result.

4. "/p" indicates a conjunctive where both elements are to be found within the same paragraph and they need not be in any order.

5. ‘‘/n’’ indicates the conjunctive, where both words are contained within a given case (in any order), but are no more than ‘‘n’’ words apart. This is known as a ‘‘proximity limiter.’’

EXAMPLE:

Ford /10 Pinto

Would return cases where the two terms were within 10 words of one another. The search *would* yield a case containing this paragraph:

> ‘‘The owner of the Ford vehicle sustained severe injuries. The pintos, though in the barn, became upset.’’

6. The time limiter-DATE (after 19xx) is a special command that limits the cases to those issued after the date specified within the parentheses. A ‘‘before’’ could have been used in place of ‘‘after,’’ to obtain older cases.

EXAMPLE:

Ford Pinto (Before 1988)

Will yield cases containing ‘‘Pinto’’ or ‘‘Ford,’’ but *only* if the case’s date is earlier than 1988.

7. Quotation marks can be used for character strings that contain blank spaces; this avoids having the computer treat the blank as disjunctive (i.e., ‘‘or’’).

EXAMPLE:

‘‘Ford Pinto’’

Will *only* yield cases that have the two words together in the above order.

8. ‘‘+s’’ means that the words are in the same sentence and in the same order; the ‘‘+p’’ connector means that they are in the same paragraph in the same order; and the ‘‘+n’’ connector means that they are in the same order but can be separated by up to ‘‘n’’ words. The ‘‘n’’ can represent any number of words less than or equal to 255.

9. ‘‘%’’ followed by a word or phrase will do a ‘‘but not’’ limitation. For example, the search command ‘‘Pinto % Horse,’’ might eliminate cases involving equestrian problems.

Lexis

The connectors for Lexis work in a similar fashion; Lexis defines some of its operators as follows:

1. ''W/n'' is a proximity limiter whereby ''n'' can be up to 255 words.

2. ''PRE/n'' means, once again, that the little ''n'' can be up to number 255. However, the ''PRE'' means that the word to the left must precede the word to the right.

3. In applying the first two rules, Lexis does not count article adjectives, such as ''an,'' ''the,'' or ''a.''

Both Lexis and Westlaw

Both Westlaw and Lexis have other connectors that can be used. Most common and notable is the ''AND NOT'' (similar to Westlaw's ''%''), which can be read as a limiter that excludes all terms that follow this particular connector.

In addition to the foregoing, for both Westlaw and Lexis the ''and'' takes priority over the ''or''; consider this example:

Pinto or Ford and tank

Can the above query provide a case that does *not* contain the term ''tank''? The answer is ''no.'' Even if a case contains the character string ''Pinto,'' it must *also* contain ''tank'' because the ''and'' predominates over the ''or.''

Veralex

Veralex has two basic services titled: SHOW ME and AUTOCITE.*

When the SHOW ME service is selected, you have a choice of receiving the full text of all of the federal and state citations, and administrative law decisions that are contained in the American Law Reports (ALR 3rd or 4th). When the AUTOCITE option is chosen, you can quickly check the status of virtually any American case. It provides parallel citations and identifies cases that directly affect the validity of the requested case as precedent.

Phinet

As previously indicated, Phinet has a link to Westlaw. But, when it comes to key words, phrases, and connectors, tax research presents some special problems.

Compare litigation, for example; searches often involve situations that may be narrowed down to specific words or phrases. In some situations, a

---

* Autocite is a registered trademark of Veracorp, which is a wholly owned subsidiary of the Lawyer's Cooperative Publishing Company.

single term or word can zero in on the desired case law. For example, the term "toxic shock syndrome" provides a single term that may provide all needed cases for a particular matter, and *only* those cases.

Other fields of research, however, are not quite so fortunate as to have product terms that serve to identify the subject matter. Normally, however, they have their own peculiar phrases and terms to narrow a search.

Conducting tax research is another matter entirely. Tax practitioners have a propensity to speak in terms of numbers, and, when they are not, they are using certain words and terms repeatedly. It is the endless combination of these particular tax terms that must be used to zero in on a particular matter. For example, consider these: depreciation, basis, income, taxpayer, commissioner, capital gain. Such is the jargon of the tax practitioner.

The problem is this—Try to find a tax case that does *not* contain the terms just listed. This creates a problem with respect to general research. Therefore, it was necessary for Phinet to provide some special functions and search capabilities for the tax firms. So Phinet presents, in addition to the general Boolean search capabilities, some special *user-defined keys* and terms to assist the location of cases involving particular types of tax matters.

HOW TO OBTAIN ASSISTANCE

Representatives and vendors of the Big Four are not difficult to locate. They advertise quite frequently in the major bar association journals. Once contacted, the representative will be quite pleased to bombard you with a substantial quantity of brochures and information pertaining to the particular service. If you have a computer with a modem, the representative will come out to your office and provide a demonstration free of charge. Even if you do not have a modem, the rep will often carry a portable.

They are normally quite eager to answer any questions that you may have pertaining to the Data Bank. But, if you really want to compare, don't ask the representative about the benefits of his or her particular system; that kind of information can be found in the brochures. Rather, ask why you should *not* buy a competing system. Then you will truly find out the key distinctions, benefits, and disadvantages of the respective systems.

To be specific, I do not ask a vendor to degrade the system of a competitor; I only ask the question—"Why should I *not* buy this other system which is bigger, cheaper, etc.?" The salesperson will be sure to tell you the reasons.

Keep in mind that the legal databases are relatively new and highly competitive. Pricing, formats, and research methods can be expected to change quite a bit. Therefore, you will want to keep abreast of the latest developments.

Generic Research Methods

1. You may go from the general to the specific, or the specific to the general. But better yet, a third method suggests that you pick the right words and phrases as soon as possible to zero in on a given research problem. This saves both time and money. If in doubt, start with a general or ''broad'' query. The computer screen should tell you how many cases satisfy the parameters *before* you search the cases. If the number is too great, then gradually narrow the query until the number of cases is manageable.

2. Pick words and terms that the Court would use during the course of litigation. For example, the term ''Civil Rights lawsuit'' would, to the average researcher, seem to be a term common to all civil rights cases. However, in truth, *no* judge, in issuing any ruling, would ever use the term ''civil rights lawsuit.'' That is because everyone involved in the litigation already *knows* that it is a ''civil rights lawsuit.''

Here is a word of *caution*—Computers are not forgiving with respect to spelling errors. Therefore, if a word is misspelled, it *will* destroy the search. You might, therefore, inquire as to features that might allow ''proximity searches,'' which only require that you ''get close.''

Practical Considerations

It is not time to burn your books; and it may never be. The computer database is the library of the future, to be sure. But books will always have their place.

There is something relaxing and, at times even comforting, about browsing through books. You do so at your own pace and in your own choice of place. Reading is not quite the same as being glued to some computer terminal, racing the clock in order to avoid excessive charges, while staring at a glowing screen. It is, therefore, far more likely that the law library of the future will consist of a compatible blend of law books and access to various databases. It is quite predictable that as the databases become cheaper, smaller firms will have access to several databases.

The time will come, perhaps sooner than predicted, when lawyers will maintain gigantic libraries on their own personal, privately owned databases. As more and more data is compressed into smaller spaces (through advancing technology), it is increasingly likely that large libraries may also be maintained in-house, without the corresponding cost and space requirements of paper libraries.

With the foregoing prognostications in mind, let's examine some of the ''dos'' and ''don'ts'' with respect to the manner in which your firm should integrate access to the commercial databases:

● Do contact the commercial legal databases for information and brochures. The services should be investigated since they could save your firm substantial dollars and increase your research capabilities; but

☐ DON'T recommend discontinuance of any of the updating services for your existing library until you have had a chance to test and use the corresponding new service;

● DO inquire as to whether or not any of your poor research tools can be replaced by an up-to-date database. Databases now have programs whereby they provide rapid updates and advance sheets in certain areas of law. Hard copies are provided via computer; the rates are significantly below those costs and charges that pertain to general research; but

☐ DON'T get rid of any good or important services that you may have. You will always need your State Reporter System and your State Statutes.

● DO take plenty of time to use, test, and research the various databases before making any decisions with respect to your library; and

☐ DON'T entertain the purchase of any *new* books until you have thoroughly considered whether or not the database can be used to provide a better or more cost effective substitute.

● DO shop for used sets of books on the *used book market*; there are a lot of bargains to be obtained; but

☐ DON'T sell any of your books or give them away cheaply. The older books may prove to be effective research tools with respect to providing basic law which can thereafter be updated instantly and electronically.

● DO keep your good digests, particularly those that key into the service that you may be obtaining. For example, if you are going to subscribe to Westlaw, by all means keep all of those books that are keyed into the West system. Likewise, if you are going to subscribe to Phinet, under no circumstances should you discontinue your Prentice Hall services; for, Prentice Hall maintains special rates for those practitioners who integrate Phinet with an existing PH tax service; but,

☐ DON'T subscribe to any new costly services just because they may be compatible with the database that you are using or considering.

ABA/net—A DATABASE OF ASSISTANCE FROM THE ABA

You may recall from our prior discussions that virtually any person or group can create a commercial database with nothing more than a computer, modem, telephone, and some information that is worth selling. The American Bar Association has entered the scene with a very beneficial database for all law firms; that term—ABA/net—is an acronym for American Bar Association Network. Though relatively new on the legal database scene, it is destined to spread in popularity.

ABA/net is more than just a database. It provides a variety of services for firms. Interestingly, this may be the reason why ABA/net has gotten off to a slow start. For, the services that it provides are *so varied*, that it has been very difficult to learn exactly what ABA/net is.

You need *not* be a lawyer to subscribe to the services offered. However, as might be expected, discounts are available if a lawyer in your firm happens to be a member of the American Bar Association.

What Exactly Is ABA/net?

For the moment at least, let's get away from computerese and acronyms. They didn't help me at all when I was trying to figure out the purpose of ABA/net; and I doubt seriously that they will help you. Moreover, terms such as ''network'' or ''electronic mail'' are very vague concepts for those who have not been involved with the services. So let's specifically consider the makeup of ABA/net. By doing so, you can gain some familiarity with the manner in which databases and user groups operate, and the way that they are structured. After all, it is easy to talk about soap; we can see it, feel it, and smell it. That is an easy product to purchase. Electronic impulses are not quite as easy to see, feel, smell, or talk about. So we will consider things at a very basic and concrete level.

Definition: ABA/net is a *service* that is managed and directed by the American Bar Association. It is available to both members and non-members of the ABA; however, members obtain special rates. To use the service, you need a computer, a modem, and a telephone.

The basic service involves access to the ABA/net databank and a variety of other databanks that are linked to it. But there are other services. We are going to cover them.

The Specific Services Offered by ABA/net

The items offered by ABA/net can be expected to change and expand as time goes on. For it is certain that more and more firms will eventually subscribe; and perhaps it may form one of the most important communication links among the lawyers of the United States, in addition to various other third parties, such as expert witnesses and other databases.

By understanding the various services of ABA/net, you can become quite familiar with the manner in which the ''broad service'' databases operate. It is for these reasons alone that I want to thoroughly consider the ABA/net roster:

Welcome to ABA/net *—The Lawyer's Network

Copyright 1988

The American Bar Association

* A Registered Service Mark of The American Bar Association

* 0 QuickMail
* 1 ABA/net Assistance
* 2 Electronic Communication Services
* 3 ABA Section Services and Conferences
* 4 Information Services
* 5 Law-Related Services
* 6 Court Services
* 7 Legal Research Services (BNA, Lexis, Westlaw)
* 8 Lawmart (SM) Electronic Marketplace (Lawmart)
*96 Command Level
*99 Sign Off ABA/net Services

Figure 8-1

The contents of the menu will, of course, change as time goes on, as new services are added or altered. But, at this time, here are the basics.

0
Quickmail

This particular service provides a rapid way to communicate with other members of the ''network.'' In essence, it provides a fast, but abbreviated portion of the Electronic Communication Services appearing later in the menu (i.e., Menu Item 2).

1
Assistance

As the heading indicates, the database provides on-line instruction and direction with respect to the numerous items that are provided. Such assistance can be particularly important for this database because of its diverse variety of topics and services. The following sub-menu selections are somewhat self-explanatory:

(1) General Information

(2) ABA/net User Tips

(3) ABA/net Phone Access Numbers

(4) Future Releases

(5) User Feedback

(6) Change Your Password

(7) Learn-on-Line Tutorial

2
Electronic Communications Services

Imagine sending messages, documents, and pleadings to any attorney throughout the United States, at any hour, without postage stamps, without calling private carriers, and without trying to beat the five o'clock rush to the post office. With ABA/net, either you or your secretary can push a few buttons on your computer and immediately communicate with other lawyers throughout the United States. As a matter of fact, we can now file pleadings with some courts electronically. Quite simply, this means that the only thing you will use will be your computer and your telephone lines. Consider these services:

- Electronic messages
- Electronic document delivery
- Telex, telegrams, and mailgrams
- Electronic file transfer
- Electronic meetings and bulletin boards
- Electronic mailing lists
- On-line tutorials
- Assignable mail boxes

3
ABA Section Services and Conferences

The latter two items in this particular set of services are geared toward specific areas of practice, such as Litigation, Estate Planning, and others. The first two items are somewhat self-explanatory:

(1) Available Conferences

(2) Teleconferencing

(3) Bulletin Board Categories

(4) Bulletin Boards

4
Information Services

Each listed item contains its own separate list of information services:

(1) Major News Wires

(2) Airline Information

(3) Stock Market Information

(4) ABI/INFORM (Business Journal Library)

(5) Electronic Clipping Service (News Headlines)

(6) Dow Jones/News Retrieval

5
Law-Related Services

Here is an additional list of informational services:

(1) ABA Newsletters

(2) AMBAR (ABA Directory)

(3) Comprowise Legal Settlement Models

(4) Continuing Legal Education Catalog

(5) Washington Summary of Congressional Record and Federal Register

(6) Bureau of National Affairs Advance Line

(7) ABA Section of General Practice Hotline

(8) ABA Calendar

6
Court Services

A variety of expanding services are available for firms that conduct litigation. Court forms, rules, and recent (slip) opinions can be found under this heading.

7
Legal Research Services

The two heavyweight databases (Lexis and Westlaw) can be accessed directly through ABA/net. You would still have to pay for the individual services, of course; but the monthly subscription rates are cheaper if you go this route.

8
LawMart—Electronic Marketplace

Termed ''lawmart,'' this facility permits attorneys to use their computers or word processors to choose law-related products and services that are offered by independent vendors. The list is ever-expanding, but consider these:

- Review of the United States Supreme Court decisions, including discussions of upcoming High Court cases by legal scholars.
- Network reporting services; these avoid the expenses of transporting a local court reporter to a distant location by arranging nationwide court reporting via your computer.

- Expert/net; this consists of resumes of highly qualified medical-legal consultants, primarily those practicing physicians who provide services to lawyers at a fraction of the cost of referral services.
- Automated legal forms; these are the general-purpose legal forms in 80 areas of law: wills and trusts, corporations, stock purchase agreements, real estate sales contracts, and options and exchanges.
- Lawmug newsletter; this teaches you how to increase productivity and efficiency in the practice of law through the newsletter of the lawyer's microcomputer users group.

* * *

For more information about this service, contact:

ABA/net
4795 Meadow Wood Lane, Suite 300
Chantilly, VA 22021

In order to subscribe to ABA/net, you merely write and request membership. You pay a subscription fee; it is a modest one, which can be used as credit for your first month's invoice. You can pay by way of credit card or direct billing.

You will pay as you would for any other database. The charges, of course, vary. But the minimum session is one minute in duration.

DO-IT-YOURSELF DATABASES

There is nothing to stop you from creating your own database with nothing more than the tools which we have previously discussed. As a matter of fact, that is precisely what you have done if you happen to employ the computer document system discussed and described in Chapter 4.

When we spoke of "working files," and saving those files to disk, we were, in effect, creating our own database for specific clients. We had no help from any software, other than our own word processing program.

In addition to the simple databases that we constructed in accordance with the comprehensive computer document system, there is software available that will permit you to create a database that is quite capable of performing some rather sophisticated sorts, in addition to providing a variety of specialized reports. If you decide to give it a try, you may be quite surprised at your own ability to manipulate data, while operating the seemingly complex, yet truly simple, program instructions.

For those who do not have database software already built into your hard disk, you may want to consider one of two programming languages that are devoted entirely to the creation of databases. The first is the ubiquitous Lotus (and its recent successor Lotus 1-2-3). The name Lotus™ is recognized as being a pioneer in the area of spreadsheets and numerical databases. For more power and size, a recognized brand such as dBase III (and now IV) ™ is recommended.

9

Training Your Computer to Draft Your Documents

DOCUMENT ASSEMBLY

In this simple, two-word term (i.e., document assembly) lies the future of document production for the law firms of the world. It also presents a gold mine of opportunity for those of you who are willing to learn about it; lawyers refuse to invest the time required to learn to use this software.

Pretend for a moment that you, and a small handful of your peers, were the *only* people in the entire country who could operate a word processor. What would your skill be worth? Even without your newly discovered systems

(Chapters 3 through 5), your output could replace several typists; and that would make you better than the best. Well, now there is a tool that can dwarf the document production capabilities of the best word processor. Instead of "just" reproducing saved text, it will "*decide*" what boilerplate is appropriate and then *automatically* insert it and produce a finished product! But the capabilities go far beyond that. In addition to its text selection features, the program will perform any required calculations, provide prompts and reminders, and also present information to guide the user's input.

Because of its apparent complexity, the tool has been picked up by relatively few entrepreneurs. With some simple skills that you probably possess, and the introductory information contained in this chapter, you could be among the first to develop the skills and then "name your price."

What It Can Do

You probably already have a pretty good idea of what your "simple" word processing software can do. If you have no word processor, then Chapter 7 will explain those capabilities. In any event, we might summarily state that your word processor permits you to rapidly manipulate, "switch around," change, and arrange text. It also allows you to store portions of text, however large or small, for instant reuse at some future date.

With any word processing program, *you* must make the decisions about the specific text that is to be used, and how the document is to be structured and formatted. And you must make those decisions repeatedly, for *each* separate instrument. But with a document assembler program, you can move up a step in technology.

From Level III which involves the creation, arrangement, and use of computer-stored text files, you now move to Level IV; here the computer asks a few relevant questions (in simple, plain English), and you answer them (again in simple, plain English). The computer takes over from there, making "its own" decisions as to appropriate language, required calculations, and comments to guide your minimal input. And while all of this is happening, the computer is preparing its finished document.

What It Is

A "document assembler" is software that can assume several different shapes and forms, depending upon the manufacturer. It may consist of a simple utility contained in a word processor, or a powerful language consisting of several components.

The document assembler, in essence, combines the logic capabilities of a language compiler with your word processing utilities to deliver a very powerful result. It is a high-level programming language (i.e., uses commands similar to English) that blends word processing and conditional logic (i.e., "if-then" statements). The result fits snugly into your Computer Document System. You may assign numbers to your programs (sometimes referred to as "scripts") just as you would any other forms or masters.

Where to Get It

Advertisements for software packages claiming to have document assembly capabilities are appearing in legal journals. Particular attention should be directed to publications of the Computer Division, Section of Economics of the American Bar Association. It regularly publishes newsletters pertaining to document assembly products. Included among those publications are the "NETWORK" newsletter and the "Document Assembly User Group News."

As I indicated, you may also expect to see "document assembly" features showing up in word processors. While these capabilities are an undisputed plus for the word processing software, they do not have anywhere near the power or capabilities of the separate document assembler programs. Such a package was developed several years ago.

The pioneer in the area is Legalware Inc., a Toronto-based subsidiary of Altimiri Corporation of Montreal; it developed the first commercial document assembly program with the legal profession in mind. Its product is known as "Document Modeler," which is perhaps the most powerful document assembler of its kind. So I am going to use it as a basis for the examples and tutorial that follow. If you can grasp the concepts behind this particular item of software, you should have no problem adapting to the simpler assemblers destined to fill the marketplace.

DOCUMENT MODELER

Historically, if ever there was a programming language designed and structured to meet the document preparation needs of the legal profession, it is DOCUMENT MODELER. Technically, it is a heavily structured, high level language; and it is one which is specifically designed for the swift, accurate, and efficient preparation of any type of document. But its capabilities extend far beyond our state-of-the-art word processing programs. For it is truly a first major step on the road to Programmed Intelligence.

As a purchaser, remember that innovators are not necessarily perfectors. Just as the Ford may not necessarily be today's most perfect car, Document Modeler may not necessarily be the best document assembler. It is to your benefit that competition to produce better assemblers is increasing. But for purposes of familiarization with the basics of this new science, Document Modeler is the most perfect place to start. It will provide the best learning tools and examples.

EXAMPLE:

For the moment, we are going to assume that you've already written the program (or "script") that is going to generate our example. It is over-simplified; but with a little imagination, you should be able to appreciate the amount of time and effort that might be spared if a more complex document were involved. In essence, the tool is capable of constructing every manner of writing.

With the foregoing in mind, the following program is designed to produce a simple promissory note. Assume that you have given it an Identifier—"Prom Note.Simp."—and assigned it a file name (in this case a "program name")—363,000 (the last three zeros should signal the user that the program is *generic* and capable of producing a numerous variety of different types of notes). After you have called for document 363,000, the computer monitor will provide some introductory comments and salutations; then:

Your Monitor Asks:	What is the date of the note?
You Key In:	January 1, 1988 (or if you wish—01/01/88)
Your Monitor Responds:	What is the face amount?
You Key In:	5,000
Your Monitor Asks and Explains:	Select the type of note: 1. Demand Note 2. Order Note 3. Installment Note

A *Demand Note* is payable, upon demand, by the Payee, at any time after the date of issuance. An *Order Note* is payable (with all accrued interest and principal) at some date in the future; and an *Installment Note* is similar to an Order Note, but principal and interest are paid in periodic installments. What is your choice?

You Key In:	3
Your Monitor Says:	What Annual Rate of Interest? (Enter "0" for a non-interest note)
You Key In:	25
Your Monitor Says:	Is the payee a loan shark??! That rate is clearly usurious—meaning they may come haul the payee away; and it is possible that principal and

	interest may be judicially forfeited. Do you want to reconsider?
You Key In:	Yes
Your Monitor Says:	What Annual Rate of Interest? (Enter "0" for a non-interest note)
You Key In:	10
Your Monitor Says:	How many months?
You Key In:	60
Your Monitor Says:	When does first payment begin?
You Key In:	February 1, 1988
Your Monitor Says:	What is the Name of the Maker?
You Key In:	Joe Smith
Your Monitor Says:	Are there any provisions that you want pertaining to the following matters—if so, select: 1. Acceleration (This should always be placed in the note.) 2. Personal Guarantee, if maker is Corporation. 3. All Endorsers Liable (This is normally included.) 4. No partial waiver shall be deemed to waive other provisions. (Always put this in.) 5. Method of Payment (This is recommended—i.e., the address of mailing.) 6. Penalties (additional menu). 7. Specials (You add text.) 8. No—I am ready to print.
You Key In:	1

Then your monitor would repeat the preceding statements and you would, at this time, enter an 8.

Your Printer Immediately Prints:

PROMISSORY NOTE

$5,000 January 1, 1988

THE UNDERSIGNED MAKER hereby agrees to pay to the order of Joe Smith, the sum of FIVE THOUSAND ($5,000.00) DOLLARS AND 00/100, together with interest and the rate of ten (10%) percent per annum; the interest and principal shall be paid in monthly installments of ONE HUNDRED AND SIX ($106.24) DOLLARS AND 24/100 per month until paid.

The first installment shall be due on February 1, 1988, and each subsequent installment shall be paid on the first day of each month thereafter, until the note is completely paid.

In the event of a default on the part of the payee, the entire indebtedness including all principal and interest, evidenced hereby, shall be accelerated, and shall be due and payable immediately upon demand.

____

Joe Smith

Some Valuable Benefits

Our example was a simple one, and easy to follow. But imagine the incredible amounts of time and effort that may be saved for lengthy or complex documents. Here are some of the potential benefits:

- You prepare, direct, and ''script'' every function that the monitor and printer will perform.
- The programs that you will create can *fit right in* to your Direct Reference System; the program-naming process permits you to follow the rules set forth in Chapter 3.
- As the example indicated, you can personally program your own *checklist* of items to be included or considered for any document.
- As a non-lawyer, you need only program or key in alternative clauses; you need not actually decide which is to be used until you actually run the program. (At that time you can make use of any needed legal assistance.) *Note:* The writing of some algorithms or scripts may require legal research, but results will be perpetuated.
- Your program can provide and limit your list of hints, tips, and suggestions to *only* those that are relevant; this is a peculiar benefit that the computer has over other types of forms. Consider the preceding example—There would not have been any need whatsoever for the computer to waste time telling you about ''Usury'' *unless* the selected rate warranted it. Thus, no time is wasted considering matters that are not directly germane.
- The ability to store ''language'' is a benefit of this system, as it is in general, for your Level III system. But here, the language is available to be plugged in by the computer, automatically, with minimal decisions and fewer keystrokes.
- Speed is an obvious system characteristic; the program not only makes text selection choices, but it also performs necessary calculations as *you* answer the prompts and questions appearing on the monitor.
- You need never be required to ''think through'' a complex situation more than once, except, of course, for purposes of update and revision. In effect, the

computer is *not only* duplicating stored text, it is copying your very own thought processes, and those of the lawyers from whom you obtain assistance.

- The program will act as a reminder of minor ''oddball'' problems which you might otherwise overlook.

What follows may seem a bit technical, but I urge you to ''stay tuned.'' As with anything new, the content will be strange and unfamiliar. The examples are short; they will teach you the logic and structure of the language, but only after you have stared at those examples, and reviewed them. Repeated examination is to be expected.

Hopefully, the simplicity of the programming language will eventually become apparent. I want our brief tutorial to seduce your interest in learning a potentially priceless skill.

A Short Course

It is safe to say, that no computer will come with a document assembler built in; therefore, you must obtain your own compiler. However, during the course of the tutorial, you do not need to have the equipment right in front of you. For we will conduct the lesson in the form of a simulation. And I promise that you will understand it.

Even if you do not intend to buy the equipment or the peripherals necessary to handle the software, you should nevertheless review the tutorial. The knowledge won't hurt. And, you may decide, after all, that such a program is worth purchasing.

Keep in mind that the tutorial is based upon ''Document Modeler'' software. The compiler contained within that software consists of a powerful programming language which may require some upgrading of your equipment (i.e., at least 512 K of RAM, Microsoft Windows, and a Graphics card). Several compilers (with no special hardware requirements) are certain to appear on the market that will be simpler to operate. Some sacrifice of ''power'' or special features may be the trade-off for such simplicity.

The Lesson Begins

We will start with some relatively simple commands, and consider them one by one, providing examples. By the time that you are finished, you will have a working knowledge of the language. For, in essence, all that a programming language consists of is a list of commands and some rules for using them.

As we examine the important commands, notice the distinct manner in which a period immediately precedes each. This unique type of syntax should assure that you may use any words that you wish, without encroaching upon some reserved word or command that has special meanings for the computer. So with that in mind, let us begin:

The .name Command

As the title of this introductory command suggests, it is used simply to provide a name for your program. To be precise, you should refer to your "program" as a "script." This will avoid confusion between all of the other "programs" that interact, such as your word processing program or your compiler. As might be expected, the .name command will form the start of your script.

You are allowed a fairly large number of alphanumeric characters in composing your name (the precise number depends upon the brand of compiler). Regardless of make or brand, you should be able to utilize the Direct Reference Numbering System developed in Chapter 3. I suggest that, in addition to using the command to name your file, you also use it to create your identifier, just to the right. For our example, we are going to be creating a simple Notice of Deposition. I therefore suggest that the following be used to start the script:

```
.Name 183,600—Notice of Deposition;;
```

There are a few important things that you should take notice of right now. First, look at the dash in between the file name and the identifier. Most software would limit you to *only* alphanumeric characters; this is particularly true when using a standard word processing program. But with DOCUMENT MODELER, you may use not only alphanumeric characters but also any other characters that you may have available (such as dashes).

Next notice the double semi-colon. By using the two semi-colons together, you tell the computer that a particular command (and all of its components) has come to an end. Such will be the format for most of the remaining commands.

The .command Command

The .command instruction is very important, even though by itself it does absolutely nothing. Its purpose is twofold.

The appearance of the .command, for the first time in the program, signals that it is a separator that is used to divide the preliminary material of the program from the actual text-printing portions. More precisely, it separates the assignment-of-variables portion from the parts that pertain to actual execution.

Secondly, when used in tandem with other instructions, most notably the .generate command, it will execute its print functions. Example 4 provides a simple but typical use of the .command—.generate duo.

The .reference Command

This is another one of those directives (just mentioned) that is used in tandem with the .command. Quite simply, the .reference command causes reference material to be placed on the screen to aid the person *using* or running the program. This command alone does *not* cause anything to be printed out on paper.

Very similar to the .reference command is the .display command. Both perform the same basic function; that is, to provide some important comments for the user. The difference lies in the fact that the .display command will *stop the program* until the user has read the material and indicated such by striking a key or pushing the mouse, thereby causing the program to resume operation. Common sense suggests that the .display command should be preferred where the "comments" material is very important.

Consider this brief portion of script:

EXAMPLE:

.name 183,600—Notice of Deposition;;
.command
.display "You are now preparing a Notice of Deposition; this form was last revised on June 1, 1986.";;

As the program operator (be it a secretary or paralegal) uses or runs the above program, nothing will yet be printed out on paper. However, the monitor will display this:

> You are now preparing a Notice of Deposition; this form was last revised on June 1, 1986.

At this time, it might be wise to resolve a problem that is certain to arise with respect to numbering your scripts. By now, you probably recognize the "8" in 183,600 as limiting the form to state court matters. Perhaps you are thinking that it may be somewhat of a waste of time to create two separate programs, just so that you can have one for federal court and one for state court, particularly when the very same script can generate both. Our file numbering system uses an "8" (as the second digit) for state court, but a "3" for federal court. There is an easy way to take care of this problem. In particular, the script that you are now creating, if you choose, can be used to create a Notice of Deposition for *any* court.

Assume, for example, that you chose to file the program pursuant to number 183,600 as indicated. You might not be aware of its location when trying to prepare a *federal court* Notice of Deposition. You may go to 133,600, not 183,600. To solve the problem, the following additional *simple* entry should be made in your Master Form Book Index:

133,600 Notice of Dep IV Use 183,600

The .generate Command

Instead of directing that material be placed on the screen (like the .display command), this particular command orders text to be printed on paper. However, an intermediate step is required before the printer starts to click. The program will always return the user back to a menu, so as to provide the option of merely saving the text for future use, or delivering an immediate document.

The command may appear by itself on a line, or it may have a number after it. In either case, it will refer to some specific text that will follow. Before presenting another example, we should go directly to the next very important command.

The .text Command

At this juncture, we are going to consider a very simple example, and assume that there is only one portion of text to be printed. The .text command is, in effect, more like a label or line number. In some instances, it may also be used for branching operations where alternative portions of text are involved.

With the information and simple commands that we have at our disposal, we may now create a rudimentary document. While our example is somewhat oversimplified, it nevertheless constitutes a complete program:

EXAMPLE:

```
.name 183,600—Notice of Deposition;;
.command
.generate
;;

.text

                    NOTICE OF DEPOSITION

    PLEASE TAKE NOTICE that you must appear at our office for a
deposition upon oral examination, ten days from the date hereof.

        ____________________________________________

;;
```

Notice that this completed program contains no variables whatsoever, it has utilized word processing capabilities only; no logic-based decisions are yet involved. As might be expected, the material between the ".text" command and the double semicolons will be printed out on paper. As simple as the above script may be, it will give you a foothold, or basic idea, of the direction in which we are headed.

But now things are going to get a little bit more complicated. Pay careful attention at this point, because we are going to make a very important move from our word processing capabilities, into the realm of the logic capabilities of the compiler.

The .data Command

This particular command provides the "meat" for the logic-based decisions that you are going to program into your script. Please try not to be confused by the use of the developer's choice of the term ".data" to identify it. In truth, the command operates much more similar to an INPUT command than a typical data command.

If you think of "data" as just laying "there" waiting to be used, your perceptions are correct, but not for this language. (In most programming languages, the term "data" does nothing more than identify such text.) For, as we shall see in the examples that follow, this command generates the prompts that cause the computer to interact with the user. In terms of program structure, it falls in between the ".name" command and the ".command" command.

In essence, after the .data command appears a series of questions will be presented. These questions will appear on the screen as the program is run, and thereafter the computer will pause, waiting for the user to answer them. I find it particularly bright on the part of the developers, to have defined a method of structuring the responses into one of six specific types, each with its own individual identifying term; those types of answers are as follows:

1. Yes or No (.yesno)
2. Number (.number (,.2)*
3. Date (.date)
4. Free Form (no identifying name is used for this)
5. Singular selection—Multiple choice (.oneof)
6. Multiple selection—Multiple choice (.someof)

Based upon all of the information that we have acquired so far, please consider the following example *very* carefully. If you understand it, then you will have a good working knowledge of the manner in which the DOCUMENT MODELER program (script) is written:

---

* The "(,.2)" indicates that the number in question is to have a comma after every three digits to the left of the decimal point, and also is to have two decimal places.

EXAMPLE:

```
.name 183,600—Notice of Deposition;;
.data
Deponent "What is the name of the Deponent?"
Date_____of_____Dep. "What is the date of the Deposition?" .date (2)
Documents "Do you want the Notice to include a duces tecum?" .yesno
Taker_____of_____Dep. "Which attorney will take the Dep?"
.oneof "Coleman" "Lipson" "Bradford"
;;
.reference—Note that this is a general form, which may be used for all
federal and state proceedings.
;;
.command
.generate
;;
.text

                    NOTICE OF DEPOSITION

TO: <<Deponent>>

     PLEASE TAKE NOTICE that <<Taker_____of_____Dep>> will
take sworn testimony upon the deposition of said deponent, on
<<Date_____of_____Dep>>, at the law offices of Coleman, Lipson and
Bradford, Professional Corporation.

;;
.command
.if Documents:
   .generate
.endif
;;
.text You are hereby commanded to bring with you all documents, letters,
writings, and memoranda pertaining to the above action.
;;
.command
.generate
;;
.text

                                   ______________________________

                                   <<Taker_of_Dep>>
```

Explanation of Previous Example: The real trick to learning any programming language is to very carefully consider a thorough example, such as that presented. Every minute that you spend studying a good example, should be worth ten minutes of studying vague explanations contained in manuals or textbooks. So I urge, that if you want to understand this language, carefully study the example line by line, until the overall picture becomes clear.

Notice that the program starts with a name assignment, which is followed by the .data command. The line of questions that appear under the .data command are signals to the user that the computer is asking for information. Each time that a question is asked, the computer will stop to permit that user to answer that question. Notice that each question is preceded by a string variable that is joined together by lower case dashes ("-"). This method tells the computer that only one variable is involved. If there were actual blank spaces between the words, the compiler would not know whether or not separate variables were intended. Notice that there should be only one variable on each line; although syntax rules do not require this, avoiding "eye strain" does.

The series ".command, .generate, and .text" are somewhat self-explanatory. But notice the use of the condition ".if." This tiny word (i.e., ".if") is the "giant" of all logic-based intelligence. The particular command has its greatest usefulness when dealing with a .yesno situation or a multiple choice question.

When the user arrives at the .yesno command, there are only two possible choices. If a "yes" is selected, then the "if" condition is satisfied. If not, it is not; and the .generate command pertaining to the document request will not be executed.

Whenever studying an example, you should always try to "simulate" the actual running of the program. Try to anticipate what it will print out as different variables are entered. Based on our preceding examples, you should be able to determine the precise manner in which the above program would run and what the output would look like.

Review

We have by no means exhausted all of the features that are available for the Document Modeler language. There are numerous other specific commands that were clearly designed with the legal profession in mind. Some, for example, perform transformations from words to numerals (.ordinal), or vice-versa (.word). Another provides automatic section numbering (.section).

Our prior example was a simple one. But even lengthy complicated programs can be "broken up" or divided into blocks (programmers of other languages sometimes refer to the blocks as ''subroutines,'' ''functions,'' or ''macros''). The purpose is to take a large, or otherwise unmanageable, project and break it down into several simple ones. For Document Modeler, there is a special command (.block) used for creating such subdivisions. With the added command, the programs follow this order:

Script

1. .name
2. .data
3. .reference

Blocks

4. .reference
5. .command
6. .text

I can only hope that the above discussions have increased your curiosity to the point of further investigation. If you don't get the ''gist'' of the language immediately, consider yourself normal. If you keep staring at the examples, you are guaranteed to pick it up.

Readers who wish to obtain additional information about Document Modeler should write or contact:

VERALEX, Inc.
One Graves Street
P.O. Box 92824
Rochester, NY 14692

10

Tying It All Together

LOOKING BACK

With nothing more than a good, though rudimentary, typewriter, some labels, and folders, you now know how to create a logic-based, polished operation. The addition of a photocopier will, of course, save a lot of outside trips to the printer, and a computer will save trips to the copier. As we continue the chain, we might add that good software will save trips to the computer and a good document assembler may save trips to work. These successive steps might be thought of as "automation."

As we move from the bottom to the top of the automation ladder, there is a tendency to become detached from the printed word, as paper producers become more concerned about the procedural aspects of rapid production while giving less attention to their substantive effects on the printed page. This book has emphasized "substance," as it presented unique "procedures" for document production and storage. Indeed, your "direct reference methods" are intertwined with the content and substance of your office paper. Your logic-based arrangements are predicated solely upon content, as opposed to titles and names. This applies, not only to your form files (Chapters 4 and 5), but also to your client file system (Chapter 2).

With *this* effort comes the first book-length system to classify, analyze, and catalogue every manner of legal text pursuant to a logic-based structure, so that it encompasses *all* of law as we know it. Perhaps there has been no other such effort since the dawn of Jurisprudence. Standardization of the system may eventually lead to greater efficiency with respect to commercial transactions, pleading preparation, and document draftsmanship in general. Because this is the first full-length description of the direct reference system, you are in a position to get a head start.

Today, it is fair to say that we will never read most of the copied, or machine-produced, print that finds its way onto important documents and pleadings. It is therefore that much more important that with your advanced systems, you should concentrate on the construction and content of your words, particularly those that are to be duplicated or mass-produced. With that kind of care and attention, and your newly discovered logic-based methods, your combined skills will certainly be priceless.

LOOKING AHEAD

The law firm of the future belongs to the microprocessor. For some of you, computerization has been too slow-moving into the practice of law; for others it has been fast and disruptive. Still others refuse to even acknowledge the computer's existence as an office tool. Nevertheless, the eventual conquest of the profession promises to be accelerated and complete.

The non-lawyer should think of the computer as the greatest equalizer that the profession has ever seen. Paralegals and secretaries can expand the use of these tools well beyond their presently employed limits.

Getting a Headstart

Out of the maze of methods, systems, software, and equipment, you may be wondering about which steps to take and in which order. Much, of course, will depend upon whether you are an administrator, paralegal, or secretary; and, perhaps even more will depend upon whether you are trying to improve your own skills and personal worth, or trying to bring order to some chaotic law practice.

For the administrator, or anyone trying to put an office "in order," I recommend a review and implementation of the chapters, one by one, in their respective orders. For those desiring personal improvement, I would summarize with a brief list of the skills of the future:

1. Grammar

The ancient skill is far too often overlooked in this, the age of the microprocessor. But as long as the legal profession deals in words, this discipline will remain paramount. Your new methods and systems will allow you to deal with words on a "wholesale" basis; they will provide speed like never before. But quality is another matter.

I can only hope that by spending less time on wasteful searches for information and duplications of effort, more time can be devoted to the preparation of polished, grammatically perfect documents. Mass production and duplication of text are valuable assets; multiplication of errors, however, can lead to disaster.

2. Technical Skills

I would be reluctant to hire any secretary or paralegal without some word processing experience. But beyond that I consider general computer aptitude to be a major asset. Those who are willing to learn about, or experiment with, new software are *most* valuable. The ability to set up and use this book's file systems, should increase in value as the direct reference methods become more ubiquitous.

3. Software Expertise

Herein lies the greatest opportunity for every member of the legal profession, to increase his or her power tenfold. For the neophyte, I would recommend taking the time to learn and use a state-of-the-art word processing program, such as WordPerfect. Then, I would suggest that an attempt be made to learn and use a state-of-the-art brand of document assembler.

CONCLUSION

With this book's emphasis upon the simple, but critical, elements of document construction and storage, we have brought the most advanced technologies "full circle." Microprocessors and software have given you the power to mass-produce text like never before. Hopefully, this book has instilled in you an ability to find what you need amidst the multitude.

With your direct reference systems and a willingness to try new software, your position in the legal field should be secure. Moreover, if you follow the suggestions and learn the mentioned skills, you should be running the law office of the future—not just working in it.

Appendix A
SAMPLE INDEX

OFFICE FORMS
(0XX,XXX)

	1X,XXX Status and Control Sheets		
10,010	Status Sheet	I,II	Basic Form
	2X,XXX Time and Billing Sheets		
20,000	Instructions	I, II	Details of Billing System
20,010	Time Sheet.Att.	I, II	For Attorneys
20,020	Time Sheet.Par.	I, II	For Paralegals
20,100	Reimbursement.Sheet	I, II	For All Personnel
	3X,XXX Retainer Agreements		
30,010	Hourly Rate	I, II	Straight Hourly
30,020	Hourly Credit	I, II	Credit for Retainer Included
30,030	Contingent	I, II	Contingent Fee Agreement
30,040	Combined	I, II	Contingent and Hourly
	4X,XXX Authorizations		
40,010	Medical	I, II	Release of Medical Records
40,020	Wage	I, II	Release of Wage Info
	5X,XXX Reserved		
50,000	Other Office Forms		

LITIGATION
(1XX,XXX)

U.S. SUPREME COURT

11X,XXX

111,XXX Commencement

111,000	Checklist.Pleadings	I	All Matters Before Court
111,001	Pet.Writ.Cert.Samp.	I	Petition-Writ of Certiorari
111,002	Appeal.Appl.Leave.Samp.	I	Application for Leave

112,XXX Response

112,000	Brief.Respond.Samp.	I	Brief of Respondent

113,XXX Interim Proceedings

113,000	Checklist.Motions	I	All Motions
113,101	Mot.Ext.Time.Brief	I	Extension to File Brief

114,XXX Rehearing

114,000	Pet.Rehearing	I	Petition for Rehearing

U.S. CIRCUIT COURT OF APPEALS

12X,XXX

121,XXX Commencement

121,000	Checklist.Pleadings	I	All Appeals
121,001	Claim Appeal	I	28 USC 1295
121,050	Brief.Sample.Tax	I	Tax Case
121,060	Brief.Sample.Labor	I	Labor Case

122,XXX Response

122,001	Brief.Resp.	I	Sample Response
122,010	Mot.Dismiss.Appeal	I	Motion to Dismiss

126,XXX Judgment

126,000	Judgment.Sample	O	Always Prepared by Court

127,XXX Remand

127,000	Remand.Sample	O	Always Prepared by Court

128,XXX Appeal to U.S.S.C.

128,000	Appeal to U.S.S.C.	O	Always Prepared by Court See 111,000

FEDERAL DISTRICT COURT

13X,XXX

131,XXX Commencement

131,007	Pet.Bank.Ch.7	I	Pet.Bankrupt.-Chap.7
131,011	Pet.Bank.Ch.11	I	Pet.Bankrupt.-Chap.11
131,013	Pet.Bank.Ch.13	I	Pet.Bankrupt.-Chap.13
131,020	Proof.Claim	I	Bankruptcy
131,101	Service Form.Mars.	I	Marshall's Form
131,102	Summons	I	Standard Form
131,103	P.O.S. Mail.Sum.	I	Proof of Service by Mail
131,104	Face Sheet	I	For Every New Suit
131,201	Comp.Interpleader	I	Sample

132,XXX Response

132,010	Mot.More Def State	I	Filed Instead of Answer
132,100	List.Aff Def.J.D.	III	Defenses to Federal Juris.
132,101	Ans.Sample	I	Basic Form Answer
132,110	Removal Package	III	Removal, Bond, Joinder
132,201	Mot.Dis.Lack J.D.	III	Lack of Fed. Jurisdiction

133,XXX Discovery

133,100	Brief.Disc.Sanc.Fed.	I	Refusal to Attend Dep.
133,201	Mot.Compell.Int.	I	Federal
133,600	Notice of Dep.	IV	Use 183,600
133,801	Mot.Disc.Willful	III	Motion for Sanctions

134,XXX Pre-trial

134,010	Pretrial Stat.Jt.	I	Joint P.T. Statement

135,XXX Trial

135,301	B.Hearsay Bus.Rec.	I	Brief-Bus. Record Rule
135,741	Jury Charges.Pd.Liab.	I,II	Product Liability
135,761	Jury Charges.Fair Rep.	II	Labor-Fair Rep Case

136,XXX Judgment

136,012	Dismissal	I	Based upon Rule 12

136,056	Order of Dismissal	I	Based upon Rule 56
136,156	Summary Judgment	I	Based upon Rule 56
	137,XXX Execution		
137,010	Affid.Garnish.	I	Affidavit-Garnishment
137,020	Writ.Garnish.	I	Writ of Garnishment
137,030	Execution	I	Sample Execution
	138,XXX Appeal		
138,000	Appeal to U.S.C.A.	I	Sample Appeal Package
	139,XXX Substantive Law		
139,000	Substantive Law		

FEDERAL COURT OF CLAIMS

14X,XXX

	141,XXX Commencement		
141,001	Art.Proc.	I	Article; See CC Rule 21
141,010	Pet.Auto Neg.	I	Mail Truck Collision
	142,XXX Response		
142,000	Response	O	Filed by Government
	143,XXX Discovery		
143,010	Sample Interrog.	III	See CC Rule 73
	144,XXX Pre-trial		
144,010	P.T.State.Samp.	II	Samp.Joint P.T. Stat.
	145,XXX Trial		
145,000	Art.Trial	I	See CC Rule 131 et Seq.
	146,XXX Judgment		
146,000	Judgment.Sample	O	Issued by Court
	147,XXX Execution		
147,000	Execution		

148,XXX Exceptions and Appeals

148,010	Appeal.Gen.	I	Sample Appeal Package
148,100	Writ of Cert.Sample	I	Appeal to USSC

149,XXX Substantive Law

149,000	Substantive Law		

TAX COURT

15X,XXX

151,XXX Commencement

151,000	Entry of Appearance	I	Rule 24
151,003	Power of Attorney	I	Rule 191
151,010	Cert.Ret.Serv.	I	Return of Service
151,101	Pet.Red.Deficiency	I	Pet. to Redetermine Def.
151,102	Pet.Small Tax Case	I	See Rules 170-179

152,XXX Response

152,000	Response	O	Filed by Government

153,XXX Discovery

153,000	Article.Discov.	I	Treatice-Tax Court Disc.
153,010	Subpoena	I	Rule 147
153,020	Appl.to Take Dep.	I	Rules 81-84

154,XXX Pre-trial

154,001	Request Trial.Place	I	Rule 24
154,100	Motion.Sample	I	Motion-Basic Form
154,101	Mot.Postpone Trial	I	See Rules 51(e) and 134

155,XXX Trial

155,000	Brief.BP	III	Burden of Proof

156,XXX Judgment

156,000	Judgment	O	Always Issued by Court

157,XXX Execution

157,000	Execution	O	Always Issued by Court

158,XXX Appeal

158,002	Notice Appeal	I	Rules 190, 191
158,003	Bond.Appeal	I	Rule 191
158,010	Appeal to U.S.C.A.	I	Sample Appeal Package

159,XXX Substantive Law

159,010	Carrying Charges	III	§212(2) IRC
159,100	Profit -v-Pers Mot.	III	§162(a), §212, §261
159,101	Legal Expenses	III	§212(1)

STATE SUPREME COURT

16X,XXX

161,XXX Commencement

161,010	Claim.Appeal	I	Claim of Appeal
161,020	Claim.Appeal.Emerg.	I,III	Emergency Appeal

162,XXX Response

162,101	Brief.Resp.	I	Sample Brief-Appellee
162,201	Mot.Dis.Appeal	I	Motion to Dismiss

163,XXX Interim Proceedings

163,000	Mot.Extend Time.Brief	I	Extension of Time to File

166,XXX Judgment

166,000	Judgment	O	Always Prepared by Court

167,XXX Remand

167,000	Remand	O	Always Prepared by Court
167,001	Mot.Clarify Decision	I	Nec. for Poor Decisions

168,XXX Appeal

168,000	Appeal to U.S.S.C.	I	Sample Package

STATE COURT OF APPEALS

17X,XXX

171,XXX Commencement

171,001	Claim.Appeal.Sample	I	Sample Package

171,010	Claim.Appeal.Fin Ord.	I	Appeal from Final Order
171,020	Claim.Appeal.Int.	I	Interlocutory Appeal
171,030	Claim.Appeal.Emerg.	I	Emergency
	172,XXX Response		
172,010	Brief.Resp.Fin Ord.	I	Appeal—Final Order
172,020	Brief.Resp.Int.	I	Resp. Interloc. Appeal
172,030	Brief.Resp.Emerg.	I	Resp. Emergency Appeal
	173,XXX Interim Proceedings		
173,001	Mot.Extend Time.Brief	I	Extension Time.File Brief
173,011	Mot.Oral Argument	I	To Permit Oral Argument
	176,XXX Judgment		
176,000	Judgment.Samp.	O	Always Prepared by Court
	177,XXX Remand		
177,000	Remand.Samp.	O	Always Prepared by Court
177,010	Mot.Clarif.	I	Motion for Clarification
	178,XXX Appeal		
178,000	Appeal	O	See 161,XXX
178,010	Claim.Appeal.Right	I	Appeal to Supreme Court

STATE SUPERIOR COURT

18X,XXX

	181,XXX Commencement		
181,000	Appearance	I	Appear. & Notice of
181,001	Summons	I	Civil Summons
181,002	Compl.	I,II,III	Auto Neg. Complaint
181,003	Compl.Div.	I,II,III	Complaint for Divorce
181,005	Jury Demand	I,II,III	Jury Demand
181,010	Writ.Habeas Corpus	I	Writ of Habeas Corpus
181,014	Prelim.Injunc.	I,II,III	Preliminary Injunction
181,301	Compl.Breach Contract	I	Complaint
181,402	Compl.Battery	I	Assault and Battery
181,403	Compl.Prod.Liab.	I	Products Liability
	182,XXX Response		
182,010	Ans.Assault	I	Answer-Assault Case

182,101	Aff.Def.Assault	III	List Affirmatives-Assault
182,102	Aff.Def.Slander	III	Slander
182,103	Aff.Def.Libel	III	Libel
182,104	Aff.Def.Breach.C.	III	Breach of Contract
182,105	Aff.Def.Prod.Liab.	III	Products Liability
	183,XXX Discovery		
183,010	Lost.Wage.Auth.	I	Lost Wage Author.-Letter
183,101	Interrog Face Sheet.PS	II	To Singular Plaintiff
183,102	Interrog Face Sheet PC	II	To Corporate Plaintiff
183,104	Interrog Face Sheet PP	II	To Plural Plaintiffs
183,106	Interrog Face Sheet DS	II	To Singular Defendant
183,108	Interrog Face Sheet DC	II	To Corporate Defendant
183,109	Interrog Face Sheet DP	II	To Plural Defendants
183,201	Demand.B.P.	I	Bill of Particulars
183,202	Demand.Prod.Doc	II	Production of Documents
183,203	Motion.Compel.Int.	I	Compel Interrog.Answers
183,310	Interrog.BC	II	Breach of Contract
183,403	Interrog—Auto Drive	III	To Driver of Auto
183,405	Interrog—Employ Hist.	III	Employment History Only
183,407	Interrog—Med. Hist.	III	Medical History Only
183,411	Interrog.Injury.Plain.	I	Lost Wages/Injuries to Pl.
183,600	Not.Dep	IV	All Dep Notices
183,601	Not.Dep.	I,II,III	Notice of Deposition
183,602	Not.Dep.D.C.	I,II,III	Duces Tecum
183,603	Not.Dep.Rec.Cop.	III	Record Copy Dep.
183,604	Not.Dep.Corp.Dir.	III	To Corporate Director
	184,XXX Pre-trial		
184,001	Witness List	III	
184,010	PT State.	I	Pre-Trial Statement
184,011	Wit.List	I	List of Witnesses
184,101	Mot.Strike.J.D.	I	Strike Jury
	185,XXX Trial		
185,010	Mot.Adj.	I	Motion to Adjourn Trial
185,101	Brief.Mary Cart.	II	Mary Carter Agreement
	186,XXX Judgment		
186,001	Default.Judg.Div.	I,II,III	Judgment of Divorce
186,002	Aff and Default	I,II,III	Affidavit and Default
186,010	Default.Application	I	Entry Affidavit
186,020	Dismissal	I	Voluntary

186,030	Dismiss.Non-Service	I	No Progress
186,090	Plea.Guilt.No Contest	I	No Contest by Mail
186,990	Settle.State.	I	Settlement Statements

187,XXX Execution

187,001	Summons.Debtor	I	Summons-Debtor Proceed.
187,101	Garnish.Writ	I	Writ. of Garn.-State
187,102	Garnish.Aff.	I	Aff. for Garn.-State
187,110	Gran.Forms	I	Filled-in Samples
187,111	Garn.Discl.Calc.Sheet	I	Discl. and Calculation
187,112	Garn.Discl.Indiv.	I	Individual Disclosure
187,113	Garn.Discl.Foreign	I	Foreign Corp.
187,115	Garn.Discl.Mich.Corp.	I	Domestic Corp.
187,201	Execution	I	Standard Form
187,901	Garn.Release	I	Garnishee Release

188,XXX Appeal

188,010	Claim.Appeal.Right	I	Claim of Appeal-Right
188,020	Bond.Appeal	I	Bond on Appeal
188,030	Ord.Trans.Rec.Appeal	I	Order of Transmittal
188,201	Rep.Cert.Trans.Appeal	I	Reporter's Certificate
188,202	Notice.Filing.Trans.	I	Certificate of Service

189,XXX Substantive Law

189,001	Def.Fraud.	I,II,III	Defending Fraud
189,002	Judgment	I	Judgment
189,100	Brief.Assault	I	Brief-Assault
189,401	Dismiss.Lack.Speed.	I	Lack of Speedy Trial
189,710	Brief.Free.Speech	I	Leaflet Passers

STATE MUNICIPAL COURT 19X,XXX

191,XXX Commencement

191,001	Aff.Claim	I	Small Claims
191,100	Complaints.All	O	See 181,XXX-All Complaints

192,XXX Response

192,000	Plea.DUIL	I,II,III	Drunk Drive Plea
192,001	Pet.Ord.Removal.Civil	I	Removal-Civil Division
192,002	Appear.	I,II,III	Appearance

193,XXX Discovery

193,000	Discovery.Generally	O	See 183,XXX
193,001	Dem.Breath.Result.	I,II,III	Demand for Results

194,XXX Pre-trial

194,101	Mot.PT Conf.	I	Motion for Pre-Trial Conf.

195,XXX Trial

195,101	Brief.Rules of Ev	I	Appl. of Evidence Rules

196,XXX Judgment

196,001	Judgment.Small Cl.	I	Small Claims

197,XXX Execution

197,112	Garn.Discl.Indiv.	I	Individual
197,115	Garn.Discl.Mich.Corp.	I	Corp.
197,201	Execution	I	Standard Form
197,901	Garn.Release	I	Garnishee Release

198,XXX Appeal

198,001	Appeal Package	I	Appeal to Superior Court

199,XXX Substantive Law

199,xxx	Substantive Law		

PROBATE
(2XX,XXX)

INTER VIVOS

21X,XXX

211,XXX Gifts

211,001	Gift.Decl.	II	General
211,002	Gift.Decl.Minor	II	Declar. Gift for Minor

212,XXX Powers of Attorney

212,001	Powers of Attorney	II	General Forms
212,101	Pow.Att.Special	II	Special Power

212,201	Pow.Att.General	II	General Power
212,301	Pow.Att.Durable	II	Durable Power

213,XXX Private Annuities

213,001	Private Annuities		

214,XXX Revocable Living Trusts

214,001	Trust.Rev.Living	II,III	Revocable Living Trust

215,XXX Revocable Life Ins. Trusts

215,001	Trust.Rev.Life Ins.	II,III	Life Insurance Trust

216,XXX Irrevocable Living Trusts

216,001	Trust.Irrev.Living	II,III	Living Trust

217,XXX Irrevocable Life Ins. Trusts

217,001	Trust.Irrev.Life	II,III	Life Insurance Trust

218,XXX Irrevocable Short Term Trusts

218,001	Trust.Irrev.Short Term		

219,XXX Charitable Trusts

219,001	Charitable Trusts	II,III	Charitable Trusts

TESTAMENTARY

22X,XXX

220,XXX Single Male Simple Will

220,001	Will.Simp.Male.Sing.	I	Single Simple Male Will
220,100	Intro.Will.Simp.Sing.	III	Introduction
220,200	Appoint.Will.Simp.Sing.	III	Standard Appointments
220,201	Appoint.Non-relative	III	Appointment of Friend
220,300	Pay Debts.Will	III	Standard Pay Debts
220,301	Don't Pay Debts	III	Unique Provision
220,400	Powers.Will.Sing.	III	Powers Clause
220,510	Mindful.Prov.Will	III	Give Nothing
220,520	Gen Pers Prov.Will	III	Minor Personalty
220,530	Specific Bequest.Will	I	Sample Language
220,540	Demon.Bequest.Will	I	Sample-Demon.Bequest
220,550	Gen.Bequest.Will	I	Sample-General Bequest

220,560	Resid.Dec.Will	III	Residuary to Descendants
220,561	Resid.Par.Will	III	Residuary to Parents
220,569	Resid.Intest.Will	III	Intestate Distribution

221,XXX Single Female Simple Will

221,000	Will.Simp.Sing.Fem.	I	Single Simp. Female Will
221,100	Intro.Will.Simp.Sing.	III	Introduction
221,200	Appoint.Will.Simp.Sing.	III	Standard Appointments
221,201	Appoint.Non-relative	III	Appointment of Friend
221,300	Pay Debts.Will	III	Standard Pay Debts
221,301	Dont Pay Debts	III	Unique Provision
221,400	Powers.Will.Sing.	III	Powers Clause
221,510	Mindful.Prov.Will	III	Give Nothing
221,520	Gen Pers Prov.Will	III	Minor Personalty
221,530	Specific Bequest.Will	I	Sample Language
221,540	Demon.Bequest.Will	I	Sample-Demon.Bequest
221,550	Gen.Bequest.Will	I	Sample-General Bequest
221,560	Resid.Dec.Will	III	Residuary to Descendants
221,561	Resid.Par.Will	III	Residuary to Parents
221,569	Resid.Intest.Will	III	Intestate Distribution

222,XXX Single Male Pourover Will

222,001 Single Male Pourover Will

223,XXX Single Female Pourover Will

223,001 Single Female Pourover Will

224,XXX Single Male Will-Test. Trust

224,001 Single Male Will-Test. Trust

225,XXX Single Female Will-Test. Trust

225,001 Single Female Will-Test. Trust

226,XXX Married Male Pourover Will

226,001	Will.Pour.Male.Mar.	I	Married Pour. Male Will
226,100	Intro.Will.Pour.Mar.	III	Introduction
226,200	Appoint.Will.Pour.Mar.	III	Standard Appointments
226,201	Appoint.Non-Relative	III	Appointment of Friend
226,300	Pay Debts.Will	III	Standard Pay Debts
226,301	Dont Pay Debts	III	Unique Provision
226,400	Powers.Will.Pour.	III	Powers Clause
226,510	Mindful.Prov.Will	III	Give Nothing

226,520	Gen Pers Prov.Will	III	Minor Personalty
226,530	Specific Bequest.Will	I	Sample Language
226,540	Demon.Bequest.Will	I	Sample-Demon. Bequest
226,550	Gen.Bequest.Will	I	Sample-General Bequest
226,560	Resid.Dec.Will	III	Residuary to Trust

227,XXX Married Female Pourover Will

227,001 Married Female Pourover Will

228,XXX Married Male Will-Test. Trust

228,001 Married Male Will-Test. Trust

229,XXX Married Female Will-Test. Trust

229,001 Married Female Will-Test. Trust

ESTATE ADMINISTRATION (Minors)

23X,XXX

231,XXX Pre-Administration

231,010	Pet.Appt.Guard.Minor	I	Appointment of Guardian

232,XXX Appt. of Fiduciary

232,000	Ord.Appoint.Lim.Guard.	I	Limited Guardian of Minor
232,010	Pet.Appt.Lim.Guard	I	Limited Guardian of Minor
232,020	Pet.Appt.Cons.	I	Conservator of Minor

233,XXX Marshaling Assets

233,001	Inventory	I,II,III	

234,XXX Claims

234,001	State.and P of C.	I,II,III	State. Proof of Claim

235,XXX General Administration

235,001	Subpoena	I,II,III	
235,701	Pet.Remov.Fiduc.	I,II	Appointing Successor
235,702	Order.Remov.Fiduc.	I,II	Appointing Successor

236,XXX Accounting

236,001	Account of Fiduciary	I,II	
236,101	Order Allowing Account	I,II	

237,XXX Distribution & Discharge

237,901	Order.Allow.Acct.	I	Fin.Acct.Assign.Res.
237,901	Receipt of Dist.Share	I	
237,991	Order of Discharge	I,II,III	

238,XXX Appeal

238,001	Claim of Appeal	I,II,III	To Superior Court

ESTATE ADMINISTRATION (Mental Inc.)

24X,XXX

241,XXX Pre-Administration

241,010	Pet.Appt.Guard.M.I.	I	Appoint Guardian for M.I.

242,XXX Appt. of Fiduciary

242,001	Pet.Appt. of Fiduciary	I	Appoint Fiduciary for M.I.

243,XXX Marshaling Assets

243,001	Inventory	I	Standard Form

244,XXX Claims

244,001	Claims	I	Use 264,101 and 264,102

245,XXX General Administration

245,001	General Administration	I	Use Forms 266,000 et Seq.

246,XXX Accounting

246,001		I	Use Forms 267,000 et Seq.

247,XXX Distribution & Discharge

247,001	Distrib. & Discharge	I	Use Forms 267,000 et Seq.

248,XXX Appeal

248,000	All Appeals	O	See 268,000
248,001	Claim of Appeal	I	To Superior Court

ESTATE ADMINISTRATION (Phy. Inc.)

25X,XXX

251,XXX Pre-Admin.

251,010	Pet.Appt.Guard.P.T.	I	Appoint Guardian for P.I.

	252,XXX Appt. of Fiduciary		
252,001	Appt. of Fiduciary	I	Appoint Fiduciary for P.I.
	253,XXX Marshaling Assets		
253,001	Marshaling Assets	I	Standard Forms
	254,XXX Claims		
254,001	Claims	I	Use 204,101 and 264,102
	255,XXX General Administration		
255,001	General Administration	I	Use Forms 266,000 et Seq.
	256,XXX Accounting		
256,001	Accounting	I	Use Forms 267,000 et Seq.
	257,XXX Distribution & Discharge		
257,001	Distrib. & Discharge	I	Use Forms 267,000 et Seq.
	258,XXX Appeal		
258,000	All Appeals	O	See 268,000
258,001	Claim of Appeal	I	To Superior Court

ESTATE ADMINISTRATION (Decedents)

26X,XXX

	261,XXX Pre-Administration		
261,000	Probate Proc.List	I	Procedural Checklist
261,001	Retainer Letter	I	Standard Form
261,002	Pet.Comm.Proceedings	I	First Pleading-Opens Estate
261,010	Pet.Open Box	I	To Open Safe Deposit Box
261,011	Waiver and Consent	I	Standard Form-All Proceed.
261,220	Notice of Hearing	I	Standard Form-All Proceed.
	262,XXX Appt. of Fiduciary		
262,901	Pet.Admit Will. Probate	I	Petition to Admit Will
262,902	Order—Admitting Will to Probate & Appointing Personal Rep.	I	Standard Order Form
262,910	Bond of Fiduciary	I	Personal Bond Form
262,920	Letters of Authority	I	Sample-Issued by Court

	263,XXX Marshaling Assets		
263,101	Inventory	I	Standard Form
263,102	Invent.Amend.	I	Amended Inventory Form
	264,XXX Claims		
264,101	Claim.Notice.	I	Notice of Claim
264,102	Claim.Not.Hear.	I	Notice of Hearing-Claims
	265,XXX General Administration		
265,010	Not.Spouse.Election, Proof of Service	I	Right to Election
	266,XXX Accounting		
266,001	Account of Fiduciary	I	Standard Form
266,091	Order Allowing Account	I	Standard Form
	267,XXX Distribution & Discharge		
267,100	Deed.Exec.Admin. Guard.	I	Deed of Fiduciary
267,800	Rep.Sale.Mort.Estate	I	Report of Sale
267,901	Rec.Distrib.Share	I	Receipt for Share
267,910	Ord.Allow.Final Acct.	I	Assign Residue
267,920	Ord.Assign.Small.Est	I	Assign Residue
267,990	Order of Discharge	I	Discharge Fiduciary
	268,XXX Appeal		
268,000	Guide to Probate Appeals & Forms	I	All Appeals-Probate Court

POST ESTATE TRUST ADMINISTRATION

27X,XXX

270,010	Declin.Trust & P.R.	I	Desig. of Per. Rep.

OTHER

28X,XXX

280,001	Pet.Name Change	I	Pet. to Change Name

CORPORATE AND BUSINESS
(3XX,XXX)

CORPORATIONS

31X,XXX

311,XXX Pre-Incorp. Agreements

311,001	Request.Corp.Forms	I	Request Forms from State
311,101	Written Consent.Name	I	Consent to Use Name
311,102	Name Reservation Form	I	File with State

312,XXX Incorp. Documents

312,101	Arts of Incorp.Profit.	I	Domestic Profit
312,102	Arts of Incorp.D.C.	I	District of Columbia
312,108	Arts of Incorp.Rest.P.	I	Restated—Profit
312,121	Cert.Appt.Res.Agent	I	Appoint Resident Agent
312,125	Cert of Incorp.S.D.	I	State of Delaware
312,126	Cert of Res.Agent	I	Dom. & Foreign Corp.
312,131	Cert of Amendment.Inc.	I	By Incorporators
312,132	Cert of Amendment.Sh.	I	By Shareholders
312,135	Cert.Change.R.Off. R.A	I	Change of Reg. Office or Resident Agent
312,138	Cert.Assume.Name	I	Corp. & Limited Part.
312,201	Arts of Incorp.P.C.	I	Professional Corp.
312,301	Arts of Incorp.N.P.	I	Non-Profit
312,401	Arts of Assoc.Ecc	I	Ecclesiastical

313,XXX Minutes

313,100	Consent Resolution	III	Standard Form
313,101	Min.AD.Ret.Plan	III	Adopt Erisa Plan (Retire)
313,110	Min.AP.Expend	III	Approve Expenditures
313,111	Min.AP.Res.	III	Approve Resolution
313,120	Min.Rat.Act.	III	Ratification-Past Action

314,XXX Employee Benefit Plans

314,101	Pens Plan.Intro	III	Intro., Pension Plan
314,201	Proft.Shar.Intro	III	Intro., Profit Sharing
314,501	Ret.Plan.Dist.	III	Distribution Method 1

315,XXX Employee Agreements

315,000	Employee Agreements		

316,XXX Shareholder Agreements

316,010 Assignment of Stock

317,XXX Mergers, Reorganizations, and Dissolutions

317,001	Cert.Term.Assume. Name	I	Corp. and Limit. Part.
317,101	Cert.Renewal.Corp. Stock	I	Renewal Exist. Stock
317,102	Cert.Merger.For.Dom.	I	Foreign and Domestic
317,103	Cert.Merger.Par.Sub.	I	Parent and Subsidiary
317,104	Cert.Aband.Merger. Cons.	I	Domestic Corporation
317,800	Cert.Appl.Author.Bus.	I	Transact Bus. in Mich.
317,801	Cert.Appl.Withdraw. F.C.	I	Withdraw. For. Corp.
317,802	Cert.Withdraw.F.C.	I	Withdraw. For. Corp.
317,808	Dissol.Tax.Clear.Corp.	I	Tax Clear. Request
317,901	Cert.Dissol.Dom.Corp.	I	Domestic Corp. or Dir.
317,902	Cert.Dissolution	I	Shareholders
317,903	Cert.Dissol.Provisions	I	Specific Provision
317,910	Cert.Revoc.Dissol.Dir.	I	Domestic Corporation
317,920	Cert of Abandonment	I	Domestic Corporation

LIMITED PARTNERSHIPS

32X,XXX

320,011	Lim Part.Suppl.L	I	Supplement-Contrib. Info.
320,012	Lim Part.Suppl.O	I	Continuation Page
320,013	Lim Part.Suppl.P	I	Partners' Names, Addresses
320,101	Cert.Restate.L.P.	I	Domestic Limited Part.
320,102	Cert.Amend.	I	Dom.Limited Partner.
320,105	Appl.Reg.Trans.Bus. MI	I	Transact Bus. in Mich.

CO-PARTNERSHIPS

33X,XXX

330,101	Cert.Co-Partnership	I	General
330,102	Cert.Co-Partnership	I	Oakland County
330,103	Cert.Co-Partnership	I	Washtenaw County
330,104	Cert.Co-Partnership	I	Wayne County
337,901	Not.Diss.Co-Part.	I	Bus.Under Assumed Name
337,902	Cert.Discon.Co-Part.	I	Oakland County
337,903	Cert.Discon.Co-Part.	I	Wayne County

JOINT VENTURES

34X,XXX

34X,XXX Joint Ventures

SOLE PROPRIETORSHIPS

35X,XXX

350,101	Cert.Pers.Assum.Name	I	Assume Name-General
350,102	Cert.Pers.Assum.Name	I	Assume Name-Macomb
350,103	Cert.Pers.Assum.Name	I	Assume Name-Oakland
350,104	Cert.Assumed Name	I	Washtenaw County
350,105	Cert.Bus.Assum.Name	I	Assume Name-Wayne Cty.
357,901	Cert.Dis.Bus.Name	I	Discont.Name-Oakland

U.C.C. MATTERS

36X,XXX

361,XXX General

361,000	Request.Info.Copies	I	Uniform Comm.Code

362,XXX Sales

362,101	Offer Pur.Prop.Pers.	III	Offer Purch.-Per.Prop.
362,201	Offer Pur.Bus.Gen.	III	Purch. Bus.-Gen. Form
362,202	Offer Pur.Prof.Prac.	III	Purch.Prof.Practice
362,203	Offer Pur.Gas Stat.	III	Purchase Gas Station
362,204	Offer Pur.Car Wash	III	Purchase Car Wash
362,205	Offer Pur.Restaurant	III	Purchase Restaurant
362,206	Offer Pur.Retail Shop	III	Purchase Retail Shop
362,501	Bill Lad.	II,III	Bill of Lading-Gen
362,502	Bill Lad.Order	II,III	Order Bill of Lading
362,601	Ship Receipt	I	Shipping Receipt

363,XXX Commercial Paper

363,101	Note.Demand.Simp.Sing.	II, III	Simple Demand Note
363,102	Note.Demand.Simp.Plur.	II, III	Plural Payees
363,121	Note.Demand.Full.Sing.	II, III	All Forfeiture Prov.
363,122	Note.Demand.Full.Plur.	II, III	Plural Payees
363,201	Note.Order.Simp.Sing.	II, III	Simple Demand Note
363,202	Note.Order.Simp.Plur.	II, III	Plural Payees
363,211	Note.Order.Accel.Sing.	II, III	Accel.Clause-Sing.Pay.
363,212	Note.Order.Accel.Plur.	II, III	Plural Payees
363,221	Note.Order.Full.Sing.	II, III	All Forfeiture Prov.
363,222	Note.Order.Full.Plur.	II, III	Plural Payees
363,301	Note.Install.Simp.Sing.	II, III	Simple Demand Note
363,302	Note.Install.Simp.Plur.	II, III	Plural Payees
363,311	Note.Install.Accel.Sing	II, III	Accel.Clause-Sing.
363,312	Note.Install.Accel.Plur	II,III	Plural Payees

363,321	Note.Install.Full.Sing.	II,III	All Forfeiture Prov.
363,322	Note.Install.Full.Plur.	II,III	Plural Payees
	364,XXX Bank Deposits & Collections		
364,101	Notice.Wrong.Dis.	III	Not. Wrongful Dishonor
	365,XXX Letters of Credit		
365,101	Letter of Credit.Gen	III	Gen. Letter of Credit
365,201	Letter of Credit.Spec.	III	Special Letter Credit
	366,XXX Bulk Transfers		
366,101	Bulk Trans.Notice.	II	Notice to Creditors
366,201	Inventory	II	Inven. of Bulk Assets
	367,XXX Warehouse Receipts		
367,101	Warehouse Receipts	I	Warehouse Receipt
	368,XXX Investment Securities		
368,000	Investment Securities		
	369,XXX Secured Transactions		
369,001	U.C.C.Fin.Code	I	Form UCC-1
369,003	U.C.C.Contin.,Etc.	I	Form UCC-3
369,011	U.C.C.Finan.State.	I	Form UCC-1A
369,101	Sec.Agreement	I	Comm.Stock or Business
369,101	Sec.Agreement	I	Indiv.,Part., or Corp.

CONTRACTS

37X,XXX

	371,XXX General Provisions		
371,000	Stand Recitals	III	Standard Recitals
371,100	Clause.Int.Gen	III	General Integration
371,101	Clause.Int.Strict	III	Strict Integration
371,102	Clause.Mod by Write	III	Modif. by Writing Only
	372,XXX Sale of Business		
372,000	Checklist.Sale.Bus	I	Comprehensive Checklist
372,001	Article.Sale.Bus	I	Law Review Art.

372,101	Sale Bus.Gen.Buyer	III	General Contract-Buyer
372,111	Clause War.Sale.Bus	III	Warranty Clause-Buyer
372,121	Sale.Bus.Gen.Seller	III	General Contract-Seller
372,201	Sale.Car Wash	I	Bus. and Comm. Lease
372,202	Sale.Art Supply	I	Goodwill, Name, Supplies

373,XXX Sale of Practice

373,000	Checklist.Sale Pract.	I	Sale-Professional Pract.
373,101	Sale Pract.Buyer	III	Favors Buyer
373,111	Sale Med Pract.Buyer	III	Med. Practice, Pro Buyer
373,121	Sale Law Pract.Buyer	III	Law Practice, Pro Buyer
373,131	Sale Vet Pract.Buyer	III	Vet. Practice, Pro Buyer
373,201	Sale Pract.Seller	III	Favors Seller
373,211	Sale Med Pract.Seller	III	Pro Seller
373,221	Sale Law Pract.Seller	III	Pro Seller
373,231	Sale Vet Pract.Seller	III	Pro Seller

REAL ESTATE
(4XX,XXX)

FEE SIMPLE ESTATES

(41X,XXX)

411,XXX Options to Purchase

411,010	Option Pur. Rep Buyer	II,III	Buyer's Favor
411,020	Option Pur. Rep Seller	II,III	Seller's Favor
411,101	Option	II	Purchase Real Estate
411,201	Option.Ex.	II	Exercise of Option

412,XXX Offers to Purchase

412,010	Offer Pur. C21	I,II	Century 21 Form
412,011	Offer Pur. LT	I,III	Lawyer's Title Form
412,012	Offer Pur. Form A	I	Alternative Form
412,013	Offer Pur. Form B	I	Alternative Form
412,021	Offer Pur. Comm	I	Commercial Property
412,201	Receipt.Dep.	I	Deposit Receipt

413,XXX Brokerage Forms

413,010	List.Agree.Open.2 Mo.	I	2-Month Listing
413,011	List.Agree.Open.3 Mo.	I	3-Month Listing

413,020	List.Agree.Exc.	I	2-Month Listing
413,021	List.Agree.Exc.	I	3-Month Listing

414,XXX Disclosure Forms

414,101	Appraisal Aff.	III	Appraisal Affidavit
414,102	Appraisal Certif.	III	Appraisal Certificate
414,201	Inspection Report	I	Inspection Report

415,XXX Lending Institution Forms

415,011	Loan App. Conv. BA	I	Convent. Loan B of A
415,012	Loan App. Conv. FF	I	First Federal
415,013	Loan App. Conv. FBB	I	First Benevolent Bank
415,014	Loan App. Conv. BB	I	Bank B
415,021	Loan App. FHA. BA	I	FHA. Bank of America
415,022	Loan App. FHA. FF	I	First Federal
415,023	Loan App. FHA. FBB	I	First Benevolent Bank
415,024	Loan App. FHA. BB	I	Bank B
415,031	Loan App. VA. BA	I	Veterans Admin. Loan
415,032	Loan App. VA. FF	I	First Federal
415,033	Loan App. VA. FBB	I	First Benevolent Bank
415,034	Loan App. VA. BB	I	Bank B
415,101	TIL	O	Truth-in-Lending Form
415,201	Escrow. Inst.	I	Escrow Instructions

416,XXX Closing Statements

416,100	Closing Stat. Buyer	I	Buyer's Closing State.
416,101	Closing Stat. Buyer	I	Alt. Form
416,200	Closing Stat. Seller	I	Seller's Clos. State.
416,300	Closing Stat. Lender	I	Lender's Clos. State.

417,XXX Escrow Forms

418,XXX Deeds

418,110	Deed Warr. Indv.	I	Warranty Deed Ind.
418,120	Deed Warr. Pshp.	I	Partnership (Grantor)
418,130	Deed Warr. Corp.	I	Corporate (Grantor)
418,220	Deed QC Pshp	I	Quit Claim Deed Part.
418,230	Deed QC Corp	I	Quit Claim Deed Corp.
418,310	Trust Deed Indiv.	I	Trust Deed Individual
418,320	Trust Deed Pshp.	I	Trust Deed Partnership
418,330	Trust Deed Corp.	I	Trust Deed Corporation
418,410	Deed QC Indv.	I	Quit Claim Deed Ind.

419,XXX Use

419,201	Cont.Const.	III	Construction Contract
419,401	Agree.Manage.	II	Management Agreement

LAND CONTRACTS

42X,XXX

421,001	Land Cont.	I	Form 1
421,002	Land Cont.	I	Form 2
421,004	Notice.Intent.Forfeit	I	
421,005	Notice of Forfeiture	I	
421,011	Comp.Aff.Recover Land	I	

CONCURRENT ESTATES

43X,XXX

430,100	Stand.Lang.T in C	I	Tenants in Common
430,200	Stand.Lang.J T	I	Joint Tenancy
430,300	Stand.Lang.T E	I	Tenancy by Entirety
432,101	Off.To.Pur.Jt.	I	Joint Purchase

DIVISIBLE ESTATES

44X,XXX

448,101	Deed.Life of Grantor	II	Deed Life of Grantor
448,201	Deed.Life.Grantee	II	Deed Life of Grantee

EASEMENTS AND SERVITUDES

45X,XXX

458,101	Eas.Grant.Travel	II	Right Ingress & Egress
458,102	Eas.Grant.Util.	II	Easement for Utilities

LEASES

46X,XXX

460,001	Business Property	I	Business Property
460,100	Lease.Res.	I	Residential Lease
460,101	Identifier Lease.Off.	II	Office Lease
460,102	Lease.Shop.Cent.	I	Use with 460,103
460,103	Lease.Shop.Cent.Add	II	Addendum
460,201	Lease.Ogm	II	Oil, Gas, & Mineral
460,601	Sub-Lease	II	Sub-Lease

460,701	Lease.Surrender	II	Surrender of Lease
461,110	Notice.Quit.Non-Pay.	I	Non-Payment of Rent
461,120	Notice Term.Tenancy	I	Terminate Tenancy

MORTGAGES
47X,XXX

470,010	Mortgage	I	
470,011	Mortgage Note	I	
470,100	Mortgage.Short	I	Short Form Mortgage
470,101	Mortgage.Long	I	Long Form Mortgage
470,201	Agree.Subord.	II	Subordination Agree.
470,202	Assignment—Part.	I	Mortgage Assignment
470,203	Assignment—Corp.	I	Mortgage Assignment
470,204	Assignment—Escrow	I	Mortgage Assignment
479,001	Discharge—Indiv.	I	Mortgage Discharge
479,002	Discharge—Part.	I	Mortgage Discharge
479,003	Discharge—Corp.	I	Mortgage Discharge

LIENS
48X,XXX

480,001	Claim	I	
480,002	Claim of Lien	I	
480,003	Indemnity Agree.Mech.	I	Indemnity—Mechanical
480,010	Notice of Commence.	I	Notice of Commencement
480,011	Proof of Service.Claim	I	
480,012	Notice of Furnishing	I	
480,013	Sworn Statement	I,II,III	
480,100	Partial.Cond.Waiver	I	Lien
480,101	Lien.Claim.Affidavit	II	Claim of Lien (Aff.)
480,102	Partial.Uncond.Waiver	I	Lien
480,103	Lien.Claim.Notice	II	Claim of Lien (Not.)
480,109	Full.Uncond.Waiver	I	Lien
480,901	Release of Mechanic's	I	Lien
482,001	Full.Uncond.Waiver. Lien	I	
482,002	Full.Cond.Waiver.Lien	I	
482,003	Part.Uncond.Waiver. Lien	I	
482,004	Part.Cond.Waiver. Lien	I	
489,101	Lien.Discharge.	II	Discharge of Lien

OTHER
49X,XXX

490,010	Appl.Condo	I	Initial Appl. for Condo

TAX
(5X,XXXX)

This index configuration varies slightly from standard practice. The identifiers will not follow the recommended noun-adjective order. Because most of the forms are recognized as "returns," there is no need to repeat that particular noun. The letters appearing in the comments column represent schedules.

As indicated in Chapter 3, the comma is placed after the second, as opposed to the third digit of the form number. Also, due to numerosity, an alphabetical cross-index for important Federal Tax Returns may be warranted.

FEDERAL RETURNS

51,XXXX

Returns 51,0001 Through 51,0099

51,0001	CT-1 Emp. R.R. Retire.	I	CT-1 Emp. R.R. Retire.
51,0002	W-2	I	Income Tax Withheld Wages
51,0002	W-2C	I	Correction of W-2 Form
51,0002	W-2P	I	State. Annuities, Pension
51,0003	W-3	I	Trans. Income & Tax State.
51,0004	SS-4, Appl. I.D. Numb.	I	Appl.-Employee I.D. No.
51,0004	W-4	I	Withholding Exempt.Certif.
51,0004	W-4P, Pension Annuity	I	Request for Withholding
51,0004	W-4S, Sick Pay	I	Request for Withholding
51,0005	Appl. S.S.	I	S.S. or Tax Acct. No.
51,0009	W-9, Req.Tax I.D.	I	Tax Payer's Request
51,0010	Consent.Extend.Time	I	Assess. Extension
51,0023	Appl.Pract.IRS	I	Appl. Practice before IRS
51,0056	Not.of Fid.Rel	I	Fiduciary Relation

Returns 51,0100 Through 51,0599

51,0211	Appl. Reward	I	Squealer's Reward
51,0433	Financial Statement	I	433-A, B, D, F, G

Returns 51,0600 Through 51,0899

51,0637	Reg.Tax Free. Trans.	I	637, A
51,0656	Offer.Compromise	I	Settle Claim
51,0668	Not.Lien	I	A, A(c), B, C, D, E, F, H, J, W, W(C)
51,0669	Discharge Certificate	I	A, B, C, D, E, F
51,0720	Return.Q. Excise	I	Quarterly Excise Tax

51,0730	Tax Wagering	I	Tax on Gambling
51,0843	Refund.Claim	I	Refund.Employ.Stamp.Estate
51,0866	Agree.Final.Deter.	I	Agreement and Settlement
51,0870	Waiver of Restrict	I	AD, E, P, S
51,0875	Accept.Exam.Findings	I	Acceptance of IRS Findings
51,0885	Adjust SS Tax Tips	I	Tips Not Report.to Employ.
51,0895	Not.Statute.Expir.	I	Notice of Expiration St.L.

Returns 51,0900 Through 51,0999

51,0900	Tax Collection Waiver	I	Agreement to Waive
51,0906	Closing Agreement	I	Re: Final Determinations
51,0907	Agree.Extend.Limit.	I	Extend Period Lim.by Agree
51,0940	Emp.Annual.Fed. Income	I	B, C
51,0941	Quartly.Fed.Tax	I	E, M, SS
51,0942	Emp.Quart.Tax	I	Return Household Employ.
51,0964	Elect.Shareholder	I	Taxed Per 333 on Liq.Gain
51,0966	Information.Diss.	I	Info Return-Dis.of Corp.
51,0970	Appl.Adopt.Elect.Inv.	I	Elective Inventory Method
51,0972	Cons.Shareholder.Div.	I	Consent to be Taxed Div.
51,0973	Ret.Info.Cons.Div.	I	Consent Dividend Deduction
51,0976	Claim.Def.Div.Cr.	I	Deficiency Dividend Credit
51,0982	Cons.Adjust.Basis	I	Consent to Adjust Basis
51,0990	Return of Organization	I	A, C, PF, T

Returns 51,1000 Through 51,1039

51,1001	Ownership.Cert	I	Reduced Rate Certificate
51,1023	Exemp.Appl.	I	Charity 501

Returns 51,1040 and 51,1041

51,1040	Ind.Tax Return	I	A, B, C, D, E, F, G, R, SE, W, A, C, ES, ES(NR), EZ, NR, X
51,1040	Short 1040	I	1040 Short Form
51,1041	Fid.Return	I	D, J, K-1, A

Returns 51,1042 Through 51,1999

51,1045	Appl.Tax Pay.Carryback	I	Tentative Carryback Adj.
51,1065	Partnership Return	I	D, K-1
51,1078	Cert.Alien	I	Claims Res.In U.S.
51,1096	Annual Summary.Transm.	I	1099 Series
51,1098	Mortgage.Int.State.	I	Interest Statement
51,1117	Bond.Income.Foreign	I	Income Bond-Foreign Taxes
51,1118	Comp.Foreign Tax Credit	I	F; Computation Form

51,1120	Return.Corp.Income	I	D, PH, A, DISC, K, N, P, Q, F, FSC, P, H, IC-DISC, K, P, L, M, POL, S, D, K-1, X
51,1122	Consol.Ret.Subsid. Corp.	I	Info, Author. & Consent
51,1127	Appl.Ext.Time.Pay Def.	I	Extend Time Pay Deficiency
51,1128	Appl.Change.Acct.Per.	I	Appl.to Change Fiscal Year
51,1310	State.Refund.Dead.	I	Claim.Decedent's Refund
51,1363	Export Exemp.Cert.	I	Export Exemption Cert.
51,1902	Rep.Indiv.Income Tax	I	B, C

Returns 51,2000 Through 51,2999

51,2106	State.Emp.Bus.Exp.Trav.	I	Travel Expense Statement
51,2119	State.Sale.Exch.Res.	I	Sale or Exchange-Residence
51,2120	Mult.Support Agreement	I	Multiple Support Agree.
51,2159	Payroll Deduct.Agree	I	Payroll Ded.Agreement
51,2190	Change.Comp.Net. Earn.	I	Self Employment
51,2210	State.Underpay.Est.	I	Underpay. of Estimated Tax
51,2220	State.Underpay.Cor.	I	Underpay.Estimate.Tax.Corp
51,2222	Sealed Bid Seized Prop	I	6335
51,2261	Collateral Agreement	I	A, B, C, D
51,2271	Depreciation Agree.	I	Dep.Agreement
51,2290	Veh.Heavy Use Tax Ret.	I	Heavy Vehicle
51,2333	Request.Blank Tax Forms	I	B, E, P, R, S, T, X
51,2350	Appl.Exten.Time.Ret.	I	Application for Extension
51,2433	Notice of Seizure	O	
51,2434	Public Auction Sale	I	A Sealed Bid, B Not.Lien
51,2436	Seized Prop.Sale Rep.	O	Sales Report
51,2441	Credit for Child Care	I	Care & Dependent Expenses
51,2553	Election.Sub S	I	Small Bus.-Elect Sharehold.
51,2555	Deduct.Inc.Earn. Abroad	I	Income Earned Abroad
51,2678	Not.Appoint.Agent	I	Not.Appoint. by Employer
51,2688	Appl.Exten.Time.Ind. Ret	I	Application for Extension
51,2848	Power of Attorney	I	D

Returns 51,3000 Through 51,3999

51,3115	Appl.Change Acct.Meth.	I	Change Accounting Method
51,3363	Accept.Disallow. Claim	I	Accep. IRS Dissallowance
51,3559	State.Alimony.Maint.	I	Statement of AL. or Maint.
51,3621	Net Oper.Loss Comp.	I	A, Net Operating Loss Ded.
51,3800	Gen.Business Credit	I	General Business Credit
51,3870	Request for Adjust.	I	Request for Adjustment
51,3903	Moving Expense Adjust.	I	F (Foreign Mov.Exp.Adjust.)
51,3911	Taxpayer State.Refund	I	Statement Regarding Refund

Returns 51,4000 Through 51,4599

51,4029	Appl.Exemp.Tax.Self.	I	Appl-Self Employ Tax Exemp.
51,4070	Empl.Report on Tips	I	A (Daily Record of Tips)
51,4089	Not.Def.Waiver	I	Waiver of Notice
51,4137	Compu.SS Tax.Tips	I	Computation SS Tax on Tips
51,4388	Taxable Invest.Inc.	I	Taxable Investment Income
51,4405	Alternative Tax Compu.	I	Altern. Computation Ret.
51,4417	Req.Fed.Tax.Dep. Forms	I	A-Request for Dep. Forms
51,4419	Appl.Mag.Media. Report	I	Magnetic Media
51,4466	Corp.Appl.Quick Refund	I	Overpayment of Estimate.Tax
51,4491	Proof of Claim	O	By IRS for Taxes
51,4506	Request Copy.Tax Form	I	Request for Copy
51,4549	Income Tax Exam.Changes	I	A, B, C
51,4562	Depreciation.Amortiz.	I	Depreciation & Amort.Sched.
51,4563	Excl.Income U.S. Poss	I	U.S. Possessions
51,4571	Expl.Filing Return Late	I	Explanation Late Filing
51,4598	Form W-2 not Received	I	Not Recieved or Incorrect

Returns 51,4600 Through 51,4999

51,4626	Compu.Minimum Tax	I	Corporations & Fiduciaries
51,4669	Employ Wage.Not With.	I	Statement.Non-Witheld Sums
51,4670	Employ.Request.Relief	I	3402(d)
51,4684	Casual.Theft Worksheet	I	Optional Form for 1040
51,4720	Excise Tax.Priv.Found	I	Private Foundations
51,4742	Quest.Med. and Dent.	I	See 4742—4752 Quest.
51,4789	Currency Trans.Report	I	Medical and Dental Deduct.
51,4797	Suppl.Sched.Gain,Loss	I	1231, 1245, and 1250
51,4810	Req.Prompt Assessment	I	Request by payer 6501(d)
51,4862	State.Income.Changes	I	Statement.Income Tax Change
51,4868	Appl.Auto.Exten.Time	I	Application-Automa. Exten.
51,4952	Invest.Expense Ded.	I	Investment Interest Deduct.
51,4972	Lump Sum.10Yr. Ave.	I	ERISA Plan Distributions

Returns 51,5000 Through 51,5499

51,5227	Split-Int.Trust.Info.	I	Split Interest Trust Return
51,5300	Appl.Determ.TEFRA	I	TEFRA Approval, Schedule T
51,5302	Census Sched.ERISA	I	Census for Approved Plans
51,5303	Appl.Determ.CBP	I	Collectively Bargained Plan
51,5305	Indiv.Ret.Trust Acct.	I	A, SEP 408(a)
51,5306	Appl.Approv.Proto.	I	SEP, Employer Spons.Acct.
51,5307	Appl.Deter.Short.Emp.	I	Employee Benefit Plan
51,5309	Appl.Determination.ESOP	I	Employee Stock Owner. Plan

51,5329	Ret.Indiv.Ret.Sav.Arr.	I	Retirement Savings Arrange.
51,5452	Corp.Rep.Nontax.Div.	I	Report for Nontaxable Div.
51,5471	Information Return	I	M, O
51,5498	Indiv.Retire.Info.	I	Retirement Arragement Info.
	Returns 51,5500 Through 51,5999		
51,5500	Employee Benefit Plan	I	A, B, P, C, R
51,5558	Appl.Exten.Time	I	Employee Plan Returns
51,5622	Min.Part.Standards	I	Employee Benefit Plans
51,5623	Min.Vest.Stand.DBP	I	Defined Benefit Plans
51,5625	Employee Benefit Plan	I	Joint & Survivor
51,5626	Employee Benefit Plan	I	Misc.Provisions
51,4627	Employee Benefit Plan	I	Coverage & Discrim.
51,5695	Res. Energy Credit	I	Residential
51,5701	Notice of Prop.Adjust.	I	Notice of Proposed Adjust.
51,5754	State.Persons.Winnings	I	Statement.Gambling Winnings
51,5803	Explan.Return.Prep.Pen	I	Prepare Penalty Explanation
51,5884	Jobs Credit	I	Return
	Returns 51,6000 Through 51,6499		
51,6047	Windfall Profit Tax	I	Goes with Form 51,0720
51,6088	Distrib.Benefits.EBP	I	Employee Benefit Plan
51,6118	Claim of Prep.	I	Income Tax Preparers Claim
51,6123	Verif.Fiduciary Fed.Tax	I	Verification of Deposit
51,6164	Earned Income Credit	I	Basic Schedule
51,6248	Annual Info.WPT	I	T, W, Windfall Profits Tax
51,6249	Compu.Overpaid WPT	I	Windfall Profits Tax
51,6252	Compu.Install.Sale Inc.	I	Computation Install. Inc.
51,6401	Reg.Missing Information	I	Request for Missing Info.
51,6458	Cert.Elect.Form.WFPT	I	Windfall Profit Tax
51,6466	Trans.Magnetic Tape.W-4	I	Transmittal of W-4
51,6467	Mult.Employ.Trans. W-4	I	Multiple Employer Transmit.
	Returns 51,6500 Through 51,6999		
51,6559	Trans.Magnetic Media	I	Report of Magnetic Filing
51,6560	Employ.Summary of W-2	I	Magnetic Media Wage Info
51,6561	Payer Summary of W-2P	I	Magnetic Media Pension Info
51,6620	Invest.Int.Expense. Ded.	I	Invest.Interest Deduct.
51,6637	Collect.Summons	I	Info.Statement
51,6638	Collect.Summons	I	Income Tax Return
51,6639	Collect.Summons	I	Financial Records
51,6677	Plan.Termination.Stand	I	Termination Standards
51,6681	Alloc.Tent.Carry.B.	I	Carryback Allocations

51,6781	Gain & Loss.Comp.Fut.	I	Commodity Futures
51,6800	Req.Missing Info.	I	To Complete Return
51,6847	Cons.Release.Tax Info.	I	Consent to IRS to Rel.Info.

Returns 51,7000 Through 51,7999

51,7004	Appl.Auto.Exten.Corp.	I	Automatic Ext.Corp.Ret.
51,7018	Employ.Order for Forms	I	Empl. Order Blank for Forms

Returns 51,8000 Through 51,8299

51,8007	Credit.Stock.Owner. Plan	I	Employee Owner. Plan
51,8027	Employ.Info.Return Tips	I	Employer's Return Tips
51,8038	Info.Return.Priv.Bond	I	Private Activity Bond Issue
51,8046	Change.Credit.Elderly	I	Change to Credit for Elder
51,8085	Collect.Decision Info.	I	Information Return
51,8088	Miss.Info.Nec.Adjust.	I	Necessary Info for Adjust.
51,8109	Fed.Tax Deposit Coupon	I	Coupon Book
51,8233	Exemp.Withhold.Non Res.	I	Nonresident Alien
51,8264	Appl.Regist.Tax Shelt.	I	Appl. for Registration
51,8269	Not.Dishon.Check. Mult.	I	Dishonor More than Once
51,8271	Invest.Report.Tax.Shel.	I	Tax Shelter Regist.No.
51,8275	Discl.Statement	I	§6661
51,8279	Elect.Treat. As FSC	I	Treat FSC or Small FSC
51,8282	Donee Info.Return	I	Information Return
51,8283	Noncash Contrib.Char.	I	Charitable Contrib.
51,8290	Ret.Check Repay.Not.	I	Notice of Repayment

Returns 51,8300 Through 51,8999

51,8300	Rep.Cash Payments	I	Over $10,000 in Cash
51,8308	Rep.Sale.Exchange.Part.	I	Partnership Interests
51,8330	Info. Return.MCC's	I	Mortgage Credit Certif.
51,8332	Release.Claim.Exempt.	I	For Divorced or Sep. Parents
51,8368	Notice of Deficiency	I	Worksheet-Not-Return
51,8379	Injured Spouse Alloc.	I	Damages Allocation
51,8396	Mortgage Int.Credit	I	Annual Return
51,8404	Compu.Int.Charge	I	Disc. Related-Deferred Liab.

STATE RETURNS

52,0000

52,XXX State Returns

51,1040	MI 1040	I	Individual, Michigan

LOCAL RETURNS

53,XXXX

53,1040	Det 1040	I	Individual, Detroit

FEDERAL CORRESPONDENCE

54,XXXX

54,XXXX Federal Correspondence

54,1001	Let.Inform.Rep.	I	Notice of Representation
54,1010	Let.Power of Att.	III	Enclosure Letter
54,1010	Let.Protest	I,III	Protest Deficiency
54,5005	Instruc.Protest	I	Instructions Checklist

STATE CORRESPONDENCE

55,XXXX

55,XXXX State Correspondence

55,1010	Let. Power of Att.	III	Enclosure Letter

LOCAL CORRESPONDENCE

56,XXXX

56,1002	Request Forms	III	Request for Local Returns

LABOR
(6XX,XXX)

GRIEVANCE STAGE

61X,XXX

610,001	Griev.Report.Cont.	I	Basic Form.Contract Claim
610,002	Griev.Report.Disc.	I	Discipline

PANEL OR BOARD HEARING STAGE

62X,XXX

621,XXX Basic Forms

621,001	Panel Form	I	For Specific System

ARBITRATION

63X,XXX

	631,XXX Subpoena Power		
631,001	Subpoena	I	Needs Sig. of Arbitrator
631,101	Brief.Sub.Power	I	Power of Arbitrator
	632,XXX Jurisdiction		
632,100	Arb. Lim.Authority	III	Limited Authority
632,101	Arb.Contract.Shall	III	Bound by Contract "shall"
632,102	Arb.Contract.Modify	III	Contract-shouldn't Modify
	633,XXX Arbitrability		
633,120	Arb.Grievance Untime.	III	Contractual Bar
633,121	Arb.Cont Exp.	III	Expired Contract
633,122	Arb.Cont.Bar.	III	Contractual Bar
	634,XXX Successorship		
634,101	Brief.Dissol.Co	II	Dissolution of Company
634,201	Brief.Decert.Union	II	Decertification
	635,XXX Discipline		
635,000	All Discharge Cases	III	All listings are Briefs
635,001	Burden.Proof	III	Burden of Proof
635,002	Arb. Punitive.Dam.	III	Arb. Punitive Damages
635,202	Alcohol/Drug Addic.	III	Discharge Too Severe
635,203	Alcohol/Drug	III	Non-Effect on Job
635,204	Alcohol/Drug.Disch.	III	Burden of Proof
635,301	Theft.Demin.	III	De Minimus
635,311	Theft.BP	III	Burden of Proof
635,351	Theft.Caught	III	Caught in Act
635,352	Steal Prior Permiss.	III	Prior Permission to Take
635,601	Tardiness	III	Multi-Issue Brief
635,701	Job Sleeping	III	Sleeping on Job
	636,XXX Seniority Issues		
636,001	Seniority Issues		
	637,XXX Wage Issues		
637,001	Wage Issues		

638,XXX Other CBC Issues

638,001	Contract.Construct.	III	Construction Principles
638,901	Arb.Subcont.Clause	III	Bound by Subcontract
638,902	Past Practice	III	Brief Arb. Past Practice

639,XXX Enforcement

639,001 Enforcement

MEDIATION

64X,XXX

641,XXX Subpoena Power

641,000 Subpoena Power

642,XXX Jurisdiction

642,000 Jurisdiction

645,XXX Discipline

645,000 Discipline

646,XXX Seniority Issues

646,000 Seniority Issues

647,000 Wage Issues

647,000 Wage Issues

648,XXX Other CBC Issues

648,000 CBC Issues

649,XXX Enforcement

649,000 Enforcement

COURT

65X,XXX

651,XXX Unfair Representation

651,301	Interrog.To.Plaint.	III	Base Set
651,410	Mot.Strike.Jury	III	Strike Jury Demand

652,XXX Strikes

652,000 Strikes

653,XXX Anti-Trust

653,600 Mot.Summary Judgment III Summary Judgment & Brief

654,XXX Labor-Erisa Matters

654,000 Labor-Erisa Matters

655,XXX Inter-Union Matters

655,000 Inter-Union Matters

656,XXX

656,000 Other

NLRB

66X,XXX

661,XXX Representation Elections

661,000 Representation Elections

662,XXX Refusal to Bargain

662,000 Refusal to Bargain

663,XXX Other ULP—Employer

663,000 ULP—Employer

664,XXX Other ULP—Union

664,000 Other ULP—Union

665,XXX Jurisdictional Issues

665,000 Jurisdictional Issues

666,XXX Decertifications

666,000 Decertifications

667,XXX Other

667,000 Other

WAGE AND HOUR

67X,XXX

677,XXX Wage Issues

677,000 Wage Issues

678,XXX Other CBC Issues

678,000 CBC Issues

679,XXX Enforcement

679,000 Enforcement

MOTOR VEHICLE
(7XX,XXX)

AUTOMOBILES

71X,XXX

711,XXX Private

711,101	Appl.Lic.Auto	I	Application for Lic.
711,110	Pet.Temp.Lic.	I	Petition.Temp. Driv.Lic.
711,201	Appl.Reinst.Lic.	I	Appl.Reinst.Revoked Lic.

712,XXX Commercial

712,101	Appl.Lic.Chauf	I	Application—Chauffeur's

713,XXX Government

713,001 Government

714,XXX Foreign

714,001 Foreign

TRUCKS

72X,XXX

721,XXX Private

721,101	Appl.Lic.	I	Use 711,101

722,XXX Commercial

722,000 Commercial

723,XXX Government

723,000 Government

724,XXX Foreign

724,000 Foreign

MOTORCYCLE

73X,XXX

731,XXX Private

731,000 Private

732,XXX Commercial

732,000 Commercial

733,XXX Government

733,000 Government

734,XXX Foreign

734,000 Foreign

OFFROAD VEHICLES (ORV)

74X,XXX

741,XXX Private

741,000 Private

742,XXX Commercial

742,000 Commercial

743,XXX Government

743,000 Government

744,XXX Foreign

744,000 Foreign

WATERCRAFT

75X,XXX

751,XXX Private

751,000 Private

752,XXX Commercial

752,000 Commercial

753,XXX Government

753,000 Government

754,XXX Foreign

754,000 Foreign

AIRCRAFT

76X,XXX

761,XXX Private

761,101	Appl.Pilot Lic.	I	Application for Lic.

762,XXX Commercial

762,101	Appl.Pilot Lic.Comm.	I	Commercial License

763,XXX Government

763,000 Government

764,XXX Foreign

764,000 Foreign

HOVERCRAFT

77X,XXX

771,XXX

771,000 Private

772,XXX Commercial

772,000 Commercial

773,XXX Government

773,000 Government

774,XXX Foreign

774,000 Foreign

SPACECRAFT

78X,XXX

782,XXX Commercial

782,000 Commercial

783,XXX Government

783,000 Government

784,XXX Foreign

784,000 Foreign

ADMINISTRATIVE AGENCY
(8XX,XXX)

SOCIAL SECURITY ADMIN.

81X,XXX

811,XXX Petition for Benefits

811,001 Petition.Benefits I Standard Form

813,XXX Proceedings by SS Against Applicant

813,001 Proceedings by SS Against Applicant

815,XXX Proceedings by Licensee for Relief

815,001 Proceedings by Licensee for Relief

816,XXX Appeal

816,001 Appeal from Adverse Determination

BUREAU OF PATENTS & COPYRIGHTS

82X,XXX

821,XXX Certification

821,101	Appl.Pat.	I	Application for Patent
821,211	Appl.Reg.Copy.Tx	I	Form, Tx-Written Material
821,212	Appl.Reg.Copy.PA	I	Form PA-Performing Arts
821,213	Appl.Reg.Copy.VA	I	Form VA-Visual Arts
821,214	Appl.Reg.Copy.RE	I	Form RE-Renewal
821,215	Appl.Reg.Copy.CA	I	Supplemental Regist.

822,XXX Licensing

822,000 Licensing

823,XXX Proceedings by AA Against Licensee

823,000 Proceedings by AA Against Licensee

824,XXX Proceedings by AA Against Third Party

824,000 Proceedings by AA Against Third Party

825,XXX Proceedings by Licensee for Relief

825,101	Complaint.Copyright	I,III	Copyright Infringement
825,301	Interrog.Patent.Pf.	I,III	Interrog. to Plaintiff

826,XXX Proceedings by Third Party for Relief

826,000 Proceedings by Third Party for Relief

FEDERAL TRADE COMMISSION

83X,XXX

831,XXX Certification

831,001 Certification

832,XXX Licensing

832,001 Licensing

833,XXX Proceedings by FTC Against Licensee

833,001 Proceedings by FTC Against Licensee

834,XXX Proceedings by FTC Against Third Party

834,001 Proceedings by FTC Against Third Party

835,XXX Proceedings by Licensee for Relief

835,001 Proceedings by Licensee for Relief

836,XXX Proceedings by Third Party for Relief

836,001 Proceedings by Third Party for Relief

FEDERAL COMMUNICATIONS COMMISSIONS

84X,XXX

841,XXX Certification

841,100	Pet.Construct.TV.	I	Permit Construct TV

842,XXX Licensing

842,000 Licensing

843,XXX Proceedings by FCC Against Licensee

843,000 Proceedings by FCC Against Licensee

844,XXX Proceedings by FCC Against Third Party

844,000 Proceedings by FCC Against Third Party

845,XXX Proceedings by Licensee for Relief

845,000 Proceedings by Licensee for Relief

846,XXX Proceedings by Third Party for Relief

846,101	Pet.Deny.Lic.	I	Petition to Deny

SECURITIES AND EXCHANGE COMMISSION

85X,XXX

851,XXX Certification

851,110	Offering.Oil	I,III	SEC Offering for Oil
851,111	Offering.Movie	I,III	SEC Offering for Movie

852,XXX Licensing

852,000 Licensing

853,XXX Proceedings by SEC Against Licensee

853,000 Proceedings by SEC Against Licensee

854,XXX Proceedings by SEC Against Third Party

854,000 Proceedings by SEC Against Third Party

855,XXX Proceedings by Licensee for Relief

855,000 Proceedings by Licensee for Relief

856,XXX Proceedings by Third Party for Relief

856,000 Proceedings by Third Party for Relief

STATE BUREAU OF WORKERS' COMPENSATION

86X,XXX

861,XXX Certification

861,100	Petition for Benefits	I	Initiate Proceedings

863,XXX Proceedings by AA Against Licensee

863,000 Proceedings by AA Against Licensee

864,XXX Proceedings by AA Against Third Party

864,000 Proceedings by AA Against Third Party

865,XXX Proceedings by Licensee for Relief

866,XXX Proceedings by Third Party for Relief

866,101	Pet.Hearing W.C.	I	Petition for Hearing

OTHER STATE AGENCY

87X,XXX

OTHER FEDERAL AGENCY

88X,XXX

Appendix B

ETHICALLY COPING WITH INSTANTANEOUS LEGAL SERVICES

Most of the money that lawfirms earn is, in some manner, dependent upon the ability to create paper. So it is safe to say that no area of specialization is without some reliance upon the printed word. As foolish as it may seem, some lawyers express concern that efficiency or speed may cut down on revenue. They were trained via an over-reliance upon the sacred "hourly rate."

Many historians trace voluminous briefs and writings back to the days of early England wherein it was rumored that lawyers' fees were predicated upon the weight of the documents produced. To some degree, this *charge by the pound* concept has survived.

There is nothing wrong with a desire to create thorough, complete documents, to be sure. And it is no secret that contemporary equipment can enable us to produce such voluminous writings that much more quickly and accurately. The decision to draft thick documents is a matter of individual choice and preference, and is not something to be debated at this juncture. The purpose of this book will be to place the tools into your hands; whether you produce voluminous documents or mini's is a matter of personal and professional conviction. In either case, proper "automation" should enhance not only speed of production and quality, but also personalization, regardless of volume.

There is, however, a need to dispel an attitude that has seemed to keep pace with the "charge by the pound" philosophy. Though clearly wrong, there nevertheless remains a too firmly entrenched notion that the ability to perform work instantaneously means that a firm must deprive itself of a reasonable attorney fee. This misconception is very deeply rooted, and not easily expunged.

Logically, no one would argue that even if it only took 15 minutes to produce a beautiful tailor-made 40-page brief, the firm is nevertheless entitled to charge more than 15 minutes of billable time. But for some reason attorneys and administrators have difficulty convincing themselves that there is nothing wrong in billing for more than the time actually expended on a given client matter. Instead, it still seems necessary to justify the hours in order to translate actual time into billable time, by using a number of factors.

Many law firms, particularly the larger and more traditional ones, have attorneys who grew up under the concept of the billable hour. As young associates, their only goal was to create as many billable hours as possible; they lived, died, collected bonuses, or reprimands based solely upon their billable hours. Therefore, it became necessary to "make work" in order to "make time." The computer, no doubt, came as a threat to some. For, if it could be used to create billable hours, then what need would there be for associates?

It is by habit, however, *not by mandate*, that most attorneys bill *strictly* on an hourly basis. The Canons of Ethics of the American Bar Association consider "time" to be *only* one of many acceptable factors for determining reasonable billing rates for clients. I point this out because the ability to prepare massive documents within minutes does not, and should not, require a diminution with respect to chargeable fees. As a matter of fact, the opposite should be expected; elimination of busy work should mean more time for planning, polishing, and perfecting. The result should be a far superior, and *more valuable*, product.

Under no circumstances am I proposing or advocating assembly line justice. But nevertheless, there is nothing wrong, nor is there anything inherently unethical, in expanding the firm's billing capacity well beyond the number of hours actually spent on particular documents. Therefore, while the goal may be to create documents within minutes, there is no corresponding requirement to bill by the minute. Rule 1.5(a) of the Model Rules of Professional Conduct issued by the American Bar Association sets forth the following "factors" to be considered as guides in determining the reasonableness of a fee:

(1) The time and labor required, the novelty and difficulty of the questions involved, and the skill requisite to perform the legal service properly.

(2) The likelihood, if apparent to the client, that the acceptance of the particular employment will preclude other employment by the lawyer.

(3) The fee customarily charged in the locality for similar legal services.

(4) The amount involved and the results obtained.

(5) The time limitations imposed by the client or by the circumstances.

(6) The nature and length of the professional relationship with the client.

(7) The experience, reputation, and ability of the lawyer or lawyers performing the services.

(8) Whether the fee is fixed or contingent.

Particular attention should be directed toward items (3) and (4) above, for they may be as important as the time and labor required. Moreover, it should not be forgotten that it is also legitimate to take into account the fact that some "time and labor" is always required to set up the structures and systems that enable the production of documents at a faster rate.

Consider automation's impact upon the most prevalent billing methods:

EXAMPLE 1—THE CONTINGENT FEE

Matters involving personal injuries, worker's compensation, and social security claims, along with some collection lawsuits, more often than not, are handled on a contingent fee basis. For this type of case, cutting wasted time has double-barreled importance; speed provides benefits from two different angles.

First, the attorney fee is contingent only upon gross receipts; so, the quicker and more efficiently the case moves, the better. Most contingent fee matters are defended by insurance carriers which, along with their attorneys, have perpetuated the notion that a case should settle *only* after a sufficient amount of paper has been generated. So by generating it fast and aggressively, the case can move more expeditiously and efficiently toward a successful conclusion. Clients have come to favor speed over delay.

Second, since the fee is totally unrelated to the time actually expended, why not utilize time better? The time saved can be used for planning strategy for the client, or working on other billable matters.

EXAMPLE 2—THE FEE-FOR-A-PRODUCT

Wills, trusts, incorporations, employee benefit plans, securities offerings, and real estate closings are examples of those legal services that deliver a relatively well-defined paper product for the client to carry away. Most firms charge some type of flat rate for the basic instruments (sometimes called "the package"), which is complemented by an additional hourly rate for any "extras." Here, once again, economics and quality both dictate that the basic package be prepared as fast as possible. Neither client nor lawyer can possibly benefit by redoing all of the busy-work construction of previously prepared language.

EXAMPLE 3—THE PURE HOURLY RATE

Pure hourly billings are most often predicated upon the type of matters that are (in terms of time) indeterminate and unpredictable. Usually, a mix of document preparation and non-written work are involved. Litigation matters (excluding those of Example 1) provide the most common examples.

Most law firms adjust their time for computer-prepared documents by inserting entries such as: drafting, proofing, correcting, etc. For truly efficient document preparers, these terms are "fudge factors" that compensate the firm for the time required to create the master files used for rapid preparation of the subject client documents.

Perhaps an "adjusted rate" method may satisfy both the client and the law firm. There are a number of ways to accomplish this adjustment; and so long as the client understands the concept, there should be no ethical problems. For example, a client might be informed that the firm's hours would be adjusted upward for computerized document preparation, but downward to compensate for certain types of unproductive time (drive time, waiting time, etc.). It could further be explained that the upward adjustment would not "come close" to the time required to draft documents from "scratch." So the client would still *come out ahead.*

An alternative method might involve charging a minimum fee for certain specified documents, such as briefs, interrogatories, releases, closing statements, etc. Virtually any *reasonable* billing method that a firm might devise should be proper, so long as the method is fully disclosed to the client.

COMMENT

Contingent fee, fixed retainer, or hourly rate; it makes no difference. The law firm sells its time; and that time only manifests itself in one of two forms—(1) appearances (at conferences and hearings), or (2) written output. There is little that you can do to shrink the first form. But if you can multiply your output capabilities for the second, then it would be foolish not to.

GLOSSARY

TERM	DEFINITION	PAGE
ABA/net	A series of legal databases and computerized services, managed and directed by the American Bar Association.	226-231
Accoustical Input Device	A voice-to-machine device that converts human speech directly into print.	103, 192, 193
Alphanumeric	A character set consisting only of letters and numerals; other characters, symbols, or blank spaces are not included.	95
Artificial Intelligence	Computer-created intelligence, capable of mimicking human mental processes.	127, 134
ASCII	American National Standard Code for Information Interchange—It is a method by which numbers are internationally assigned, on a standard basis, to represent computer characters. It forms the character base for most operating systems and word processing utilities.	198
Autosave	A word-processing software feature that causes text to be saved automatically when a power failure occurs.	198
Base Page	A page of text that does not change from instrument to instrument; its text remains constant.	136, 137, 140, 141
Block Move	A word processing function that involves the simple but important ability to ''pluck out'' a chunk of text and move it to another part of a document.	198

Term	Definition	Pages
Boilerplate	Standard or "canned" language that can be used repeatedly for similar documents.	140, 141
Boolean Logic	Sometimes referred to as "Boolean Algebra" it refers to a logic-system which consists of only two values ("true" and "false"), and three operators ("and," "or," and "not"). The system forms the underlying predicate for computer logic. It also forms the basis for the construction of microchips.	208, 209, 219-221
Category	One of the nine major segments of the subject of law. (In the decimal structure of the Direct Reference Filing System, it is represented by the first digit from the left.)	3-5
Compiler	A translater that converts computer languages (sometimes referred to as "source code") into symbols that are capable of being understood by the computer (sometimes referred to as "machine language").	234, 235
Conjunctive	In a Boolean Logic setting, it simply refers to the word "and."	220, 221
Copy Function	A word processing function that allows you to copy a block of text into another document, or another portion of the same document, without erasing the original block.	198
Cutting and Pasting	In a word processing context, it is the ability to move blocks of text from one part of the document to another electronically.	198
Databank	The "place" on your computer disks where you store text.	213-232
Database	A place where you put, store, and periodically retrieve data.	94
Decimal System	A number system that consists solely of numbers, wherein each digit represents a particular trait of the item that is being numbered or classified.	5-8

Term	Definition	Pages
Default	A process whereby computer software will automatically perform a given operation or function, unless instructed otherwise.	207
Delete	A word processing function that erases text.	198
Desktop Publishing	A term used to describe a popular software function, that gives the user the ability to create ''newspaper-like'' publications, with multiple columns, and text that is automatically adjusted to allow for photographs and figures.	187, 210
Digital	Refers to the computer's ability to reduce images to numbers (particularly binary code), so that they can be manipulated and processed by a computer.	171, 175
Directories	Divisions or subdivisions of the computer's hard disk.	112
Disjunctive	In a Boolean Logic setting, it simply refers to the word ''or.''	220
Document Assembler	Software or word processing utilities that are designed to enable the computer to automatically select boilerplate language, based upon the user's response to certain ''plain English'' questions.	198, 236-246
Document Modeler	A powerful document assembler that utilizes its own programing language; this particular software was developed by way of a grant from the American Bar Association.	235-246
Download	A transmission process whereby text is electronically sent from some database, however distant, to your computer's disk.	94
Electronic Mail	A service of ABA/net which allows its subscribers to transmit documents to one another by way of modem.	228, 229
Extender	In a word processing context, it consists of additional characters that can be tacked on to the end of a file name.	116

Term	Definition	Page
File	A single unit of text to be stored on a computer disk.	93
File Name	The official ''Name'' that the computer will recognize and identify with a given file.	93
Final Copy	As distinguished from a ''hard copy,'' this is a final, complete, formatted document ready to be signed or used.	93
Floppy Disk	It serves the same function as a hard disk, except that you can touch and move it about; in general, a single floppy disk will never have as much storage capacity as a hard disk.	93
Font	The size and style of print to be used for a given document.	198
Footnote Spacer	A feature which arranges pages containing footnotes; i.e., pages are automatically ended at an appropriate point so as to allow enough room for footnotes at the bottom.	199
Format	To provide the computer ''layout'' or structure for the print that appears on the pages of a given document.	93
Formate	To take a pleading, contract, or any writing and develop from it a master or prototype, designed for repeated future use when creating similar documents.	93, 156
Function	Similar to a subroutine, it is a segment or portion of a larger computer program that performs a specific operation upon numerical or character data.	246
Global Search and Replace	A function that permits you to direct the computer to automatically change a word, term, or character string everywhere that it appears in the document, without tracking down each individual item.	199
Hard Copy	A paper ''printout'' of all of the text contained in a given computer file.	93, 133
Hard Disk	As the name implies, it is a disk-shaped ''Storage Bin'' for Computer storage of your files and file names.	93

Term	Definition	Pages
Hardware	A collection of devices, such as personal computers, printers, expansion cards, etc., which, when combined with software, make up a computer system.	185
Headers and Footers	Page numbers and whatever additional text you may require at the beginning or the end of every page of text for a given document, or portion thereof.	199
Identifier	A concise, short statement, written in abbreviated English, indicating the precise nature of the text contained in a given form or master.	49, 50, 93, 94, 95, 126
Insertion	In a word processing context, it is the ability to ''plug'' blocks of text into the middle of paragraphs or sentences.	199
Interface	To connect computer components to one another.	186-193
Justification	The ability to ''line up'' the right-hand margins of a document by causing a proportional spacing between the words on each line.	199
LAN	Acroynm for Local Area Network. It refers to interconnecting, stand-alone computer systems within a given office or specific area.	186
Level	One of five Levels of Technology used to identify the physical makeup of a form or document creation device.	8-10, 127, 133, 149
Level I	The first of the five ''levels of techonology''; it refers to those forms which do not require any equipment or technological skill, but rather refer to forms that are supplied from outside sources, such as printed forms multipart-carbons, impression forms, summonses, and sample pleadings.	8, 9, 127, 133, 149
Level II	Refers to forms that are ''created'' by the use of a photocopier.	9, 127, 133, 134, 149
Level III	Refers to forms that are stored on a computer hard disk or floppy disk, under the auspices of some word processing program.	9, 127, 134, 153, 154

Term	Definition	Pages
Level IV	Forms (or more accurately "scripts") which are used to generate final documents.	9, 127, 134
Level V	Refers to documents that are devised through artificial intelligence; they are actually programs that reside in a computer's memory. We use the term to refer to any software or hardware, the technology of which is beyond document assembler capabilities.	10, 127, 134
Level Indicator	A Roman Number, or numbers, indicating the level and location of a given form. It is used on the index pages of your Master Form Book. See "Level."	8, 9, 127
Macro	When used by a programmer, the term refers to a standardized subroutine or function; in a word processing environment, it refers to the ability to save sets of repeatedly used keystrokes for future use.	199
Master	A media used to create documents.	89-118, 119-166
Master File	A file to be saved and used to create more than one document.	94
Master Form Book	A single looseleaf book that serves as a guide and locator for all of your masters, forms, stored text, identifiers, and sample documents.	119-134
Master Index	A component of your Master Form Book which lists all of the forms in your office.	123-132, Appendix A
Merge	A word processing feature that permits you to take data from two computer files, and blend them into a single document.	200
Micro-Floppy	A smaller, heavier, more compact 3 1/2″ square disk; in truth, it does not bend or flop, but *does* hold more text and protects that text better than a standard floppy.	9

Micro-Processor	Sometimes synonymously referred to as a computer, it is really the processing unit upon which the computer's design is predicated.	177-186
Modem	A link between a telephone and computer which enables data to be transmitted from the latter, via telephone lines, to other computers.	188, 189
Mouse	A piece of hardware that permits you to provide information to a computer by pressing a single button instead of typewriter keys.	191, 192
Multifacing	Creating several alternative pull pages (for a Master) that vary according to gender, plurality, sex, etc.	150, 151
Multi-User Terminals	Several computer terminals that are connected to a single disk system or databank.	186
On-Line	Connected to a database by way of a modem.	214
Optical Scanner	A computer-connected device that has the ability to "look at" a page of printed material and feed the images into the computer's storage disks.	103, 189-191
Program	A list of instructions for the computer.	235
Proportional Spacing	See Justification.	
Prototype	A completed document used as a sample or guide for the preparation of a similar document.	8
Proximity Search	When conducting a "free text" search of a database, this particular utility or function will cause the computer to return data that is "close" though not identical to the character string that is sought.	225
Pull Sheet	One of several alternative pages of text to be inserted into an otherwise complete instrument.	137, 141, 151, 152

Script	Programs or instructions that are written by one who uses Document Modeler software.	235, 240
Search and Replace	See Global Search and Replace.	200
Second-Generation Typos	"New" mistakes created as "otherwise" perfect text is retyped.	91
Sort Commands	Computer utilities for arranging lists in numerical or alphabetical order.	200
Spell-Checker	A built-in computer dictionary that signals the user as to any spellings that do not appear in it.	200
Spreadsheet	An electronic matrix of cells, each of which is identified by a row and column number. Each cell can be filled with numerical data or characters.	203, 204
Subroutine	A block, segment, or portion of a larger computer routine; a subroutine is actually a miniature program within a larger routine or program.	246
Syntax	Rules governing the structure and use of commands for particular programming languages.	239
Dummy Terminal	Simply a video display connected to a keyboard and communications equipment. Its sole function is to communicate with the central computer.	186
Text Conformity	A measure of the degree to which the text on the computer screen matches the text on the printed page.	200
Windows	A method of implementing multi-tasking. By hitting a certain key, the user's screen may be saved as the job is placed in the background, and another screen, or "window," is made available for use. Several jobs can be performed at the same time with this utility.	200
Wordwrap	See Wraparound.	200

Working File	A temporary file to be created in conjunction with one document, then removed from the hard disk after that document has been executed, finalized, and is no longer likely to be modified.	94, 104-118
Wraparound	A feature whereby the word processor automatically places words on lines in such a manner that none are split between two lines.	200
WYSIWYG	(Pronounced "wiswig") An acronym for "what you see (on the monitor) is what you get (on paper)." It refers to the software's ability to make the screen look like your actual printed page.	200

BIBLIOGRAPHY

BOOKS

1. *ABA/NET The Lawyer's Network* (Pocket Guide), ABA/NET is a service mark of the American Bar Association, ITT Dialcom, Inc., 1984.
2. Altman Maryann, and Robert I. Weil, *How to Manage Your Law Office*. Matthew Bender Company, Inc., 235 East 45th Street, New York, NY 10017, 1985.
3. Barnes, Kate, *Using MultiMate*. Que Corporation, 7999 Knue Road, Indianapolis, IN 46250, 1985.
4. Borgerson, Mark J., *A Basic Programmer's Guide to PASCAL*. John Wiley & Sons, Inc., 605 Third Avenue, New York, NY 10158, 1982.
5. Bove, Tony and Cheryl Rhodes, *The Art of Desktop Publishing*. Bantam Books, New York, NY, 1987.
6. Braeman, Kathryn and Fran Shellenberger, *From Yellow Pads to Computers*, The American Bar Association, 1987.
7. Brandon, Dick H., and Sindey Segelstein, *Boardroom's Complete Guide to Mini-Computers*. Boardroom Books, 500 Fifth Avenue, New York, NY 10110, 1981.
8. Brown, Jerald R., and Leroy Finkel, *IBM PC: Data File Programming*. John Wiley & Sons, Inc., 605 Third Avenue, New York, NY 10158, 1983.
9. Collins, Anna, *Document Maker Manual*. Legalware, Inc., 49 Wellington Street, E., Toronto, ONT M5E 1C9, 1986.
10. Cook, William J., *The Joy of Computer Communication*. Dell Publishing Company, Inc., 1 Dag Hammarskjold Plaza, New York, NY 10017, 1984.
11. Dunning, Kenneth A., *Getting Started in GPSS*, Engineering Press, Inc., P.O. Box 1, San Jose, CA 95103, 1981.
12. Greenberg, Phillip and Rita, *The Complete Guide to dBase III, a Self-Teaching Guide*. John Wiley & Sons, Inc., 605 Third Avenue, New York, NY 10158, 1986.
13. Hirsch, Seymour, Basic: *A Programmed Text*. John Wiley & Sons, Inc., 605 Third Avenue, New York, NY 10158, 1975.

14. McClure, Rhyder and Mary Abdill, *Fast Access/Lotus 1-2-3*. Simon and Schuster Inc., Gulf & Western Plaza, New York, NY 10023, 1988.

15. Remer, David, *Computer Power for Your Law Office*. Sybex, Inc., 2344 Sixth Street, Berkley, CA 94710, 1983.

16. Rhoads, Forrest Dean and John Edwards, *Law Office Guide to Small Computers*, Shepard's/McGraw-Hill, 1984.

17. Staudt, Ronald and Bernard J. Farber, *The Dow Jones—Irwin Handbook of Microcomputer Applications in Law*. Dow Jones—Irwin, Homewood Ill. 60430, 1987.

18. Soloman, Samuel A., *IBM PC Assembly Language is Fun and Easy*. Reston Publishing Company, Inc., a Prentice Hall Company, Reston, VA 1984.

19. Templeton, Harley M., *From Basic to 8086/8088 Assembly Language*, p. 26, 27. Wordware Publishing Inc., P.O. Box 1747, Plano, TX 75074, 1985.

20. Thomas, Terry, and Marlene G. Weinstein,*Computer-Assisted Legal and Tax Research*. Prentice Hall Information Services, Paramus, NJ 07652, 1986.

PERIODICALS

1. *ABA Software Reviews*, The Legal Technology Advisory Counsel of the American Bar Association (LTAC).

2. Davies, Owen, ''Voicewriters—Artificial Intelligence,'' *Omni*, November 1986, p. 34, Vol. 9, no. 2.

3. Dickinson, John, ''Survey of Printers,'' *P.C. Magazine*, November 11, 1986, p. 135, Vol. 5, no. 19.

4. Gary, Leon, Jr., ''Getting and Staying Computerized,'' *Legal Economics*, May/June 1985, p. 21.

5. *Legal Economics*, ABA Section of Economics of Law Practice.

6. Lipson, Ashley S., ''Direct Reference Legal Filing System,'' *Legal Economics*, July/August 1983, p. 39, Vol. 9, no. 4, Section of Economics of Law Practice of the American Bar Association; *The Michigan Bar Journal*, July 1981, p. 451, Vol. 60, no. 7; *Law Office Economics and Management*, Spring 1982, p. 20, Vol. XXIII, no. 1; *Law Office Economics and Management*, Fall 1982, p. 286, Vol. XXIII, no. 3; *Trial, the National Legal News Magazine*, October 1982, p. 16, Vol. 18, no. 10; *Hawaii Bar Journal*, 1982, p. 135, Vol. XVII; *The Docket*, National Association of Legal Secretaries, December/January 1983, p. 8, Vol. 31, Issue 3; *Tennessee Bar Journal*, February 1983, Vol. 19, no. 1; *The California Lawyer*, June 1983, p. 52, Vol. 3, no. 6; *The Colorado Lawyer*, September 1983, p. 1465, Vol. 12, no. 9.

7. Lipson, Ashley S., ''Lawyers's Short Course in the 'Basic' Computer Language,'' *Law Office Economics and Management*, Fall 1983, p. 283, Vol. XXIV, no. 3; *The California Lawyer*, October 1983, p. 47, Vol. 3, no. 10; *Trial, the National Legal News Magazine*, December 1983, p. 24, Vol. 19, no. 12; *Jurimetrics*, Winter 1984, p. 154, Vol. 24, no. 2; *The Arkansas Lawyer*, April 1984, p. 104, Vol. 18, no. 2.

8. Lipson, Ashley S., ''Computerizing Your Document System,'' *Trial, The National Legal News Magazine*, January 1985, p. 28, Vol. 21, no. 1; *The Profitable Lawyer*, November 1984, p. 15, Vol. 1, no. 4; *Of Counsel*, November 1984, p. 10, Vol. 3, no. 11; *Economics and Management of Law Practice Section Newsletter,* January 1985, Entire Edition, Issue No. 2; *The Maryland Bar Journal*, February 1985, p. 4, Vol. XVIV, no. 2; *Baltimore Association of Legal Assistants, Newsletter*, March 1985; *Law Office Management Digest*, May/June 1985, p. 1, Vol. XV, no. 3.

9. Poor, Alfred, ''Networks (LAN Software Comes of Age),'' *P.C. Magazine*, October 28, 1986, p. 285, Vol. 5, no. 18.

10. Robbins, Richard L., and James Sproll, ''Up-Grading Your Law Office Computer System,'' *ABA Journal*, August 1985, p. 54, Vol. 17.

11. Schneider, Allan H., ''Copiers for Law Offices—New Technology,'' *ABA Journal*, February 1986, p. 66, Vol. 72.

12. Tunick, David C., ''How to Acquire a Computer Painlessly,'' *California Lawyer*, November 1986, p. 53, Vol. 6, no. 11.

13. ''Westlaw—A Guide to Legal Research,'' West Publishing Company, 50 W. Kellogg Blvd., P.O. Box 64526, St. Paul, MN 55164-1003, 1986.

14. Wiswell, Phil, ''Word Processing,'' *P.C. Magazine*, August 20, 1985, p. 112, Vol. 16.

Index